T0042996

CAMPAIGNS, ELECTIONS, AND THE THREAT TO DEMOCRACY

WHAT EVERYONE NEEDS TO KNOW®

CAMPAIGNS, ELECTIONS, AND THE THREAT TO DEMOCRACY

WHAT EVERYONE NEEDS TO KNOW®

2nd Edition

DENNIS W. JOHNSON

OXFORD
UNIVERSITY PRESS

OXFORD
UNIVERSITY PRESS

Oxford University Press is a department of the University of Oxford.
It furthers the University's objective of excellence in research, scholarship,
and educationby publishing worldwide.

Oxford is a registered trade mark of Oxford University
Press in the UK and certain other countries.

"What Everyone Needs to Know" is a registered trademark of
Oxford University Press.

Published in the United States of America by Oxford University Press
198 Madison Avenue, New York, NY 10016, United States of America.

© Oxford University Press 2022

All rights reserved. No part of this publication may be reproduced, stored in
a retrieval system, or transmitted, in any form or by any means, without the
prior permission in writing of Oxford University Press, or as expressly
permitted by law, by license, or under terms agreed with the appropriate
reproduction rights organization. Inquiries concerning reproduction outside
the scope of the above should be sent to the Rights Department, Oxford
University Press, at the address above.

You must not circulate this work in any other form
and you must impose this same condition on any acquirer.

Library of Congress Cataloging-in-Publication Data
Names: Johnson, Dennis W., author.
Title: Campaigns, elections, and the threat to democracy :
what everyone needs to know / Dennis W. Johnson.
Other titles: Campaigns and elections
Description: Second edition. | New York : Oxford University Press, 2022. |
Series: What everyone needs to know |
Includes bibliographical references and index.
Identifiers: LCCN 2022023703 (print) | LCCN 2022023704 (ebook) |
ISBN 9780197641972 (hardcover) | ISBN 9780197641989 (paperback) |
ISBN 9780197642009 (epub)
Subjects: LCSH: Political campaigns—United States. | Campaign
management—United States. | Politics, Practical—United States. |
Elections—United States. | Democracy—United States.
Classification: LCC JK2281 .J622 2022 (print) | LCC JK2281 (ebook) |
DDC 323.70973—dc23
LC record available at https://lccn.loc.gov/2022023703
LC ebook record available at https://lccn.loc.gov/2022023704

1 3 5 7 9 8 6 4 2

Paperback printed by Lakeside Book Company, United States of America
Hardback printed by Bridgeport National Bindery, Inc., United States of America

For Pat, with all my love

CONTENTS

4 Statewide, Local, and Congressional Elections   53

5 Presidential Elections 65

8 Money, Mega-Donors, and Wide-Open Spending   123

9 Inner Workings of Modern Campaigns   151

10 Direct Democracy—Ballot Campaigns   163

11 How Campaigns Have Changed   178

12 Threats to Democracy   189

PREFACE TO THE SECOND EDITION: WHY YOU NEED TO KNOW ABOUT CAMPAIGNS, ELECTIONS, AND THE THREAT TO DEMOCRACY

So much has changed in American elections since the first edition of this book was published just three years ago. Even the title has changed, to reflect not only our concern about campaigns and elections but also the threats to democracy that have recently surfaced. In this edition, there are two new chapters on the extraordinary 2020 presidential election between incumbent Donald Trump and challenger Joe Biden. Under normal circumstances, this book would not focus on just one presidential election, but the events surrounding the 2020 election were so unique, so contentious, and in the end such a threat to democratic norms and standards that this election deserves special treatment in this volume. In chapters 6 and 7 we will look at the extraordinary campaign events, the impact of the pandemic, the shift to mail-in voting, the attempts by President Trump to raise substantial doubt about the election before it even occurred, and, most consequentially, the Big Lie—the attempt by Trump and his allies to subvert the vote of the people and upset the Electoral College vote.

The final section, chapter 12 on the threats to democracy, is greatly expanded and updated. It focuses on the growing distrust in American institutions and the flurry of laws passed by Republican-dominated state legislatures to restrict access to voting and to trim the powers of state election officials. We look at the Democratic responses to these attempts at voter suppression and the struggle in Congress to protect voting rights and the integrity of the voting process.

American democracy is indeed under threat and we all need clear, authoritative, unbiased answers about campaigns, elections, and the integrity of our democratic systems and institutions. This updated and thoroughly revised edition will help us sift through the noise and false narratives of those trying to undermine democratic values and institutions.

The right of all citizens to vote and participate in elections is a bedrock principle of American democracy. It has been a hard-won right, overcoming prejudice, stubborn resistance, and blatant discrimination grounded in state law and practice. In our textbook versions, citizens are given the opportunity to choose their representatives and to vote on issues without fear of intimidation, knowing that the elections will be fairly conducted, and the decision of the voters will be abided by. Citizens also are assured that elections will be held on a frequent and regular basis, usually every two or four years. Our concept of democracy also assumes that citizens will be active in public affairs—not just voting, but also learning about issues, supporting candidates for office, even donating money and working on campaigns.

But now, in the third decade of the twenty-first century, our campaign and election systems are not working the way the textbooks taught us. We have seen profound changes in how campaigns are conducted, how voters get their information, who gives money to campaigns, how the highest court has interpreted the relationship between money and free speech, how campaign consultants have used their influence, how a president and his followers have denigrated the electoral process and have pushed a Big Lie about the 2020 election results, and how outside forces have tried to impact—and sometimes have succeeded in impacting—elections.

Before we move on, let's define two key words: *elections* and *campaigns*. Through an *election*, citizens have the chance to choose from among candidates for public office who will, if elected, vote on policy issues. Usually, elections are held on a fixed day, very often in early November for a general election. Sometimes there are special elections (often to fill a seat vacated by a death or resignation), primaries (to determine which of several candidates will represent a political party), and, occasionally, runoff elections (when the leading primary candidates have not reached a certain percentage of voters during the first round). In over half the states, an election can also include ballot issues, where there is no candidate, only policy issues at stake (for example, whether to have a lottery or permit marijuana for recreational use). Elections are conducted and monitored by state and local officials, candidates are chosen to fill government jobs, and policy issues are decided.

A *campaign* is the active side of an election: announcing a candidacy, raising and debating issues, scheduling meet-and-greet dinners and rallies, raising campaign funds, identifying potential voters, communicating through social media and television, and getting voters out to the polling stations. Much of what we'll discuss in this book deals with the changing dynamics and mechanisms of campaigning.

But over recent years, unfortunately, we've seen some disturbing trends.

- Thanks to federal court decisions, the federal campaign-finance laws have been almost entirely blown out of the water. We used to require transparency; now millions of campaign dollars can be hidden. We used to have limits on the amount of money that can be donated or spent; that's almost all been taken away.

- The result is that a handful of mega-donors, those willing to give $25 million or $50 million of their own money (often hidden from public view) to a campaign, can have a major impact on statewide and other races.
- Campaigns are no longer contests between one candidate and another. Organized interests (many of them hidden behind innocent-sounding names) have flooded campaigns with their pitches, ads, and organizational muscle.
- In the 2016 presidential election, more adults sat at home than voted for either Donald Trump or Hillary Clinton. In many big-city mayoral elections, little more than 15 percent or 20 percent of the voters cast ballots. While the 2018 and 2020 elections saw big increases in voter participation, the United States still lags far behind most democracies in citizen involvement.
- Many voters simply don't know what media to trust anymore. Fake news found on social media sites, much of it coming from other countries, confuses voters and distorts reality. A president barking "fake news," pushing false information about the elections, and disparaging the mainstream press certainly doesn't help.
- Mistrust of government and its institutions is at an all-time high, and partisanship and the ideological divide are as corrosive as they have ever been. That mistrust has been fueled by the 2020 Big Lie, former president Trump's refusal to accept the reality of his defeat, and his efforts to punish those Republicans who defy him.

This book will try to sort out what is real, what is confusing, and what everyone should know about campaigns and elections. It poses 157 questions and answers that are based on federal law and court decisions, the findings of scholars and campaign practitioners, and an analysis of historical events.

The book is divided into twelve chapters, with questions and answers focused on a common theme. Chapter 1 concerns voting and participation. We'll look at how our elections work; how our participation rates compare with other countries; the long, tortured history of gaining the right to vote for women and minorities; voting fraud; and how we protect our electoral process. In chapter 2, the focus is on the creation of legislative districts. We'll look at how state legislatures create districts, the ongoing battle over gerrymandering and creating districts favorable to one party or the other, and how states lose or gain congressional districts following every ten-year census. Chapter 3 is devoted to the role of political parties and elections. How have the Democratic and Republican parties changed over the years? Why don't we have other parties popping up to challenge them? How many people consider themselves independents, and how do they vote during elections? Is the Republican Party basically the Trump Party? We'll also ask whether political parties have surrendered their role in campaigning to wealthy donors and super PACs.

In chapter 4, we'll look at statewide, local, and congressional elections. We start with a simple question: how many local and state government offices require election by voters? We'll also look at how local candidates communicate with voters when television is too expensive. Historically, women have not run for office in the same numbers as men; has this changed in the era of Donald Trump? In chapter 5, we look at presidential elections. Several questions surround our cumbersome and antiquated Electoral College system: Why do we have this system in the first place? How and when did it break down? Is it a fair system? Who wants to change it and how could it be changed? We'll also look at questions about our lengthy primary system: How did we get to the point of having all these primaries, and aren't there ways to shorten the process? Why don't we have a straight-up-and-down nationwide vote where whoever gets the most votes wins?

Chapter 6 is new to this edition, and we explore in detail the 2020 presidential election. President Trump lost by 7 million votes but, thanks to our antiquated Electoral College system, came within an eyelash of winning. We'll look at the impact of Covid, the massive use of mail-in balloting, and the surprising turnout of voters on both sides. In chapter 7, we will look at the "Big Lie," the repeated attempts by President Trump to deny the legitimacy of the contest, even before any votes were counted. And we'll go into the "Stop the Steal" effort, showing who was behind it, who aided and abetted the effort, and how courageous state and local officials—many of them Republican—blocked the falsehoods. We now know that Trump's own advisers knew that the so-called steal was nothing but a sham. We'll look at those elected officials who, either by their aggressive actions or more usually by their silence, were complicit.

In chapter 8, we examine the impact of money in campaigns, with the influence of mega donors and wide-open spending. So much has changed in the past few years. What's the difference between "hard" money, "soft" money, and "dark" money? How have Supreme Court decisions profoundly changed the way we regulate campaign financing? We'll look at the agencies responsible for overseeing federal campaign financing, especially the Federal Election Commission and the Internal Revenue Service. We'll identify some of the wealthiest donors and see what their impact may have been, but we'll also look at what average citizens can contribute.

In chapter 9, we look at campaign consultants. What are the roles of campaign managers, pollsters and media specialists, big-data consultants, get-out-the-vote specialists, and a legion of other campaign operatives? We'll ponder the question, if Hillary Clinton had an all-star team of consultants, why was she beaten by Trump's team, which could at best be described as "second tier"? How do campaigns and political consultants run a political campaign during a Covid pandemic? Chapter 10 is devoted to direct democracy and ballot campaigns. How do ballot campaigns work, and what kinds of issues typically appear on ballots? We'll also look at why ballot issues are a gold mine for political consultants, especially in California. We'll look at the attempt to recall the California governor in 2021. And we'll explore the dicey issue of whether there should be a system for holding nationwide ballot elections.

In chapter 11, we'll look at how campaigns have changed since the beginning of the digital age. We'll look at the revolution in microtargeting and big data, explore the impact of social media, and look at the role of that tried-and-true communications tool, television. Finally, chapter 12 wraps up our exploration of campaigns and elections by asking whether our system and our actions pose a threat to democracy. We'll look at the attempts by Republican-controlled state legislatures to restrict voting access and at Democratic-dominated state legislatures attempting to broaden the right to vote. We'll look at Russian hacking, "fake news," the vulnerability of our election system to cyber warfare, home-grown terrorism, and other issues. We'll probe the question: which is worse—Russian and other foreign actors attempting to mess with our elections or homegrown attempts to subvert the will of the people and cast doubts on our electoral system? We'll also tackle the question: what can citizens do to better understand how money is spent and how they can better participate in these most important components of citizenship?

In all, we'll gain a much better understanding of how elections and campaigns work, the strengths and weaknesses of our democratic institutions, and how we can make our system better.

ACKNOWLEDGMENTS

Many colleagues, friends, and associates helped me develop this volume on campaigns and elections. As with several of my previous works, I turned to my colleagues at the George Washington University and its Graduate School of Political Management. I especially thank Michael Cornfield for his insights and analysis. I also turned to several of our adjunct faculty and friends; specialists in the art of electioneering and politics, especially Tom Edmonds and Michael Malbin; along with the anonymous reviewers of this project.

I also recruited friends and colleagues who have no real background or specialized knowledge of campaigns and elections. This book is written for them and people like them— engaged and concerned citizens—and is designed to answer their questions and give them a better understanding of the inner workings of campaigns and the importance of elections. These friends have acted in one way or another as my informal focus group for the first edition of this book, giving me advice on the questions presented here and posing some questions that I had not thought of earlier. Special thanks to Jeanine Draut, Sunny Early, Lollie Goodyear, Erik Johnson, Phyllis Kester, Christina Dykstra Mead, David Mead, Pat Miller, Danny Poole, Mike Saunders, Trish Saunders, Helen Shreves, Susan Wright, and Haskell Thomson and the wise folks (especially Elliott Jemison, Mary McDermott, and John

Woodford) at the Chocolate Sparrow Coffee Club in Orleans, Massachusetts.

My special thanks to senior editor Angela Chnapko, who encouraged me to write a second edition of this book, and who, along with senior project editor Alexcee Bechthold, made the whole process run smoothly. In addition I would like to thank the fine production team headed by project managers Lavanyanithya Kathirvel and Ponneelan Moorthy, production editor Katherine Schminky, and the copyediting of Danielle Michaely.

Most of all, thanks to my wife, Pat, who read every word of this text, both in its first and second editions; gave me some very helpful suggestions; and, more than anything, was my best cheerleader and support through all the burdens and joys of writing this volume.

1

VOTING AND PARTICIPATION

Compared to other democracies, the United States has a mediocre record of voter participation. Our interest usually peaks during presidential elections. In 2020, there were a record number of voters, reaching 67 percent of eligible citizens, but that was far above the usual rate of voting. For local elections and ballot measures, voter participation is often much lower. The United States has had a long history of denying citizens the right to vote, and today there is pressure to clamp down against alleged voter fraud. Elections are administered at the state and local levels, but despite federal assistance, many of the state systems are fragile and vulnerable to electronic fraud and political chicanery.

How does the United States conduct elections?

The most familiar method of conducting elections is called the *single-winner* system—the candidate with the most votes wins. There are two versions of the single-winner system. The first is the *plurality-voting* method, which means that no matter what percentage of the vote the top vote-getter receives, that candidate is declared the winner. This is how our federal elections (for the House of Representatives and the Senate) work, as well as many gubernatorial and other statewide contests. The winning candidate doesn't need a majority of votes (50 percent plus one vote), just the most votes. The second version is the *majority-voting* method, in which the winning candidate must receive a majority of the votes. When there are many candidates and none receives a majority, states and other jurisdictions with majority systems will hold a runoff between the top two candidates.

Our presidential election system, of course, is also a single-winner system, but the outcome depends not on popular vote but on having the majority of electors from the Electoral College. We'll see in much more detail how the Electoral College works in chapter 5 and examine in depth the problems found in the 2020 election in chapters 6 and 7.

We also have a *multiple-winner* system. This usually occurs at the local level in cities and counties, and the chief feature is that several candidates are declared winners. For example, there might be four available seats in a local at-large election and seven candidates. The top four vote-getters will be declared the winners.

Another system, called *ranked-choice voting* (RCV), is used in a number of municipalities, including San Francisco and Minneapolis, and it is employed statewide in Maine. In total, RCV has now been adopted in fifteen states, from Alaska to Florida. Instead of just choosing one candidate, voters rank their preferences. When there are multiple candidates, if the top vote-getter doesn't receive a majority, then the candidate with the lowest number of votes will be eliminated. At that point, the voters' second choices will be considered. Ultimately, a winner will emerge with a majority of the votes. In 2018, a congressman from Maine lost his bid for re-election under a newly installed RCV system. He had the highest number of votes, but not a majority. When the votes were calculated using the RCV method, his opponent gained more than 50 percent of the vote and was declared the winner. The effect is very similar to a runoff election, and has the benefit of ensuring that an outlier candidate who gains perhaps only 15 percent to 20 percent of the vote doesn't come in first in a multicandidate race.

The biggest recent test of RCV was in the New York City mayoral primary, held in June 2021, with eight candidates vying for the Democratic nomination. In this very public contest, RCV may have been confusing to voters, but even more so to city election officials, who struggled to come up with the eventual winner.

What's the historical background on the right to vote in America?

We pride ourselves that nearly every American adult is eligible to vote. Right now, the only people who cannot vote are convicted felons, those with mental incapacities, and residents who are not citizens. But as we will see, many Americans fail to register, are somehow blocked or intimidated, or simply do not take advantage of the right to vote, particularly in state and local elections.

The history of extending the right to vote in this country has been long and tortuous. As historian Alexander Keyssar reminds us, "At its birth, the United States was not a democratic nation. The very word 'democracy' had pejorative overtones, summoning up images of disorder, government by the unfit, even mob rule."[1] And for many years to come, very few people had the right to vote. Women, nearly all free African Americans, slaves, Native Americans, and White adult males who couldn't meet the property requirements were excluded from the vote. Later, Asian Americans and Hispanic Americans were routinely denied the right to vote.

The Civil War brought an end to slavery and also established citizenship for former slaves, through the Thirteenth Amendment. African American men obtained the right to vote under the Fifteenth Amendment, in 1870. In the South, this was carried out under military-enforced Reconstruction. By 1890, some 147,000 African American men were on the voting rolls in Mississippi. Altogether, 1,500 African Americans were appointed or elected to office in the South from 1870 to 1890.

Ironically, several northern states still prohibited Blacks from voting. Then came the resurgence of southern White domination and the purge of Black voting rights. Starting with Mississippi in 1890 and spreading throughout the South, there was a massive effort to remove Blacks from the voting rolls—through intimidation, so-called grandfather clauses, literacy tests, poll taxes, and other devices. It worked: before the purge, 67 percent of Mississippi Blacks were registered to vote; by 1892, just 4 percent remained on the rolls. The US Congress did nothing to stop the wholesale elimination of voting rights—so much for the protections of the Constitution. North Carolina governor Charles Aycock, whose remains rest in the US Capitol crypt, said in 1903 that he was "proud" of his state for solving the "Negro problem": "We have taken him out of politics and have thereby secured good government under any party and laid foundations for the future development of both races. . . . Let the Negro learn once [and] for all that there is unending separation of the races, that the two peoples may develop side by side to the fullest but that they cannot intermingle."[2] One estimate found that in the 1940s, only 5 percent of all African Americans living in the South were voting. Full voting protections for African Americans—men and women— did not come until the Voting Rights Act of 1965.

Women battled for decades to secure the right to vote. Starting in 1848, at the Women's Rights Convention held in Seneca Falls, New York, women activists began to fight throughout the states and in Congress to obtain the right to vote. Carrie Chapman Catt, leader of the principal woman's suffrage organization, bitterly recounted those battles: 56 referendum campaigns, 480 campaigns to urge state legislatures to submit suffrage amendments to voters, 47 campaigns to include woman suffrage in state constitutions, 277 fights to have state parties include woman suffrage in their platforms, 30 platform fights during presidential elections, and 19 campaigns in each of the Congresses, spanning thirty-eight years.[3] Finally, in 1920, women gained the right to vote through the Nineteenth

Amendment. There was concern, mostly among opponents, that women would form a bloc, even a Women's Party, to vote their interests, but as women settled into voting, they soon occupied the whole spectrum of ideology and partisan ties.

The right to vote was expanded twice more. The Twenty-Third Amendment (1961) extended the right to vote for president and vice president to the citizens of the District of Columbia. Eighteen-year-olds were granted the right to vote by the Twenty-Sixth Amendment (1971). The overwhelming sentiment was that if we are asking eighteen-year-olds to fight in the Vietnam War, then we should allow them to vote as well. The saying was "old enough to fight, old enough to vote."

Why was the Voting Rights Act of 1965 important? What's the importance of the 2013 Shelby County and the 2021 Brnovich decisions?

The Voting Rights Act of 1965, together with the Civil Rights Act of 1964, was one of the most important pieces of legislation passed during the twentieth century. The Deep South had continued to block or intimidate African American voters, keeping them from exercising one of democracy's most important rights. After civil rights protestors were beaten and jailed in Selma, Alabama, in 1965, an exasperated President Lyndon Johnson ordered his attorney general: "I want you to write me the goddamnest toughest voting rights act that you can devise."[4]

The Voting Rights Act suspended for five years all sorts of voting registration requirements that had impeded minority voting in six southern states (Alabama, Georgia, Louisiana, Mississippi, South Carolina, and Virginia) and several counties in other states (North Carolina, Arizona, and Hawaii). To back up the law, federal examiners (mostly southern federal bureaucrats) were sent to those states to monitor the elections. Any new voting requirements or restrictions these states proposed had to be approved by the Justice Department, in a process called *preclearance*. Once the voting restrictions were removed, African American registration increased by a million during the first four years, and the number of southern Black elected officials doubled.[5] Still, White citizens and groups tried in many ways to circumvent the requirements of the Voting Rights Act and dilute or minimize Black voting strength.

The Voting Rights Act was renewed several times. The last time was in 2006, when its protections were extended until 2033. But in June 2013, the Supreme Court ruled, in *Shelby County v. Holder*,[6] that Congress had exceeded its authority in 2006 when it reauthorized the section of the Voting Rights Act that required the preclearance of state election laws. In *Shelby County*, the court said, basically, that the stringent requirements in the original law had been the right thing to do back in 1965, but that "things have changed dramatically" since then. Congress should have updated the law, said the conservative majority on the court. Chief Justice John Roberts wrote the opinion. Congress had failed to make any updates, and thus the preclearance provisions—the real heart of the law's enforcement—were ruled unconstitutional.[7] The Supreme Court essentially defanged the Voting Rights Act. Within a few hours of the *Shelby County* decision, Texas attorney general Greg Abbott announced that the state's voter-identification restrictions would be implemented immediately. Those stringent restrictions had previously been blocked by a federal court. Soon, similar action was taken in Alabama, North Carolina, and Virginia and attempted in Florida.[8]

Then came the 2020 presidential election, the Big Lie, and in the aftermath Republican-controlled state legislatures, eighteen in all, passed legislation to restrict voting rights and decrease voter access. Arizona was one of those states. Its legislature passed two restrictive laws: one law required election officials to throw out ballots that were cast in the wrong precinct, and the second law barred most people and groups from collecting absentee ballots and dropping them off at polling places. When the inevitable lawsuit appeared, a lower federal court determined that there was clear evidence that these two laws made it harder for persons of color to vote. But when the case reached the Supreme Court, in *Brnovich v. Democratic National Committee*,[9] the majority of justices ruled otherwise.

The 6-to-3 conservative majority determined that the states have a legitimate right to root out voting fraud and that the Voting Rights Act, through Section 2, provided just limited power to overturn state law or practice. Through Justice Samuel Alito, the court reasoned that the Voting Rights Act could be used to strike down measures only when they imposed substantial and disproportionate burdens on minority voters.

"Where a state provides multiple ways to vote, any burden imposed on voters who choose of the available options cannot be evaluated without also taking into account the other means available," wrote Alito. Thus, the Arizona laws, and presumably many of the other restrictive laws winding their way through state legislatures, could not be considered violations of the now watered-down version of the Voting Rights Act.

This did not sit well with the three liberals on the court. In her dissenting opinion, Justice Elena Kagan wrote that the majority had done great harm to the Voting Rights Act, stating that the majority ruling was a devastating blow to the nation's ideals. "Whenever it can, the majority gives a cramped reading to broad language. And then it uses that reading to uphold two election laws from Arizona that discriminate against minority voters. . . . What is tragic is that the court has damaged a statute designed to bring about 'the end of discrimination in voting.' "

President Joe Biden weighed in, stating that the court "has now done severe damage" to the Voting Rights Act. "After all we have been through to deliver the promise of this nation to all Americans, we should be fully enforcing voting rights laws, not weakening them."[10]

In the final section of this book, chapter 12, we'll look further at the efforts to dismantle the Voting Rights Act and the counterattempts to expand and protect voting rights and access.

*Who votes more, men or women? Why is there a gap
between the voting participation of women and men? What
about Gen Xers and Millennials?*

The Center for Women in American Politics at Rutgers
University has noted that since the 1964 presidential election,
women have outnumbered men when it comes to voting.[11]
Since then, women have consistently outperformed men in
terms of both numbers and percentage of voters. In the 2016
presidential election 63.3 percent of women (73.7 million)
voted, whereas 59.3 percent of men (63.8 million) voted. In
2020, women increased their participation rate to 68 percent,
while men increased to 65 percent.

Why do women vote at a higher rate than men? Political
scientists are not clear on any one reason, but several pop up.
Women are more likely to access and manage services such as
healthcare, elder care, and childcare, for which they may look
for government support. Women are also more likely to feel
the effects of poverty than men, and to see the federal government as a source of assistance. Many women have risen up
in opposition to Donald Trump's policies and his treatment of
women, despite his boast on the campaign trail that "nobody
has more respect for women than I do. Nobody." The Supreme
Court nomination of Brett Kavanaugh and the #MeToo movement have only added fuel to the fire, giving many women a
greater impetus to become active in elections and politics.

Women voters have become more Democratic in recent decades, thanks in part to the growing right-leaning
social policies of the Republican Party. Many lawmakers
in the Republican Party used to support the Equal Rights
Amendment, extended childcare services, and part-time
and flexible work for men and women, and it was not so
rigid in its opposition to abortion. That has all changed. The
Democratic Party is more often seen as the "women's party,"
and the Republican Party as the "men's party." In 2016,
Hillary Clinton won the women's vote by 12 points but lost

the men's vote by 12 points—a total spread of 24 points, the largest gender gap ever recorded in presidential elections. In 2012, without a woman on either party's ticket, Barack Obama won the women's vote by 12 points and lost the men's vote by 8 points.

White women typically favor Republicans, but women of color, African Americans, and Hispanics have voted heavily for the Democratic Party in recent elections. Women without a college education voted heavily for Trump in 2016, whereas women with a college education voted more for Democrats.[12] And as we'll see in chapter 6, college-educated women heavily supported Joe Biden in 2020, and the most loyal women were African Americans, who gave him an 87 to 7 percent advantage over Donald Trump.

Young voters may also play an important and growing role in upcoming elections. The Pew Research Center reported that in 2016, Generation Xers (those who were then between the ages of thirty-six and fifty-one) and Millennials (between the ages of eighteen and thirty-five) together accounted for more voters in 2016 than the Silent Generation (ages seventy-one and older) and baby boomers (ages fifty-two to sixty-nine).[13] As older voters die, the Gen X and Millennial vote will become even more important. Millennials typically vote less often than older voters, but their participation rates are increasing. Furthermore, in 2016, Millennials were the group that most strongly favored Democrats over Republicans: 55 percent of Millennials were Democrats or Democratic-leaning independents, while 33 percent were Republicans or Republican-leaning independents. During the 2018 midterm elections, 31 percent of eighteen- to twenty-nine-year-olds voted, 10 points better participation than in the 2014 midterm elections, but not as strong as their participation in the 2016 presidential election, at 51 percent. In 2020, Millennials came out in record numbers and voted heavily for the Democratic Party. Again, the numbers will be looked at in greater detail in chapter 6.

What are the rates of voting for African Americans, Hispanic Americans, and Asian Americans? And what was the racial makeup of those who voted in recent elections?

In a 2020 report, the Pew Research Center observed that "in all fifty states, the share of non-Hispanic White eligible voters declined between 2000 and 2018, with ten states experiencing double-digit drops in the share of White eligible voters."[14] This was especially true in the Southwest, with California, Nevada, and Texas experiencing a significant share of the Hispanic vote; this was true in Florida as well.

Here is the racial makeup of American voters during the 2020 and 2000 presidential elections:

- White, 72.0% in 2020; 80.7% in 2000
- African American, 11.0% in 2020; 11.5% in 2000
- Hispanic, 10.0% in 2020; 5.4% in 2000
- Asian, 3.0% in 2020; 1.8% in 2000[15]

In short, the percentage of White voters is dropping, and Hispanic American and Asian American participation is growing. The US Census Bureau forecasts that Whites will constitute 50 percent of the population in 2050, that Hispanics will go from 13 percent (2000) to 24 percent (2050), that African Americans will go from 13 percent to 15 percent, and that Asians will go from 4 percent to 8 percent.[16] The shrinking percentage of White voters means trouble for the Republican Party if it keeps going down its current path of appealing to and relying heavily on White voters while losing minority supporters.

Before 2020, had there been efforts to diminish voting participation?

Unfortunately, the answer is yes. It is a long-standing democratic norm that people should be encouraged to participate and that the greater the participation, the better it is for democracy. But in reality, there have been repeated efforts to curtail participation, and the burden falls heavily on minority citizens. This is nothing new.

We have had a long and ugly history of racial discrimination and deprivation of the fundamental democratic value, the right to vote. The South, dominated by Democrats during much of the post–Civil War period through the 1960s, suppressed African American voting until the federal government intervened by passing the Voting Rights Act of 1965. The Civil Rights Act, passed the year before, and the Voting Rights Act received key support from moderate Republicans, while Southern Democrats fought vigorously against these federal protections. President Lyndon Johnson is reported to have said, "There goes the South," meaning that White Southern voters would abandon the Democratic Party in droves. He was right. President Richard Nixon, a Republican, exploited what he called the "Southern strategy," wooing White voters away from their traditional home in the Democratic Party, capturing those who supported Alabama governor George Wallace. Nixon courted White southerners with his racially coded pleas for "law and order." African Americans stayed with the Democratic Party and became its main source of political power in the South.

Minorities are increasingly voting for the Democratic Party; the Republican Party is increasingly seen as the "White party." (There is more on the political parties in chapter 3.) Gerrymandering against minorities becomes easier when "Democrat" replaces "African American." The dilution of minority voting is forbidden by the Voting Rights Act, but partisan gerrymandering is not forbidden. As a Republican lawmaker in North Carolina boasted, "I think electing Republicans is better than electing Democrats. So I drew this map to help foster what I think is better for the country."[17] It would be interesting to speculate how much gerrymandering would go on if, say, in North Carolina, the allegiance of African Americans was split evenly between Republicans and Democrats.

Do convicted felons ever get back the right to vote?

About 2.5 percent of all adults are currently disenfranchised because they have been convicted of a felony, according to a 2016 study by the Sentencing Project, a criminal-justice research and advocacy group.[18] Researchers estimate that some 6.1 million adults who are or were incarcerated have lost the right to vote; four decades ago, in 1976, that number was 1.17 million. Disenfranchisement policies are controlled by the individual states, and they vary widely. Some states restore voting rights after prison only (fourteen states); after prison and parole (four states); after prison, parole, and probation (eighteen states); or after prison, parole, probation, and postsentencing (twelve states). In some places, the restoration is automatic; in other places, it must be gained by petition. Just two states, Maine and Vermont, have no restrictions on felony voting; even those serving time in prison can vote. In four states, disenfranchisement is permanent unless voting rights are granted by the governor.

Disenfranchisement has fallen most heavily on African Americans. In four states, more than one in five African American adults have been disenfranchised: Florida (21 percent), Kentucky (26 percent), Tennessee (21 percent), and Virginia (22 percent).

There have been some attempts to restore voting rights to former felons. In Virginia, Democratic governor Terry McAuliffe signed an executive order to restore the voting rights of convicted felons who had served their sentences, a number estimated at 206,000. Republican lawmakers cried foul and sued the governor. The Virginia Supreme Court ruled that McAuliffe could restore voting rights only on a case-by-case basis, not through a sweeping executive order affecting all former felons. McAuliffe then proceeded to restore voting rights, one by one, and by the end of his term of office, he had restored voting rights to some 13,000 ex-felons. His successor, Democrat Ralph Northam, continued the restoration process. Through a November 2018 ballot measure, Florida voters restored voting rights for some 1.5 million ex-felons, but in March 2019 Florida Republicans in the legislature tried to limit the number of ex-felons who could vote, claiming they needed to pay back all court fees and fines. This legislation, signed by Governor Ron DeSantis, put as many impediments as possible in the path of felons seeking to gain full voting rights.

Why do so few voters participate in elections, especially in state and local contests?

There are more than 500,000 local elected officials in the United States, and elections are usually held every two or four years. In many of these elections, however, very few citizens bother to vote.

A recent study at Portland State University, in Oregon, examined 23 million voting records in fifty cities to see who votes and who doesn't.[19] Some of the results are astounding. Voting turnout was less than 15 percent in ten of the thirty largest cities, and the median age of those who voted was fifty-seven. Older voters were fifteen times more likely to vote in these mayoral elections than young people, ages eighteen to thirty-four.

Here are the study's results for the most recent mayoral contests in several cities, showing the percentage of voting participation and the median age of voters.

- Dallas, 6.1%; median age, 62
- Las Vegas, 9.4%; median age, 68
- El Paso, 11.6%; median age, 59
- Miami, 11.9%; median age, 68
- Los Angeles, 18.6%; median age, 59
- Denver, 22.6%; median age, 59

The one bright spot was the city of Portland, where nearly 60 percent of voters participated, and the median age was forty-nine. What are the consequences of such disparities in voting? As one reporter noted, "Elected leaders will represent the interests of retirees, if they know what's good for them. . . . Mayors and Council members will think first to the needs of constituents who turn out to the polls."[20]

The questions still remain, why do so few people vote, and why is the median age so high? Political scientists have studied this issue for years and come to a number of conclusions. For many people, voting isn't worth the time and effort it takes; elections are generally held on Tuesday, a workday for most. For some, the fear of the Covid pandemic and the need for social distancing were factors. Voter registration requirements may hold some back. Others don't keep up with local issues, choose not to or cannot vote in primary elections, are just not interested in politics, or don't trust government or elected officials. Perhaps they feel that the outcome of an election is a foregone conclusion—why bother to vote? Who, then, votes most often? The elderly, the better educated, those who have a strong sense of partisanship or ideology, and those who believe that government can be a force for the good in society.

Compared to other democracies, how does the United States rank in terms of voting participation?

American voting participation is quite low when compared to other industrial democracies. In a 2017 study by the Pew Research Center, the United States was ranked twenty-sixth in voting participation during its last election. Just 55.7 percent of American adults voted in the 2016 presidential election; but in 2020, some 67 percent of voters participated.[21] Here's how Americans compare with voters in several other countries in recent elections:

1. Belgium, 87.2% of all adults voted
2. Sweden, 82.6%
3. Denmark, 80.3%
4. South Korea, 77.9%
5. Australia, 70.9%
   . . .
14. United States, 67.0%

Interestingly, in the United States the percentage of partic-ipation among adults who had registered to vote was much higher (86.8 percent). So the key weakness in the United States appears to be low registration rates. Many American adults are not eligible to participate in elections simply because they have not registered or were somehow hindered from registering. A smaller percentage of American voters, often between 35 percent and 40 percent, participate in midterm elections. But in the 2018 midterm elections, voting participa-tion reached a fifty-year high, with 47 percent of eligible voters casting their ballots.

What would happen if every American adult were required to vote, as in some other countries?

In some countries—such as Belgium, Brazil, Australia, Argentina, Ecuador, and Peru—voting is required, and penalties, usually fines, can be levied on those who fail to par-ticipate. Some argue that voting is a duty of citizenship, like paying taxes, showing up for jury duty, and enrolling your chil-dren in school. But mandatory participation laws sometimes meet voter resistance from people who simply don't like the government telling them what to do. Some will submit blank or incomplete ballots, pay little attention to the candidates and issues involved, and do the bare minimum of thinking and preparation before casting their vote. On the other hand, compulsory voting might force those who otherwise wouldn't vote to think about the candidates and issues and register their preferences. One study in Australia found that after compulsory voting was established, more young voters and minority voters took part, and representation in Parliament of the Labour Party, the more progressive party, increased.[22]

What would mandatory voting be like in the United States? Barack Obama in his last year of office thought it would be a good idea, saying it would be "transformative" if everybody voted: "The people who tend not to vote are young, they're lower income, they're skewed more heavily towards immigrant groups and minority groups," Obama said. "There's a reason why some folks try to keep them away from the polls."[23] It would certainly be a tall order, would probably run into constitutional problems, and would meet tough challenges from those trying to suppress voting rather than expand and encourage it throughout the entire population. And it would go against the grain for many Americans, who would rebel against having a voting requirement imposed upon them.

After the 2000 presidential election exposed problems in local voting systems, Congress passed legislation to make sweeping reforms in the administration of voting procedures. Has that made any difference?

In 2002, Congress passed, and President George W. Bush signed into law, the Help America Vote Act (HAVA). The 2000 presidential contest put a spotlight on state and local election activities, and revealed that there was no uniformity in how states administered voting. We learned that in Florida, where much of the attention was focused, counties had different voting machines—some digital, some fully automated—and that some counties relied on hand-prepared ballots. Ballot integrity became a major issue. Some counties said that yes, their machines and methods might be old-fashioned (paper ballots, for example), but they worked, and besides, it would cost too much money to buy newer voting machines. In addition, there was considerable blowback from the private voting-machine vendors, who balked at providing additional security against hacking attacks.

HAVA was designed to help states improve voting administration and voting integrity. The Election Assistance Commission was created as an independent agency of the federal government, and by 2005, some $3.3 billion had been disbursed to the states to help them purchase new voting machines. HAVA also required that for federal elections all new voters had to provide a driver's license or the last four digits of their Social Security numbers. HAVA helped improve voting systems, but bigger problems became evident. As the *New York Times* reported, in September 2018, the real problem was that election security depended on unregulated private voting-machine vendors: "The mad history of election security in the United States is a history of how misguided politicians and naive election officials allowed an unregulated industry to seize control of America's democratic infrastructure."[24] In 2018, Congress added $380 million in grants under the HAVA Election Security Fund to help with cybersecurity training and audits; still, there is little assurance that hacking and meddling in the most basic act of democracy—citizen voting—has been adequately addressed.[25]

How vulnerable are state and local voting procedures to hacking and cyber threats?

As we learn more about the dangers and reality of Russia's (and perhaps others') attempts to hack into voter computer systems, state election commissions and state legislatures have responded with a wide variety of efforts. A report by the US Senate Intelligence Committee found that most state election systems were outdated. It recommended three things: switch to paper ballots or to electronic voting that leaves a paper trail; check voting results with "risk-limiting audits" (which count a sampling of ballots by hand and check them against the machine results); and better train election personnel about the risks of cybersecurity. One state, Colorado, seems to be doing the best job of protecting its election system against cyber threats, according to the Center for Democracy and Technology, because it has incorporated the recommended safeguards.[26] But many states haven't met the challenge because of bureaucratic (and legislative) inertia, not recognizing the seriousness of the problem, or a lack of funds. Chapters 7 and 12 discuss in more detail the threats of Russian meddling in American presidential and congressional races.

How accurate are voting records?

Alarm bells went off when reports were published that many of the voting records in states were outdated: the names of dead people had not been removed, files hadn't been updated after people had moved out of state or changed their addresses locally, there were typos and misspelled names, and the like. In early 2012, the Pew Center on the States reported that the voter registration system throughout the states desperately needed an upgrade.[27] "These systems," the Pew study reported, "are plagued with errors and inefficiencies that waste taxpayer dollars, undermine voter confidence, and fuel partisan disputes over the integrity of our elections." Pew investigators found the names of 1.8 million deceased persons still on the voting rolls, 2.75 million people who were registered to vote in more than one state, 24 million (one in eight) registrations that were invalid or significantly inaccurate, and at least 51 million adults (one in four) who were not registered at all.

It's clear that the states have their work cut out for them in cleaning up their voting rolls. But this mess is not voter fraud; rather, it is bureaucratic inefficiency and a waste of taxpayers' funds, and it reflects the inability of states to manage large data systems. The National Voter Registration Act of 1993 set the guidelines for purging voters from the voting rolls. States redoubled efforts to purge those who had died, moved, or been double counted. Between 2014 and 2016, the names of some 16 million voters were removed nationwide. But in a wide-ranging report, the Brennan Center for Justice at New York Law School warned that some of those aggressive state purges violated the provisions of the Voter Registration Act, citing the efforts in Florida, New York, North Carolina, and Virginia, in particular. Four other states (Alabama, Arizona, Indiana, and Maine) had written purge policies that had violated the act.[28] For example, purged voters had not been given notice of their removal, nor were they told of the federally required waiting period before their names could be removed. Sometimes, voting purges occurred within ninety days of an election, in violation of federal law. The Brennan Center also reported that a new coterie of conservative activists has been suing state election boards for not being aggressive enough in getting rid of suspect voters.

Can a person be kicked off the voting rolls for failing to vote in previous elections?

In 2018, the US Supreme Court ruled that a state could kick people off the voter rolls if they had not voted in some previous elections and had failed to respond to notices from state election officials. The case before the court came from Ohio, which has probably the most aggressive form of voter purging of all the states. Ohio election officials removed voters after they had failed to respond to a notice; the Supreme Court ruled that Ohio's action did not violate the failure-to-vote clause of the act.[29] Twelve states, generally led by Democrats, filed briefs against Ohio's action; seventeen states, generally led by Republicans, filed briefs in support of Ohio.

The *New York Times*, in an article about the court's decision, cited a 2016 Reuters investigation that found that at least 144,000 persons had been removed from the voting rolls in Cleveland, Cincinnati, and Columbus, Ohio's three largest cities. "Voters have been struck from the rolls in Democratic-leaning neighborhoods at roughly twice the rate as in Republican neighborhoods," the study found. "Neighborhoods that have a high proportion of poor, African-American residents are hit the hardest."[30] In 2016, Trump defeated Clinton in Ohio by over 446,000 votes.

Before the 2020 election, how did mail-in ballots, absentee-ballot voting systems, and early voting work out?

In 2000, Oregon became the first state to institute mail-in ballots for all elections. Other western states quickly followed suit and permitted (even encouraged) mail-in ballots. Three states—Oregon, Washington, and Colorado—began conducting all their elections through mail-in ballots, and twenty-two states permit some form of mail-in voting.[31] Supporters argued that it is cheaper to conduct elections through mail-in ballots, and that the method gives voters time to study the ballot and make more informed choices. Ballots can be long and complicated and filled with difficult choices. For example, on the 2018 Colorado ballot, Denver voters had to vote on candidates for six state offices and one congressional office, thirteen statewide ballot issues, and nine city ballot questions. Opponents point out the loss of the tradition of going to a polling station and interacting with neighbors, and the potential for coercion by family members to vote a certain way.

Twenty-one states provide absentee ballots but require voters to prove they have a valid reason for voting absentee; twenty-seven states and the District of Columbia provide absentee ballots but don't require voters to provide a reason.[32] More and more people have taken advantage of early voting, not waiting to vote in November. One study estimated that in the 2016 presidential election, 50 million votes would be cast before Election Day.[33] This can cause logistical and communication difficulties for candidates who are trying to persuade voters, only to find that many of them have already cast their vote. But campaigns with sophisticated tracking systems can also lock down votes and streamline their get-out-the-vote operations by eliminating calls and pleas to those who have already voted.

The 2020 election was a major test for mail-in voting. Many states instituted mail-in voting for the first time, as states tried to cope with the Covid crisis. There will be more on the 2020 mail-in voting issues in chapters 6 and 7.

In recent years, there have been charges of widespread voter fraud. Are those charges believable?

We have heard a lot of charges of voter fraud, most of which came from conservatives and the 2016 Trump campaign (charges of a "rigged election"), alleging that minorities were voting illegally. But according to research conducted by disinterested, nonpartisan organizations, voter fraud is a myth. The Brennan Center has taken the lead in examining alleged voter fraud and concluded that perhaps 0.0003 to 0.0025 of the votes might—might—be fraudulent. The *Washington Post* in 2014 investigated voter fraud allegations and found thirty-one credible (but not yet proven) cases of voter impersonation out of 1 billion votes studied. Similar findings have come from social scientists at Columbia University and Arizona State. The Brennan Center concluded that an American is more likely to be "struck by lightning than he . . . [is to] impersonate another voter at the polls."[34]

But one of the first things President Trump instituted was a voter fraud commission to unearth alleged voter irregularities. It's not clear what Trump's motives were. But we know this: He bought into (and encouraged) the narrative that there was widespread voter fraud in America. He also bought into the idea that he would have won the popular vote had the supposed 3 million fraudulent votes cast for Hillary Clinton not been counted (in this story, no fraudulent votes were, or would have been, cast for Trump). Again, it was a false accusation. But Trump was eager to prove that he won both the Electoral

College and the popular vote. A commission was established in 2017, with Kris Kobach, the secretary of state in Kansas and a strong supporter of Trump's views, as its vice chair. Vice President Mike Pence was nominally in charge but had little enthusiasm for the project.

The commission—officially, the Presidential Advisory Commission on Election Integrity—immediately ran into resistance from state election commissions, headed by both Republicans and Democrats, when it began asking for detailed information about voters and voter files. Election experts, state election officials, scholars, and civil rights organizations also cried foul. To them, the commission's goal was to make it more difficult for young people and citizens from minority groups to vote. A former head of the Civil Rights Division of the Justice Department, Vanita Gupta, said the commission's "entire purpose was to legitimize voter suppression." Election law scholar Richard L. Hasen said the commission "made rookie, boneheaded mistakes about handling documents used by the commission, again in violation of federal law."[35]

A year later, in January 2018, Trump abruptly disbanded the commission, without its having published any findings. But the president continued to maintain, in a tweet, that there was "substantial voter fraud." The commission was then handed over to the Department of Homeland Security to complete the task, and it has not been heard from since. Meanwhile, one of the few Democratic members of the commission, Maine secretary of state Matthew Dunlap, characterized its work as "the most bizarre thing I have ever been a part of."[36]

But a contentious congressional election in 2018 put the spotlight on another kind of possible voter fraud. The North Carolina State Board of Elections refused to certify the election of Republican Mark Harris over Democrat Dan McCready in the state's Ninth Congressional District. The reason: suspected manipulation of absentee ballots by a consultant tied to Harris's campaign, along with evidence that rigging absentee ballots had occurred during the 2016 campaign as well. In late February 2019, state officials unanimously threw out the results of the November 2018 election and ordered a new contest. Harris, citing health issues, decided not to run again.[37]

All of this, of course, was before President Trump declared massive voting fraud during the 2020 election. Despite overwhelming evidence to the contrary, Trump continued to insist on voter fraud, to refuse to concede to Joe Biden, and to whip up protest and perpetuate falsehoods among his most fervent supporters. This unprecedented assault on the integrity of the electoral system was soon dubbed the "Big Lie," and is covered in much greater detail in chapters 7 and 12.

2

CARVING OUT LEGISLATIVE DISTRICTS

Congressional districts are reapportioned every ten years. In recent years this practice has led to a great deal of criticism of overt partisanship and even charges of racial gerrymandering. What have the courts said about redistricting plans, and is there a better, fairer way to create the boundaries of elective districts?

How do some states gain and some states lose congressional seats following reapportionment?

Every ten years, the US government is required to count all persons—not just citizens—living in the country. This census is mandated in Article I of the Constitution, and the information collected is used to help determine whether a state will gain or lose a seat in the House of Representatives.

The process is called *reapportionment*, and here is how it works. There are 435 seats in the House of Representatives. That number has been fixed for nearly a century (except when two additional seats were temporarily added when Alaska and Hawaii were admitted to the Union in the late 1950s). Every state is guaranteed one seat. In addition, the District of Columbia has one nonvoting representative in Congress. After each state receives one representative, there are 385 seats left for distribution. Through a complex statistical formula, each state is given a rank ordering for the next available seat, based on the state's population.[1]

The average size of a House district has grown greatly since the 1930s. Now, the average size of a congressional district is 761,169; in smaller states, with just one representative, the size of the district depends on the population of the state. Wyoming, the smallest state population-wise, has just 538,000 persons and one seat in the House.

Compared to other democracies, the United States has many more persons represented in the average district:[2]

Country	Population	No. of Districts	Population per District
Finland	5.6 million	200	27,858
Sweden	10.2 million	349	29,233
France	67.8 million	577	117,588
Australia	25.5 million	151	168,652
United States	331.1 million	435	761,169
India	1,326.1 million	543	2,442,161

Following the 2020 census, here is how the state delegations fared.

Six states gained new seats:

Oregon (+1, now 6 seats)
Colorado (+1, now 8)
Texas (+2, now 38)
Florida (+1, now 28)
Montana (+1, now 2)
North Carolina (+1, now 14)

Seven states lost congressional districts:

California (−1, now 52)
New York (−1, now 26)

Pennsylvania (–1, now 17)
Ohio (–1, now 15)
Michigan (–1, now 13)
Illinois (–1, now 17)
West Virginia (–1, now 2)

Minnesota was lucky, obtaining the final district available. It did not lose a seat because it had eighty-nine more people than New York; that amounted to 0.0016 percent of its population. There are six states that have the minimum of one congressional district: Alaska, North Dakota, South Dakota, Vermont, Delaware, and Wyoming. Every state (except West Virginia and Mississippi) gained population since 2010; the reapportionment winners just grew much faster. California, which now represents 11.8 percent of the entire US population, grew during this time, despite all the handwringing about massive emigration. It lost a congressional district because its growth was smaller than other states.

Why has redistricting been such a problem?

Reapportionment refers to the process of deciding how many seats a state will have in the US House of Representatives. *Redistricting* refers to how those congressional seats will be carved up. Redistricting also refers to the way state and local government districts will be shaped. For decades, many legislative and other districts drawn up by the state legislatures were of unequal population size. Typically, rural counties or rural districts were given the same weight as much more populous urban districts. At one time Los Angeles County, for example, had 422 times more people than the smallest county in California, but both counties had just one senator. For much of this time, redistricting was considered a strictly political issue, to be resolved by the legislatures and the people, but not by the courts.

That all changed, however, when the US Supreme Court issued landmark opinions establishing the principle of "one person, one vote." The first case was *Baker v. Carr* (1962), which determined that redistricting was not simply a political matter but an issue that the courts could tackle (a "justiciable issue"). The second case, *Reynolds v. Sims* (1964), gave us the standard of "one man, one vote" (or "one person, one vote").

At the time of *Reynolds*, Alabama had a county-unit system; that is, each county was entitled to one representative. At first glance, this may seem fair, but it meant that urban areas were vastly underrepresented. There was as much as a 41-to-1 population disparity in the most extreme cases. The court ruled that Alabama's scheme went against the Fourteenth Amendment's equal protection clause and required that the state districts be reconfigured so that they were as close as possible in population size. Chief Justice Earl Warren wrote, "Legislators represent people, not trees or acres. Legislators are elected by voters, not farms or cities or economic interests." The Supreme Court extended "one person, one vote" to congressional districts in a separate case, *Wesberry v. Sanders*, in 1964.[3] With the exception of the US Senate, every federal and state legislative district adheres to the principle of one person, one vote, and the state's total population is the measuring device.

In 2016, the Supreme Court unanimously turned back a challenge to the way "one person, one vote" was calculated. In *Evenwel v. Abbott*, plaintiffs Sue Evenwel and Edward Pfenniger argued that children, disenfranchised prisoners or former convicts, the mentally ill, and noncitizens should not be counted in a state's population—only persons eligible to vote should be counted. Their suit was sponsored by the Project for Fair Representation, a conservative group that also was behind the successful *Shelby County v. Holder* Voting Rights Act case. What was their motivation in bringing the suit? As journalist Garrett Epps noted, if only eligible voters were counted, the redrawn political maps would show a "whiter, older, and more conservative" electorate.[4]

What are the requirements for creating legislative districts?

The federal government follows two principles in creating legislative districts. The first is that congressional districts should be as equal in population size as possible. The second principle, which comes from the Voting Rights Act of 1965 and subsequent court interpretations, is that they should not dilute the voting strength of minorities.

Professor Justin Levitt notes that at the state legislative level there are several criteria for determining district configurations: districts must (a) be contiguous—that is, all parts of the district should be physically adjacent (forty-nine states have adopted this rule; twenty-three states have adopted it for congressional districts); (b) follow political boundaries, such as counties and cities, and others (forty-two states follow this rule; nineteen follow it for congressional boundaries); (c) be compact (thirty-seven states follow this rule; eighteen require congressional districts to be as compact as possible); and (d) preserve "communities of interest," such as racial, ethnic, or economic groups (twenty-four states do this; thirteen states require this for congressional districts).[5]

Redistricting is, and always has been, a political process: the party in power in the state legislature does the best it can to protect its lawmakers and to improve its chances in upcoming elections. Redistricting battles often end up in court. In 2015, for example, the state senate and congressional district lines in Florida were ruled unconstitutional. According to Levitt's calculations, courts have recently struck down congressional districting plans in Florida, North Carolina, Pennsylvania, Texas, and Virginia, and the courts drew the lines themselves in twelve states.[6] State legislative plans have been ruled unconstitutional in twelve states, and the courts drew the lines themselves in eight states.

Who makes the decision about redistricting legislative districts?

In most states, the decision on redistricting rests with the state legislature. Sometimes the governor has veto power over the redistricting plan, but usually not. Because legislatures are the final determiners, the party in power has a great advantage in trying to manipulate the districts to its own advantage. However, the maps drawn by legislators can be challenged in federal or state courts.

Thanks to sophisticated databases, we now have much more information on where voters are, how often they vote, and their preferences. Voting maps are so granular and detailed that a legislative committee can easily see, block by block, house by house, where the possible votes are. Critics argue that redistricting thus becomes nothing more than an incumbent protection plan. The districts are gamed to give one party or the other an advantage and to protect members who are up for re-election. And much of this is the result of the increasing use of partisan gerrymandering.

What is partisan "gerrymandering"? How far can it go before it is unconstitutional?

Gerrymandering is the term used for the creation of unusually shaped legislative districts that help one party or group over another. It was named after Elbridge Gerry, governor of Massachusetts, who, in 1812, signed into law a redistricting map that would protect his party's candidates (Republicans) against their opponents (Federalists). The editor of the *Boston Gazette* proclaimed that the new district looked like a salamander. "Salamander! Call it a Gerrymander," he said. A cartoon of the gerrymandered district printed in the newspaper in March 1812 characterized the new legislative district as a "horrid monster."[7] Gerry, a signer of the Declaration of Independence, later became vice president of the United States under James Madison.

Gerrymandering is alive and flourishing in the United States today, as Republicans and Democrats carve up legislative districts to give themselves partisan advantage. In 1990, when North Carolina received an additional district, the state was under the mandate of the Voting Rights Act to create a minority-majority district if possible. The legislature, then controlled by Democrats, came up with a meandering, 160-mile-long district that mostly followed the interstate highway and picked up African American voters in various parts of the state. In a subsequent Supreme Court decision, Justice Sandra Day O'Connor called another attempt by North Carolina's Democrats to create an equally meandering minority-majority district "bizarre" and said that it "bears an uncomfortable resemblance to political apartheid." O'Connor further observed, "It is unsettling how closely the North Carolina plan resembles the most egregious racial gerrymanders of the past."[8]

Republicans at first cried foul but then realized that pushing all those reliably Democratic African American voters into one district would give Republicans a better chance in the rest of the state. For a while, there was an unspoken alliance: African Americans would get their representation in Congress, and Republicans would capitalize on the leftovers.

North Carolina, whose legislature was soon dominated by Republicans, has been the poster child for aggressive gerrymandering and voter suppression, resulting in multiple lawsuits over the decades. As was noted in chapter 1, a federal court ruled in 2016 that North Carolina's massive voter identification law repressed the rights of African American voters with "surgical precision." In 2017, a federal court ruled that it "represents the most extensive unconstitutional racial gerrymander ever encountered by a federal court." The US Supreme Court, in May 2017, struck down the North Carolina redistricting, finding that the Republican legislature had unconstitutionally racially gerrymandered to dilute minority voting. The court found that the packing of African American voters into two districts denied them the equal protection of the law guaranteed under the Fourteenth Amendment. Conservative Justice Clarence Thomas, the court's sole African American, sided with the majority.[9]

In January 2018, a three-judge federal panel again said that the North Carolina redistricting plan was a knowing, intentional, and hugely impactful violation of the US Constitution. Voting-rights expert and law professor Rick Hasen called it "the most brazen and egregious" electoral distortion yet seen in the United States. North Carolina's leaders "admitted the practice, but argued it should be seen as perfectly legal." As University of North Carolina law professor Gene Nichol observed, "Our leaders have given us the largest, most blatant and indefensible political gerrymander in American history. We're unsurprised. They're unashamed."[10] In June 2018, the US Supreme Court sent the case back to the lower courts to determine if the plaintiffs had proper legal standing. But in August 2018, a panel of three federal judges again held the congressional redistricting unconstitutional because it favored Republicans over Democrats.

The Supreme Court has also heard partisan gerrymandering cases from Wisconsin and Maryland. In Wisconsin, the Republican-dominated legislature had drawn up the controversial districts, whereas in Maryland the suspect districts were drawn up by the Democratic-controlled legislature. Rather than make a final judgment, the Supreme Court returned the cases to the lower federal courts. But in June 2018, the court upheld a redistricting plan that was implemented in Texas. Justice Samuel Alito, writing the opinion for the conservative majority, rejected arguments that Texas lawmakers, dominated by Republicans, had deliberately gerrymandered based on race. The decision in effect ended a seven-year battle over redistricting. However, in a forty-six-page dissent, Justice Sonia Sotomayor argued that Black and Hispanic voters would be hurt by this decision: "Those voters must return to the polls in 2018 and 2020 with the knowledge that their ability to exercise meaningfully their right to vote has been burdened by the manipulation of district lines specifically designed to target their communities and minimize their political will."[11]

In 2019, the Supreme Court tackled the basic question: is partisan gerrymandering unconstitutional? A five-to-four majority, under Chief Justice John Roberts, determined that partisan gerrymandering was a "political issue," and thus outside the reach of the Supreme Court. Roberts stated that "federal judges have no license to reallocate political power between the two major political parties, with no plausible grant of authority in the Constitution and no legal standards to limit and direct their decisions." The chief justice conceded that "excessive partisanship in districting leads to results that reasonably seem unjust." Nevertheless, the court should not intervene.

Justice Elena Kagan dissented, accusing the conservative majority of abdicating one of its major responsibilities. She wrote, "The only way to understand the majority's opinion is as follows: In the face of grievous harm to democratic governance and flagrant infringements on individuals' rights—in the face of escalating partisan manipulation whose computability with this nation's values and law no one defends—the majority declines to provide any remedy. For the first time in this nation's history, the majority declares that it can do nothing about an acknowledged constitutional violation because it has searched high and low and cannot find a workable legal standard to apply."

With these decisions in *Rucho v. Common Cause* and *Lamone v. Benisek*, the state legislatures were free to redistrict, with the majority party using all its partisan muscle to gain advantage.

Has there been any attempt to take redistricting and gerrymandering out of the hands of partisan legislators?

Control over the redistricting process varies throughout the states. In thirty-seven states, the legislatures have primary control over their own district lines. In five of those thirty-seven states, advisory commissions have been created to help establish the rules and boundaries. But regardless of the commissions' advice, the final decision rests with the lawmakers. In seven of the thirty-seven states, there are backup commissions that can make redistricting decisions if the state legislature fails to come up with its own plans. In seven other states, there are so-called politician commissions made up of elected officials, which can make the final determination on redistricting.

Do any states have independent bodies that make the decisions on new boundaries? Yes, nine states—Alaska, Arizona, California, Colorado, Hawaii, Michigan, Montana, Utah, and Washington—have independent commissions, whose members are neither elected representatives nor public officials. Five other states—Arkansas, Missouri, New Jersey, Ohio, and Pennsylvania—have political commissions, whose members are public officials. These commissions will be responsible for redrawing legislative district maps.[12]

Why do all states get two senators no matter how big—or small—they are?

There is an immense difference in the population of the most and the least populous states. In 2021, California had an estimated population of 39.61 million. That makes it bigger than Canada (36.2 million) and seventy times bigger than Wyoming, the least populous state, with 581,075 people. Yet California has two US senators, and so does Wyoming.

California (39.61 million people), Texas (29.73 million), Florida (21.94 million), and New York (19.30 million) have two US senators each, as do Vermont (623,251), Alaska (724,357), North Dakota (770,026), and South Dakota (896,581). The four most populous states account for over one-third of America's total population but only 8 percent of the Senate's total representation.

How did this happen? It was a political compromise hammered out by the Founding Fathers in 1787. One of the key questions was how should states be represented in a national legislature. They decided to have a House and a Senate but disagreed on how to apportion the seats. There were two proposals: The Virginia Plan called for apportionment according to population (giving big states, like Virginia, more representatives). The New Jersey Plan called for equal representation in both the House and Senate (rewarding small states, like New Jersey). Roger Sherman, a delegate from Connecticut, came up with the "Connecticut Compromise," which based representation in the House on population and gave each state equal representation in the Senate. The Connecticut plan was adopted, and its representation formula is embedded in the Constitution. At the time of its ratification, in 1789, the voting disparity between the biggest state and the smallest state was 11 to 1 (now, as we have seen, it is 70 to 1).[13]

The American population will be even more concentrated in big states in the future. The Weldon Cooper Center for Public Service at the University of Virginia noted that by 2040, nearly one-half the entire population of the country will live in just eight states—Florida, Georgia, North Carolina, New York, Pennsylvania, Illinois, Texas, and California. If the next eight most populous states are included, sixteen states will have around 70 percent of the population.[14] That distribution will be accurately reflected in the House of Representatives, but it will only exacerbate the big state–little state divide in the Senate, giving small-population states an enormous advantage.

Have there been attempts to change this system? Yes, but there is no way the small states will ever vote against their self-interest and let the bigger states have more representation. We won't be seeing Wyoming with 2 senators and California with 140 senators!

3

POLITICAL PARTIES AND ELECTIONS

At one time, the political party was the central vehicle for organizing and executing political campaigns. But by the 1960s, the party had been replaced by professional consultants, and campaigns became more candidate focused than party focused. The policies and allegiances of the two major parties have changed dramatically, and there has been a steady increase in the percentage of voters who consider themselves independents. Increasingly, the two major parties are further and further apart ideologically, reflecting the growing chasm in the so-called culture war. The Democratic Party, under the leadership of Joe Biden, strains to contain moderates and a growing support for its progressive wing. The Republican Party has been captured by Donald Trump and his fervent supporters, becoming more combative and aggressive, banking its future on rural White voters.

When did the two major political parties play an important role in elections and campaigns?

For much of American history, the political parties have been instrumental in picking candidates, giving them money, supplying volunteers to work on their campaigns, and helping to get out the vote. Candidates most often came up through the party ranks—they were known, trusted, and selected by party leaders.

During the 1960s and increasingly throughout the latter part of the twentieth century, the political party became less important for candidates running for office. Candidates, mostly at the statewide and federal levels, began turning to political consultants to assist them in their campaigns. As we will see in chapter 9, the political parties have, to a large degree, been supplanted by campaign managers, pollsters, media consultants, direct-mail specialists, and other operatives. Well-funded private interests, like the conservative network created by wealthy brothers Charles and David Koch, have also taken over many of the traditional functions of political parties.

Nevertheless, the political parties still can be important during campaigns. The most recent example is the role the Republican Party played in helping Donald Trump win the presidency. At a crucial time in the latter stages of the 2016 campaign, the Republican National Committee came through with targeted messages and get-out-the-vote resources that helped the rag-tag Trump campaign focus on the key battleground state of Wisconsin. Republicans learned a big lesson from the Obama campaigns and began investing heavily in digital, data, and field operations to assist their 2016 candidate. Then in 2020, the Republican National Committee did the same: used its extensive campaign resources to significantly boost the number of voters coming out for Trump in key battleground states.

The South was once very Democratic but now is largely Republican. What happened?

Following the Civil War and Reconstruction, southern Democratic politicians regained control of their state governments. To many defeated southerners "Republican Party" and "Lincoln" were despised words. For nearly the next hundred years, the Democratic Party dominated southern politics. As political scientists Earl Black and Merle Black noted about the Republican Party, "In 1950, there were no Republican senators from the South and only two Republican representatives out of 105 in the southern House delegation. Nowhere else in the United States had a major political party been so feeble for so many decades."[1]

That began to change with the 1960s civil rights movement, when the northern, progressive wing of the Democratic Party was challenged by southern politicians, including Alabama governor George Wallace. Eventually, Republican Richard Nixon employed his "Southern strategy"—a scheme to draw conservative White southerners away from the Democratic Party. It worked. Throughout the South, Democratic governors, senators, and House members were defeated and replaced by conservative Republicans. A number of Democrats switched parties to become Republicans. Today, the South, along with the Great Plains states, is the most reliably Republican region of the country. In the 2018 session of Congress there were 40 Democrats and 112 Republicans from southern states. The Democratic Party can rely on African American voters in these states, but the White southern Democrat is almost a dying breed. Furthermore, African Americans have been "packed" into a few districts via redistricting. In the Deep South, there are no White Democratic members of the House of Representatives, and in South Carolina, Republican Tim Scott became the first African American elected senator in the South since Reconstruction. The southern state legislatures, long dominated by Democratic politicians, are all controlled by Republicans.

Why is the White South so Republican? Or to rephrase, why is the White South so conservative? Much has to do with opposition to northern liberal Democratic policies; the most important—as it traditionally has been in the South—is race and the aspirations of African American citizens. It is also a reflection of southern conservative cultural and religious values clashing with those of the progressive northern Democratic wing of the party.

What's the difference between Republicans and Democrats?

In the 1970s and 1980s, there was a significant ideological overlap between Republicans and Democrats. There were Republican moderates, even liberals, many from the Northeast and big cities. There were also good ol' boy White, conservative southern Democrats, pleased to help fellow Democrats Jimmy Carter from Georgia and Bill Clinton from Arkansas get elected president. At one time, African Americans were loyal to the Republican Party, the party of Lincoln. For a long time, California was a Republican stronghold, as was New England.

But so much has changed. The parties and the ideologies (conservative, liberal, libertarian, progressive) have become polarized. In October 2017, the Pew Research Center did a major study of the ideology and attitudes of voters who consider themselves either Republicans or Democrats. Pew observed that the "Republican coalition is deeply divided on such major issues as immigration, America's role in the world and the fundamental fairness of the U.S. economic system."

Pew divided Republicans (and independents with Republican leanings) into four categories:

- *Core Conservatives* make up about 13 percent of the public and 31 percent of all Republicans and are the most politically engaged. This group is largely White and male and financially comfortable; 33 percent hold a college degree or more, and they believe strongly in smaller government and lower corporate tax rates.
- *Country First Conservatives* make up a smaller group (6 percent of the entire public) and are less educated (16 percent have a college degree or more) and older than other Republicans. They are more critical of immigrants and

deeply suspicious of US foreign involvement. Republicans in both categories strongly support Donald Trump.

- *Market Skeptic Republicans*, representing 12 percent of the public, diverge from the traditional Republican Party over its support of big business and lower taxes, and advocate increasing corporate taxes. They believe the economy is skewed toward powerful interests.
- *New Era Enterprisers*, representing 11 percent of the electorate, are fundamentally optimistic about the future and basically pro-business.

On the Democratic side:

- *Solid Liberals*, 16 percent of the public, are the most politically engaged of all Democrats. They are highly educated and well off, and express liberal views on virtually every social and political issue.
- *Opportunity Democrats*, 12 percent of the public, are less affluent and less educated than solid liberals but agree with them on most issues, and they emphasize hard work and individual effort as the key to getting ahead.
- *Disaffected Democrats*, 14 percent of the public, are mostly minority voters and are financially distressed. They agree strongly with the Democratic Party but are cynical about government and its responses to their needs.
- *Devout and Diverse*, 9 percent of the public, are majority-minority voters, even less affluent than Disaffected Democrats and the least politically active.

Another category, called "Bystanders," about 8 percent of the public, simply do not participate; they are mostly young and majority-minority.[2]

Both parties are in flux, but especially the Republican Party, which increasingly is in lockstep with Donald Trump. His core supporters are squarely behind him, but his policies and actions send shivers up the spines of many traditional

Republicans and create heartburn for his opponents. The 2018 midterm elections were tied directly to how people felt about Trump. "In no previous election has the linkage between opinions of the president and how the people are likely to vote been as strong as this time," observed congressional expert Gary Jacobson.[3]

Shouldn't the Republican Party really be called the "Trump Party"?

In 2015, Donald Trump, with no prior political experience, battled against established Republican Party candidates— former governors (John Kasich of Ohio, Jeb Bush of Florida, Mike Huckabee of Arkansas, and Chris Christie of New Jersey) and former or present US senators (Ted Cruz of Texas, Marco Rubio of Florida, Rick Santorum of Pennsylvania, and Rand Paul of Kentucky). He beat them all. A "Never Trump" movement fizzled, and soon President Trump became the voice of the Republican Party. Despite the turmoil and friction, his fellow Republicans publicly kept quiet, refusing to criticize or complain. Their reluctance to speak out was anchored in one stark reality: Trump's base loved him, and any perceived threat against the president could mean a swift rebuke. Republicans in Congress stood by him through two impeachments, the January 6 insurrection, and perpetuating the "Big Lie" (more on the Big Lie in chapter 7).

Even in defeat and out of office, Trump has a profound hold on his core constituencies. In an October 2021 survey, the Pew Research Center found that two-thirds of Republicans and independents who lean Republican want Trump to continue playing a leading role in the Republican Party for years to come; and this approval percentage has increased since the January 6 insurrection. A full 44 percent wanted him to run for the presidency in 2024, and nearly two-thirds (63 percent) stated that the Republican Party should not accept elected officials who criticize Trump.[4]

Trump has put on hold other possible presidential candidates, like Chris Christie, Marco Rubio, Ted Cruz, Josh Hawley, Tom Cotton, and who knows who else. It would be nearly impossible for any other potential candidates to challenge Trump in a future election. In the meantime, the more Trump is on the political stump, the better for Democrats, who see him as the best motivator to get Democrats out to vote.

Why are we so polarized today?

There has definitely been a growing ideological and political gap between Republicans and Democrats. In a 2014 study of the American electorate, the Pew Research Center found that 92 percent of Republicans are to the right of the typical Democrat, and 94 percent of Democrats are to the left of the typical Republican. That's a big change from twenty years earlier, when 64 percent of Republicans were to the right of the average Democrat and 70 percent of Democrats were to the left of the average Republican.[5]

The percentage of individuals who consider themselves "mixed" has shrunk over the decades, from 49 percent in 1994 to 39 percent in 2004, while those who consider themselves "consistently liberal" or "consistently conservative" have grown in each camp. In 2014, 79 percent of Democrats had unfavorable views of Republicans, and 82 percent of Republicans felt the same way about Democrats. And the hostility and suspicion has grown since then, and was particularly evident during the Trump years.

What's going on?

Polarization. A definition by political scientist James Q. Wilson is appropriate here. For Wilson, *polarization* is

an intense commitment to a candidate, a culture, or an ideology that sets people in one group definitively apart from people in another, rival group. Such a condition is revealed when a candidate for public office is regarded by a competitor and his supporters not simply as wrong but as corrupt or wicked; when one way of thinking about the world is assumed to be morally superior to any other way; when one set of political beliefs is entirely correct and a rival set wholly wrong.[6]

David Blankenhorn, president of the Institute for American Values, argues that polarization can cause major harm: (a) it produces policy gridlock so that nothing can get done in Congress; (b) it degrades public discussion; (c) it is likely to contribute to inequality; (d) it separates us; (e) it undermines trust; (f) it thwarts empathy; (g) it weakens the intellect; and (h) it lowers the caliber of citizenship.[7]

It's not just an ideological or cultural divide; it is also a geographic and community divide. Bill Bishop summed it up in *The Big Sort: Why the Clustering of Like-Minded America Is Tearing Us Apart*.[8] Bishop argued that Americans more than ever now live in communities of like-minded individuals, read like-minded blogs and social media sources, watch television news shows that fit their preconceived notions, and generally live in a cocoon of their own making. We might ask ourselves: If you can't stand Trump, when's the last time you watched Fox News? If Trump's your hero, when did you last flip on news analysis on NPR or CNN? When's the last time you talked with that stranger whose bumper sticker makes you gag in disgust?

Today, there seems to be little hope for reconciliation or even understanding. One recent poll, conducted by the University of Virginia Center for Politics, showed the extraordinary levels of mistrust between Democrats and Republicans. On the perceptions of voters in the other party, the question was "I believe that Americans who strongly support [the opposing party] are a clear and present danger to the American way of life." Among Biden voters, 75 percent somewhat agreed/

43 percent strongly agreed; among Trump voters, 78 percent somewhat agreed/47 percent strongly agreed.

How about seceding from the Union? The poll asked this question: "the situation is such in America that I would favor [Blue/Red] states from seceding from the union to form their own separate countries." Among Biden voters, 41 percent somewhat agreed/18 percent strongly agreed; among Trump voters, 52 percent somewhat agreed/25 percent strongly agreed.[9] (Secede from the Union? Can you imagine posing this question to voters in 1950, 1980, or even 2000?)

How much disagreement is there within the political parties?

Not only is there tension between the parties; there's plenty of internal dissension, both on the Republican and Democratic sides. Since the early 1990s and even before, conservative Republicans have denounced fellow Republicans who are moderates or even progressives on social policy and other issues. The pejorative term they used to disparage these more progressive party members is RINO (Republican in name only), meaning "they call themselves Republicans, but they sure don't act like it"—that is, they aren't conservative enough. It showed the ideological tensions within the party as it moves steadily away from moderation to a full-tilt Trump conservatism. Now, it's not simply RINO or not; it's Trump supporter or Trump traitor. Several dyed-in-the-wool Republicans, like Georgia governor Brian Kemp, Arizona governor Doug Ducey, and especially congresswoman Liz Cheney, have been targets of Trump's abuse because they have failed to support him at every move.

Democrats like to consider themselves a "big tent" party—that is, one that accommodates many different ideological stripes. Yet Democrats have experienced internal ideological tension in recent years. We've seen ardent supporters of the progressive policies of Bernie Sanders fighting against more mainstream Democratic visions embodied by Hillary Clinton. Since Trump's election, we've seen an upsurge of liberal and progressive candidates, several of whom won their seats by beating established Democratic office holders. There is now a vocal and active Progressive Caucus, composed of about ninety-five members in the House and five in the Senate. The internal ideological fight among Democrats is so critical because of the party's razor-thin margins in both the House and the Senate.

Who has more followers, Democrats, Republicans, or independents?

Since 2004, the Gallup Poll has been asking citizens which political party they identify with, and if the answer is neither, whether they consider themselves independents. In decades past, more voters allied with one of the two major political parties and fewer considered themselves independents. But that has changed. In Gallup Poll results from August 2018, 27 percent identified as Republicans, 29 percent as Democrats, and 43 percent as independents. For years now, we have seen similar results: most people saying they are independents, with Democrats sometimes taking the top party spot and Republicans in third place.[10] "Independent" isn't a political party; it refers to a voter who is unaffiliated with either major political party. Colorado recognizes this reality, and it officially refers to independents as "Unaffiliated" voters. But when it comes time for elections, these self-described independents typically will choose one of the two major party candidates over an independent or a third-party candidate. During the 2016 presidential election, 94.3 percent of the independent vote went to either Clinton or Trump; in 2020, the percentage of independent voting for Trump or Biden was even higher.

In the wake of the January 6 insurrection and the first several months of the Biden presidency, Gallup found that more Americans identified as Democrats than Republicans. An average of 49 percent of adults stated they identify with the Democratic Party or are independents leaning in that direction, while 40 percent identify with the Republican Party. This was the largest gap between parties since 2012.[11]

How did we get the labels "red states" and "blue states"?

The terms originated with network television coverage, when the networks were trying to project how a state would vote during the presidential elections. In 1976, NBC had a high-tech (for the time) map of all the states, and since most people had color television, the network experimented by calling Republican states "blue states" and Democratic states "red states." The other networks got involved over the years, but there was no consistency between which states were deemed blue and which were red. That was resolved during the 2000 presidential election, when Republican states were designated red and Democratic states blue. But these blanket statewide designations often hide voting realities. Should, for example, a state that goes 51 percent to 49 percent Republican be called a red state? News organizations started calling such states "purple" states and, better yet, started looking not at the entire state but at counties and cities as distinct political entities, giving us a more granular look and more accurate understanding of where Democratic and Republican voting strength lies.

What are the Democrats' "Blue Wall" and the Republicans' "Red Wall"?

The "Blue Wall" consists of states that are reliably Democratic during presidential elections. Starting with California (fifty-five electors—before the 2020 reapportionment), New York (twenty-nine), and Illinois (twenty), Democratic presidential candidates could count on the eighteen states (and the District of Columbia) to all vote Democratic and produce 242 electoral votes. Winning those states would mean Hillary Clinton in

2016 would need just thirty-eight additional electoral votes to win. But in politics, walls sometimes crumble, and they did so that year. Wisconsin, Pennsylvania, and Michigan went for Trump by very small margins. Those states were regained by Democrats when Biden won in 2020, again by the smallest of margins, in each of those states. Republicans likewise have their "Red Wall." But just as Trump shattered the Blue Wall in 2016, Bill Clinton shattered the Red Wall in 1992, capturing 118 of the Red Wall's 191 electoral votes.[12]

Here are the most reliable Democratic states (with 2021 electoral votes):

California (54)—Democratic since 1992
New York (28)—Democratic since 1988
Illinois (19)—Democratic since 1992
Pennsylvania (19)—Democratic since 1992, except 2016
Michigan (15)—Democratic since 1992, except 2016
Massachusetts (11)—Democratic since 1960, except for
     Reagan in 1980 and 1984
Maryland (10)—Democratic since 1992
Minnesota (10)—Democratic since 1960, except for Nixon
     in 1972
New Jersey (14)—Democratic since 1992
Washington (12)—Democratic since 1992
Oregon (8)—Democratic since 1988
Connecticut (7)—Democratic since 1997
Delaware (3)—Democratic since 1992
Hawaii (4)—Democratic since 1960, except for Nixon in
     1972 and Reagan in 1984
Rhode Island (4)—Democratic since 1960, except for Nixon
     in 1972 and Reagan in 1984
Maine (4)—Democratic since 1992, except for 1 elector each
     for Trump in 2016 and 2020
Vermont (3)—Democratic since 1992
Wisconsin (10)—Democratic since 1988, except for Trump
     in 2016

District of Columbia (3)—Democratic since 1964 (when its citizens could first vote for president)
Total: 238 (down from 242 in 2010)

Before Democrats get too confident in their Blue Wall, in several of these states Democrats barely eked out victories.
What are the most reliable Republican states?

Alabama (9)—Republican since 1964, except for Wallace in 1968 and Carter in 1976
Alaska (3)—Republican since 1968
Arizona (11)—Republican since 1964, except for Clinton in 1996 and Biden in 2020
Georgia (16)—Republican since 1984, except for Clinton in 1992 and Biden in 2020
Idaho (3)—Republican since 1968
Indiana (11)—Republican since 1968, except for Obama in 2008
Kansas (6)—Republican since 1968
Mississippi (6)—Republican since 1964, except for Wallace in 1968 and Carter in 1976
Montana (4)—Republican since 1968, except for Clinton in 1992
Nebraska (5)—Republican since 1968, except for 1 elector for Obama in 2008 and 1 elector for Biden in 2020
North Carolina (16)—Republican since 1968, except for Carter in 1992 and Obama in 2008
North Dakota (3)—Republican since 1968
Oklahoma (7)—Republican since 1968
South Carolina (9)—Republican since 1964, except for Carter in 1976
South Dakota (3)—Republican since 1968
Texas (40)—Republican since 1980
West Virginia (4)—Republican since 1996
Wyoming (3)—Republican since 1968
Total: 158 (up from 155 in 2010)

Like Democrats, Republicans should not get overconfi-
dent: Arizona and Georgia went Democratic in 2020, and, with
a surging Hispanic population, Texas may become more of a
battleground than a safe Red Wall state.

What are the states moving from one party to another?

Historically, the biggest change came when the solid conservative Democratic South shifted to the solid conservative
Republican South. In 1950, every southern state went for the
Democratic candidate. Then came the civil rights revolution,
the increasing power of northern Democrats, and, starting
in the late 1960s, the abandonment of the Democratic Party
among a majority of White voters in the South. The New
England states used to be a bastion of Republican support;
by 2020, they were solidly in the Democratic fold (except for
one district in Maine). California was consistently Republican
for many years, but now Democrats have a strong grip on
the state.

There have been other moves. Once a bastion of Democratic
votes, West Virginia (four electoral votes) has gone Republican
every election since 2000; Iowa (six) and Ohio (seventeen),
once tossups, are now consistently Republican. Once reliably
Republican, Virginia (thirteen) moved into the Democratic
column in 2008, 2012, 2016, and 2020. Colorado (ten), a long-
time Republican state, went Democratic in 2008, 2012, 2016, and
2020. For the first time since 1996, Arizona voted Democratic;
for the first time since 1992, Georgia voted Democratic.

Wasn't the Tea Party a separate political party?

When forced to compete with a third-party movement,
Democrats and Republicans will often co-opt the issues and
channel the anger of outsiders, adopting as their own some of
its positions and policies. Or the third-party movement will try
to infiltrate a mainstream party. That's what happened with

the Tea Party. The Tea Party movement sprang up in January 2009, almost immediately after Barack Obama was sworn into office. Supporters of the Tea Party movement were upset over Obama's election, over the perceived bailout of Wall Street financiers, and with regular Republicans for not standing up to the progressive drift in policymaking. The Tea Party never became a separate party organization, but it attached itself to the Republican Party, hoping to make it even more conservative than it had been. It was a smart choice to affiliate with a major party rather than strike out separately. That way, Tea Party members could exert their influence from the inside instead of being shunted aside. In the House of Representatives, a core of some thirty or so members were elected as Tea Party advocates and used their influence on the other members of the Republican delegation.

Do other political parties get involved in presidential elections?

When former president Teddy Roosevelt challenged President William Howard Taft in 1912, the Republican Party stayed with the more conservative Taft, and Roosevelt bolted to form a new party, the Progressive Party, or more commonly called the "Bull Moose" Party. Like many splinter parties, the Progressive Party was based on the personality of one individual, Roosevelt, and after Teddy lost, it soon died off. The same thing happened with other third-party challengers, such as Strom Thurmond and the Dixiecrat Party in 1948, George Wallace and the American Independent Party in the 1960s and 1970s, Ross Perot and his Reform Party in the 1990s, and Ralph Nader and the Green Party in 2000.

In 1992, Ross Perot received 19 percent of the popular vote (but no electoral votes). Perot was the second most successful third-party candidate, after Roosevelt, in gathering the popular vote. But in recent years, third parties have rarely received more than 2 or 3 percent of the popular vote. They can, nevertheless, be important factors in presidential elections.

In the past seven presidential elections, only three times did the winner receive more than 50 percent of the popular vote; and in two elections, the winner received fewer popular votes than his opponent. Considering how close some of our recent presidential elections have been, we can see the impact that even a small third-party vote can have on the outcome. For example, with the 2000 election in the balance and the vote so close in Florida, we saw some startling statistics: There were ten presidential candidates on the Florida ballot—George W. Bush and Al Gore, but also Pat Buchanan, Ralph Nader, and a bunch of other candidates. The difference between Bush (2,912,790 votes) and Gore (2,912,253) was just 537 votes; the tenth (and last) vote-getter, James Harris of the Socialist Workers Party, received 562 votes—more than the difference between Bush and Gore. Ralph Nader, whose supporters probably would have been more inclined to vote for Gore than Bush, received 97,488 votes. Many Democrats complained that Nader was the spoiler in that election, and that without him on the ballot, Gore would have won.

Third-party candidates played a critical role during the 2016 election. In three crucial states—Wisconsin, Michigan, and Pennsylvania—Jill Stein, the Green Party candidate, came in fourth, behind Trump, Clinton, and Gary Johnson, the Libertarian Party candidate. Yet in each state Stein had more votes than the difference between Clinton and Trump. Stein, whose political beliefs and message were much closer to Clinton's than Trump's, was the big spoiler in 2016. Third-party candidates gathered far fewer votes in 2020, but the Libertarian Party candidate was able to gain more votes than the difference between Trump and Biden in three crucial states (more on this in chapter 6).

Have the political parties surrendered their role in campaigning to wealthy donors and super PACs?

We'll learn more about political action committees (PACs) and super PACs in chapter 8. For now, let's look at some of their activities that go beyond just giving money to candidates. A few

PACs perform some of the campaign functions that we traditionally would expect from political parties. PAC management expert Steven E. Billet looked at some of the biggest connected PACs and characterized them as "Monster PACs."[13] He found seventy-two PACs that had spent at least $2 million each during the 2005–2006 election cycle. The largest was EMILY's List, an organization that promotes pro-choice Democratic women candidates. It spent $34 million. But these PACs weren't just spending money. They were doing things that the political parties would normally do: they recruited candidates, trained campaign operatives, mobilized support, and ran campaigns parallel to those run by the candidates themselves.

But Monster PACs wouldn't be the last word in PAC activities. They were only the precursors to the new and far richer super PACs created after the Supreme Court gave them the green light in 2010. As we'll see in chapter 8, super PACs and mega-donors, especially the Koch brothers, have taken it upon themselves to recruit, train, and promote candidates, not waiting for the political parties to do so. Political parties, especially the Republicans, may not have surrendered their traditional roles in campaigning and elections, but now they have company.

What's happened to the Democratic Party and the Republican Party?

It would seem that 2008 was a high point for Democrats. The country was just finishing up the bumpy years of the Bush presidency with a collapse of the economy, and now a Democrat, Barack Obama, had been elected to clean up the mess. Democrats added to their majority in the House (257 versus 178 Republicans) and gained control of the Senate (56 plus 2 independents versus 42 Republicans). But during the Obama years, more than 1,100 Democratic lawmakers— national and state—were voted out of office. Democrats lost 11 Senate seats, 60 House seats, 14 governorships, and over 900 state legislative seats.[14] Seizing upon citizen anger and frustration, the Republican Party had poured money and resources into capturing seats held by vulnerable Democrats. Over the years (and decades), the Republican Party has been able to outhustle and outmaneuver the Democratic Party. The loss of state legislative seats was most important because Republicans gained control over the process of reconfiguring both state and national legislative districts, and could gerrymander those seats to further increase their grip on state government.

But though the Republicans gained strength in Congress and at the state level, they were not able to capture the prize of the presidency in 2012. When it came time to nominate a presidential candidate in 2016, there was a crowded Republican field of seventeen candidates, many of whom were former governors or US senators. They were completely overwhelmed by the personality and appeal of Donald Trump, the outsider who took delight in trashing and belittling his conventional Republican opponents. A feeble and, in the end, ineffective "Never Trump" movement within the party was the last gasp against the brash outsider.

Since Trump's election, the Democratic Party has been energized by new recruits infuriated by Trump policies and behavior, engaged in leadership squabbles, and been able to regain the majority in the House of Representatives, gaining forty congressional seats in the 2018 midterm elections. While Biden won the presidency, Congress has become almost a dead heat. Democrats lost House seats in 2020 and now have the slimmest of majorities; Republicans lost Senate seats, deadlocking that body 50-50, with Vice President Kamala Harris providing the tie-breaking difference. The polarization in the country is reflected in Congress: often no Republicans will vote for a Democratically sponsored measure.

The Republican Party remains clearly in the grips of Donald Trump, fueled by the Big Lie and Trump's resentments and bruised ego. The few critics in the party who are not afraid to speak up against Trump's policies and abuses of the norms of the presidency are vastly outnumbered by Republican colleagues who support Trump or simply acquiesce.

4

STATEWIDE, LOCAL, AND CONGRESSIONAL ELECTIONS

The vast majority of campaigns and elections in the United States occur at the state and local levels and include everything from gubernatorial and big-city mayoral contests to local ordinances to electing dogcatchers. Although much of our attention is on presidential contests, it is here at the local and state levels that much public policy and many decisions that affect everyday life are made.

How many state and local elections are there?

There are nearly 520,000 elected officials throughout the country! The United States is truly the land of elections. There are

- 50 state governments, each with a state legislature, statewide elected officials, judgeships, and state boards. Altogether, a total of 18,749 seats must be filled through elections.
- 19,429 municipal governments
- 16,504 township or town governments
- 3,034 county governments
- 13,506 school districts
- 35,052 special districts

In all, there are 87,575 elective bodies at the state and local levels, with 519,146 positions to be filled.[1]

What are the rules and regulations controlling campaign financing at the state and local levels?

Campaign finance matters, because money can have a big influence on who is elected and what laws and policies are made. The individual states make their own rules and regulations on campaign financing, and those rules vary widely. This is how states decided who pays for campaigns and how.

Corporate funds to candidates:

21 states prohibit giving any corporate money to candidates;
8 states allow unlimited corporate money; and
21 states limit corporate contributions, from $1,000 to $50,000.

Labor union funds to candidates:

18 states prohibit union contributions to candidates;
8 states allow unlimited union money to candidates; and
24 states limit union contributions, from $1,000 to $50,000.

Individuals giving money to candidates:

10 states prohibit individuals from giving more than $1,000 to a candidate; and
12 states allow unlimited individual contributions to candidates.

In every state, funds donated to candidates must be disclosed, though the minimum amounts that must be reported vary from $200 to $50 or less. Only South Carolina doesn't require disclosure of donations to political parties or to political action committees.[2]

How do local candidates get out the message and let voters know about themselves?

During election seasons, we are inundated with television commercials by candidates for governor, big-city mayor, US Senate, or the presidency. But most local candidates, say, for a school board, city council, or county commissioner, cannot afford television ads. They find that the most effective way to communicate with voters is through individual meetings, yard signs, direct mail, newspaper and radio advertisements, and, increasingly, Internet advertising and social media. Even in our digital age, direct mail is probably the most effective and widely used means of communicating with voters. Direct mail is a lot less expensive than the typical midsized media market television ad, and it can target messages directly to individuals. The US Postal Service acts as surrogate for the campaign, delivering mail far and wide to addresses throughout the district—in gated communities, hard-to-reach rural areas, and high-rise apartment buildings and condominiums. And because of advances in microtargeting, a direct-mail piece sent to the thirty-year-old divorced woman in apartment 1103 can be tailored to her interests, while the seventy-five-year-old retired union man in apartment 1108 will get a very different message. Television advertising in big cities is expensive; often, 95 percent of the viewers in the audience it reaches aren't in the same district as the candidate; and it sends just a single message that must fit all. These are three strikes against television for most local candidates.

Are more women running for political office than in previous years?

"Just imagine if Congress was 51 percent women," New York senator Kirsten Gillibrand wondered in an October 2016 speech. "Do you think we'd be fighting for access to birth control?"[3] For many years the question has been asked: Why aren't there more female candidates running for elected office? Historically, the United States has been woefully behind other countries in numbers of female legislators. The International Parliamentary Union ranked countries in 2018 according to the percentage of women in their lower houses and in their upper bodies or senate.[4] Rwanda ranked first with women legislators making up 61.3 percent of its lower house and 38.5 percent of its senate. Next were Cuba, Bolivia, Grenada, Namibia, Nicaragua, Costa Rica, Iceland, Sweden, Mexico, and South Africa. All these countries had at least 40 percent female representation in their lower houses. The United States came in 102nd.

Why don't more women run for political office? Political scientists Jennifer L. Lawless and Richard L. Fox examined this fundamental question in their 2005 study, *It Takes a Candidate: Why Women Don't Run for Office.*[5] It was not a question of structural impediments to running, they argued, but rather a question of ambition. And their conclusion, after looking at the responses from more than 3,800 successful men and women who could be considered "eligible candidates," was that men were more politically ambitious than women. There was, they wrote, a "dramatic gender gap" in the attitudes toward running for office.

But circumstances have changed dramatically. Since the election of Donald Trump in 2016, the historic Women's March on the day following the inauguration, the emergence of the #MeToo movement, and the Kavanaugh Supreme Court hearings, there has been a groundswell of interest in women running for office. EMILY's List, the powerhouse organization that helps fund pro-choice Democratic women, noted that some 34,000 women contacted the organization after the 2016 election seeking information about running for office.[6] For 2018, some 257 women—Democrats and Republicans—ran for seats in the House and Senate, a record number. By contrast, 131 women ran for Congress in 1998, and 48 ran in 1978. Forty women, another record, ran for governor in 2018.[7]

In the 2021 US House of Representatives, there were 143 women (29.8 percent), a record number—104 Democrats and

39 Republicans. In the 2019 Senate, there were 24 women (24 percent), also a record number—16 Democrats and 8 Republicans. Women hold both Senate seats in four states (Minnesota, New Hampshire, Nevada, and Washington). In 2021, at the state and local levels, according to the data compiled by the Center for American Women and Politics at Rutgers University,[8] are

- 2,290 total women state legislators (31% of all 7,383 state legislators).
- 1,511 (66.0%) of these women are Democrats; 758 (33.1%) are Republicans.
- 606 (26.5%) of women legislators are persons of color.
- Since 1971, the number of women serving in state legislatures has grown by five times.
- Nevada (60%), Oregon (45.6%), and Colorado (45.0%) lead the way in having women serve in state legislatures. West Virginia (11.9%), Mississippi (15.5%), and Alabama (16.4%) are at the bottom of the list.
- 9 women serve as governors (18%).

Does it cost a lot for local candidates to run for office?

Much of the cost of running for local office depends on where the district is, how competitive the district is, the internal political circumstances, the cost of placing ads in media markets, and how much attention the campaigns receive from outside interest groups.

In many areas of the country, it doesn't cost much to run for small-town mayor, local state legislator, school board, or a variety of other offices. If one party is heavily favored, there may not be much incentive for its or the opposing party's candidate to spend a lot of money on a foregone conclusion. There are often no opponents, and the incumbent wins by default. Many of the offices are noncontroversial and don't offer any financial incentives for outside parties, and, frankly, it is fortunate that there are candidates who want to serve. In hundreds of thousands of other local contests candidates spend very little money, often out of their own pockets or from close friends and associates.

Here are campaign expenditures for some state legislative races held in 2016, showing the winning candidate, the total amount spent, and, in parentheses, the average donation:[9]

- Alabama House: Danny Crawford (R), $150,846 ($824.29)
- Kansas House: Monica Murnan (D), $38,346 ($262.64)
- Oklahoma House: Josh West (R), $74,284 ($313.07)
- New Hampshire Senate: Martha Hennessey (D), $39,770 ($290.29)
- Washington House: Shelley Kloba (D), $182,012 ($407.18)
- Wisconsin House: David Steffen (R), $66,537 ($139.19)

On the other end of the local political spectrum, however, enormous amounts of money are spent.

In some of the most expensive campaigns no candidates at all were running for public office. While most of us were concentrating on the presidential elections in 2008 and 2012, several heated and expensive battles were being waged on ballot issues, and hundreds of millions of dollars were at stake. In 2012, the campaigns for two California ballot issues cost nearly $150 million each. The first, Proposition 30, was approved: it called for a sales and income tax increase, along with a temporary tax on high-income earners. The second, Proposition 32, was defeated; this so-called Paycheck Protection initiative would have banned corporate and labor-union contributions to state and local candidates, among other things.

There were several expensive California ballot issues in 2008 as well. One, which involved four separate propositions, asked voters whether certain Native American tribes could open casinos and get a piece of the state's lucrative gambling business. The tribes spent heavily, and the organizations opposing the tribes also spent heavily. The four ballot initiatives were all approved. Native American tribes were permitted to build their own facilities, and altogether some $172 million was spent trying to convince voters.

Another $106 million was spent on California Proposition 8, which would have added an amendment to the state constitution restricting a marriage to a union between a man and a woman. The issue galvanized conservative religious groups. The Catholic Diocese of San Francisco reached out to the Mormon Church to gets its support. As the *New York Times* described it, "The Mormons were the last major religious group to join the campaign, and the final spice in an unusual stew that included Catholics, evangelical Christians, conservative black and Latino pastors, and myriad smaller ethnic groups with strong religious ties."[10] Individual Mormons poured a considerable amount of money into the campaign and did the organizational footwork, and the measure passed. But in the end, a federal district court ruled the amendment unconstitutional and the Supreme Court refused to reconsider the decision.

Altogether, voters in thirty states approved ballot issues defining marriage as solely a union between a man and a woman. Those were all struck down in 2015, when the Supreme Court ruled in *Obergefell v. Hodges*[11] that same-sex marriages were protected by the due process and equal protection clauses of the Fourteenth Amendment.

There have been some very expensive mayoral races as well. The biggest spender was billionaire Michael R. Bloomberg, who opened his very fat wallet in three very expensive New York City mayoral contests. In 2001, Bloomberg spent $74 million in his successful campaign for mayor; in 2005, he spent $85 million on his re-election campaign; and then he spent $102 million in his third campaign, in 2009. Altogether, Bloomberg spent more than $261 million and was successful in each election. Then, Bloomberg decided to run for the presidential nomination in 2020; he spent at least $1 billion but was able to gain only the four delegate votes from Guam. Any student of finance would tell us that this was a horrible return on investment.

Meg Whitman, former CEO of eBay and, later, Hewlett-Packard, spent $176 million ($144 million of her own money) running for governor of California in 2010. She lost to Jerry Brown, who had been California's governor before. Brown, with widespread name recognition, spent a "mere" $40 million (and nothing out of his own pocket) to win.[12] The Illinois governor's race in 2018 saw two new big spenders battle it out: incumbent governor Bruce Rauner spent $61 million of his own money but lost to billionaire Jay Pritzker, of the Hyatt House fortune, who spent $171 million of his own money. Altogether, $255 million was spent in that bitter election.[13]

We are also seeing record amounts of campaign money being spent in mayoral contests throughout the country, including in St. Petersburg, Florida ($2.6 million in 2017); Everett, Washington ($400,000 in 2017); Boston, Massachusetts ($6 million in 2014); Richmond, Virginia ($2.2 million in 2016); and San Antonio, Texas ($4.38 million in 2015).

Do states have public financing laws and, if so, what offices do they apply to?

Several states have public-financing provisions, which enable candidates to receive taxpayer money for elections. A report by the National Conference of State Legislatures showed that fourteen states currently have some form of public financing.[14] Usually, the financing is for elections for governor and lieutenant governor (twelve states), state legislative office (five states), and judicial office (two states). States cannot require candidates or political parties to use public funds; they can opt out of public financing and rely on private money. In this era of readily available private money, it is tempting to forego public financing.

That's what happened in Arizona. A candidate running for a statewide office in Arizona must raise $5 each from two hundred people to qualify for public financing. In 2014, Arizona offered $1.1 million in public money for its gubernatorial election. But incumbent governor Doug Ducey declined public financing and took in more than $2.4 million. (At the presidential level, recent candidates also have declined public funding; see chapter 5.)

How can an average citizen help a candidate or a cause at the local level?

Few people participate in voting. Fewer still give money or actively assist in campaigns. The most important thing is for voters to feel they have a stake in the contest, that their voice will make a difference, and that they should spend some time volunteering and giving their support. Giving money is often the easiest thing to do, and now with online donations, it is as simple as clicking a button. The best-run local elections depend on old-fashioned shoe leather: neighbors and friends knocking on doors, handing out leaflets, grabbing a telephone and calling people, giving individuals a ride to the polling station, and a variety of other efforts. These activities all require time and effort, and few campaigns can succeed without dedicated volunteer help.

How can you help? It may be as simple as finding out who is running, calling the campaign office, or volunteering through a service organization or club. Up and down the election spectrum, campaigns are becoming more professionalized, using consultants, automated telephone calls and polls, canned messages, and social media splashes. Still needed, and most appreciated by campaigns, are actual volunteers, willing to call others and to put in hours of work to get out the message and get fellow voters to the polls. When we leave it to the professionals or to others, the democratic process is diminished, and in the end, we get less than we deserve.

Electing judges has become more and more like electing regular political candidates. Is there any danger to this?

There are several ways for judges to be selected. One method is through partisan elections, in which judges (and their party affiliations) are listed on the same ballot as other candidates. Eight states choose their supreme court judges through partisan elections; nine states hold partisan elections for appellate court judges, and twenty states use partisan elections when selecting their trial judges. Another method is to hold nonpartisan judicial elections in which the political party of the candidate is not listed on the ballot. Thirty-four states use the merit (or Missouri) plan, which gives the governor the power to appoint judges from a list presented by a judicial commission. When it comes time for re-election, judges in these states are reviewed by the judicial commission or voters are asked for a yes-or-no vote to keep the judges (often with the commission's recommendation attached).

Partisan judicial elections most often appear in the South, nonpartisan elections are more likely in the Northwest states, gubernatorial appointments occur mostly in the Northeast, and the merit plan mostly is found in the Midwest.[15]

We've seen the ugly partisan maneuverings during the Kavanaugh Supreme Court hearings, and we've seen how nasty national and local elections can be. Do we really want our state judges, who are chosen directly by the people, to endure this kind of mudslinging and character assassination? Imagine that a judge with a sterling and noncontroversial record makes a difficult but very unpopular decision, upholding the basic principles of the Constitution. But when she comes up for re-election, her opponent runs attack ads against her that shout out that she's "soft on crime." Her integrity is impeached, and her reputation is smeared. Here are two examples of this: In Ohio, appeals judge Bill O'Neill reversed a rape conviction. Later came an attack ad sponsored by the Ohio Republican Party, "When Crime Occurs," which included the tag line "When crime occurs, victims deserve justice. But as a judge, Bill O'Neill expressed sympathy for rapists." Before University of Michigan law school dean Bridget McCormack ran for a judgeship in Michigan, she had served as a volunteer co-counsel for a Guantanamo detainee. In the week before the election came a series of attack ads, sponsored by the conservative Judicial Crisis Network, based in Washington, DC. The ads ran 416 times on television, with this tag line: "My son is a hero and fought to protect us. Bridget McCormack volunteered to free a terrorist. How could you?" Despite the barrage of negative ads, both O'Neill and McCormack fought back and won their elections.[16]

Following the 2011–2012 election cycle, the National Institute on Money in State Politics observed that "many of these judicial races seemed alarmingly indistinguishable from ordinary political campaigns—featuring everything from super PACs and mudslinging to millions of dollars of candidate fundraising and independent spending."[17]

This is what routinely happens in elections for Congress or the statehouse. Do we want this to be the fate of our elected judges—slammed for upholding the Constitution but making unpopular decisions?

Congressional incumbents hardly ever lose when they are up for re-election. Why is that so?

It is one of the great ironies of American politics. Citizens have a very unfavorable view of Congress (around 15 percent approval in recent polls), but individual lawmakers have at least a 90 percent certainty of re-election in the House and an 85 percent to 90 percent chance in the Senate. In 2016, 98 percent of incumbents were re-elected in the House, and 93 percent were re-elected in the Senate. Overall, since World War II, the re-election rate has been 93 percent in the House and 80 percent in the Senate.[18] There are no term limits for members of Congress, so it is possible that a savvy and politically astute lawmaker can stay in Washington for decades.

The sad thing is, only about one in three Americans can name their members of Congress. Those who can name their representatives tend to be much more positive about that individual (and tend to vote more regularly). As journalist Chris Cillizza has noted, it is easier to hate an institution (Congress) than to hate the individual member, particularly if he or she is our representative.[19]

So what advantages might a sitting member of Congress have in getting re-elected? Political scientists have come up with several possible reasons: incumbents usually have a big advantage in name identification; they can usually raise far more money than potential opponents, especially from political action committees; they have visibility (and staff to help them project visibility throughout their term); they have the perks of office, such as a full-time staff to help constituents with problems.

Thanks to gerrymandering, many congressional districts are considered "safe," meaning that the incumbent can usually expect to win by gathering 60 percent of the vote. The nonpartisan Campaign Finance Institute found that in the 2012 elections, some 256 incumbents were re-elected with over 60 percent of the vote. On average, they spent $1.3 million, whereas their opponents could only muster an average of $154,000. In 2012, the average Senate seat cost its winner over $10 million. In recent congressional battles, the cost of running for office has skyrocketed, with some congressional contests costing over $20 million and Senate races costing more than $100 million. There is more on the cost of running for office in chapter 8.

The most vulnerable time for a member of Congress is the first time up for re-election. And historically, a new president finds that support for his party drops off during the midterm elections. For example, in 1994, two years after Bill Clinton was elected president, Republicans gained a whopping fifty-four seats and regained control of the House for the first time in forty years. (But in the 2002 midterms after George W. Bush was elected president, Republicans picked up eight seats in the House and two in the Senate—a very unusual circumstance.) In 2010, two years after Barack Obama was elected president, Republicans gained sixty-three seats in the House and six in the Senate. Obama was correct when he remarked that Democrats had taken a "shellacking." In 2018, Democrats regained the majority in the House by picking up forty seats. But in the Senate, Republicans were able to pick up two seats and increase their majority.

5

PRESIDENTIAL ELECTIONS

Presidential elections are the crown jewel of American electoral democracy, but there are some very important issues looming. Is the Electoral College the most reliable way to measure a presidential election, or should we be looking at other systems? The primary and preprimary phases are long, expensive, and arduous. There are several ways our system could be made better. Will we ever create a better system?

Can anyone run for president, or is that just an old American myth?

In one sense, it's true that anyone can run for president. There are just three requirements: a candidate must be native born, a US resident for fourteen years, and at least thirty-five years old. So, although millions of immigrants cannot run for president, many millions more people are eligible. In recent presidential elections hundreds of people have filled out the paperwork, paid the filing fee, and appeared on scattered ballots throughout the states. But their chances of winning are virtually zero. It's no surprise that nearly every person who vies for the nomination of our two major parties is an elected official or a former elected official. In recent years, perhaps the closest to that "anyone" myth was Barack Obama, with his meteoric trajectory from lowly state senator in Illinois to president four years later. Occasionally, a deep-pocketed entrepreneur will try—for example, Carly Fiorina in 2016, Ross Perot in 1992 and 1996, and Steve Forbes in 1996 and 2000. Business executive Wendell Willkie became the Republican nominee in 1940, and, of course, billionaire entrepreneur and television celebrity Donald Trump broke all the barriers, having no prior government service, military service, or experience in elective office.

In 2020, the Democratic primaries were chock full of candidates (twenty-eight in all), ranging from long-serving, experienced lawmakers and governors to newcomers without any government experience. Veteran elected officials included Joe Biden, vice president for eight years and US senator for thirty-six years before that, and Bernie Sanders, in Congress since 1991. Several had been governors (Steve Bullock of Montana, Jay Inslee of Washington, John Hickenlooper of Colorado). Two were billionaires (Tom Steyer and Michael Bloomberg, who was also former mayor of New York City). Entrepreneurs Steyer and Andrew Yang and best-selling spiritual author Marianne Williamson had no elected office experience. The hopefuls ranged in age from seventy-eight (Sanders) to thirty-eight (Pete Buttigieg).

In future presidential contests, other wealthy entrepreneurs or celebrities without a lick of governmental experience may be tempted to run. But for an average person without any previous statewide elective experience, name recognition, and money, it's next to impossible to succeed.

Why do presidential elections last so long?

During the fall of 2015, about the time the nationwide Canadian elections were concluding, a local Vancouver radio station was fielding calls from voters who were disgusted with how long the elections had dragged on. People were incensed: the Canadian elections were ten weeks long! Such an outrage! But Canada's election calendar was typical. In many parliamentary systems, the elections last no more than a couple of months, or the party in power might call for a "snap" election. This happened in Canada in 2021, when Prime Minister Justin Trudeau called for a "snap" election; thirty-six days later, the election took place.

American presidential elections go on for a ridiculous amount of time. Our presidential elections aren't ten weeks long, or even ten months long. They can go easily for nearly two years. President Trump, on the day he was inaugurated in January 2017, filed papers for his re-election campaign in 2020, and by September 2018, he had accumulated over $100 million for his re-election campaign. Trump may or may not run for election in 2024. In the meantime, other Republican hopefuls are hesitant to make any moves, for fear of undercutting or offending the former president.

We could say that the official starting point of the presidential election is the first time that voters make a decision about the candidates, which is the Iowa caucus, usually held in January or February of the presidential election year. But most candidates start planning for a run at least a year before that, and those preparations culminate in an announcement speech. Political scientists call the year before the first caucuses and primaries the "invisible primaries." This is the time when candidates for their parties' nomination are flying around to key primary and caucus states, raising money, trying to win over local and state political leaders and get favorable press coverage from news outlets, participating in debates with other possible candidates, and overall, trying to show that they are solid prospects. No votes have been taken, but candidates are trying to show that they've got what it takes.

Why do we have so many primaries and caucuses?

We can go back to the reforms of the Democratic Party in 1972 to find the explosion of state primaries and caucuses. Before then, there were maybe ten to sixteen primaries across the country. Then Democrats, tired of losing presidential contests,

decided the best cure for losing was to be, well, more democratic: let the people decide, instead of the state party leaders.
The Democratic Party encouraged party members in individual
states to hold primaries and caucuses. Soon the Republicans
climbed on board, and we now have primaries and caucuses
for both parties in virtually every state and territory.

In most presidential years, the two major parties quickly
weed out second- and third-tier candidates. So the nominee
is already pretty much decided by the time of the primaries
and caucuses held after March. But in recent years, that has
changed. In 2008, Hillary Clinton and Barack Obama went
through nearly the entire calendar year of primaries and
caucuses before Obama was declared the nominee. And in
2016, when a record number of Republicans fought for the
nomination, Donald Trump didn't become the nominee until
well into May, after Ted Cruz and John Kasich finally gave
up. Incumbent presidents running for a second term usually
don't have to worry about candidates from their own party
running against them (and if they do, they're probably in a
lot of trouble). Lengthy primaries help keep a candidate in the
news, but they also can drain away precious money and result
in nasty internal fights (Hillary Clinton and Bernie Sanders in
2016 come to mind). In 2020, Donald Trump had no Republican
opponent, but the Democrats seemed to be in for a lengthy primary season until Joe Biden won the crucial South Carolina
primary. Then soon it was all over, and Biden captured the
nomination.

What's the difference between a caucus and a primary?

Whether a state political party employs caucuses or primaries,
the purpose is the same: to choose delegates to the party's national convention. Technically, when voters went to the polls
to choose, say, Kamala Harris, to use an example from the 2020
Democratic primaries, they were choosing delegates who were
pledged to vote for Harris in the first round of voting at the
Democratic National Convention.

When several candidates from the same party are running, the political parties can hold primary elections to determine which one will receive delegate votes. In some states, the vote is winner-take-all: the top vote-getter receives all the delegates for that state's party at the nominating convention. In other states, the vote is apportioned out to the candidates. For example, if a state Democratic Party has ten delegates, and Candidate A receives 60 percent of the vote, and Candidate B gets 40 percent, then six delegates will be pledged to Candidate A in the first round, and four delegates will be pledged to Candidate B.

Most state primaries are closed: only Republicans can vote in their state's primary, and only Democrats in theirs. After all, the argument goes, if you want to vote for a Republican candidate, you'd better be a Republican. A small number of states allow anyone to vote in any primary; that is, a Republican can vote in a Democratic primary, and vice versa, but not both. This gives a vote to independent (or Unaffiliated) individuals or those who don't want to commit to a political party to vote.

Caucuses are different animals. Typically, only registered party members can participate, and they must gather together and vote their preferences. It's a much more intimate process than simply going to the polls and casting a vote. The best-known set of caucuses are those in Iowa, and they go through a series of votes over a period of weeks. But what counts the most, of course, is the initial caucus, at the lowest level. Here's how it works: Let's say five Democrats are running for president. The Democrats in each Iowa caucus precinct will get together, in a church basement or a community hall; at this meeting, fifty or maybe a hundred voters might turn out. In 2016, there were about 1,100 Democratic caucus meetings in Iowa, at which 11,065 precinct delegates were chosen. Advocates for each candidate will give short speeches, and then the caucus-goers will go off to vote, often retiring to a different corner of the room and trying to persuade those supporting marginal candidates (those who got less than 15 percent of the vote in the first go-round) to join them. The whole process has been described as something like a junior-high-school dance.[1] News will get out quickly in the media about which candidate has received what percentage of votes; this, after all, is the first concrete evidence of how voters have decided. Weeks after the precinct caucuses, there will be county conventions, where the precinct delegates will be winnowed down to a smaller number, and then district conventions, and, finally, about three months after the initial caucus, the state convention, where the delegates will be pared down to the forty-four delegates to which Iowa Democrats are entitled.

Republicans go through a similar process, but there are fewer caucuses, fewer delegates chosen, and it's all done in secret, not out in the open. Caucuses bring out the truly committed voters, not the casual voter who may have decided to show up on Election Day, or the nonparty voter.

Why does Iowa go first?

For a long time, New Hampshire held the first presidential primaries.[2] The state received a lot of attention for this, and the local economy got a boost, as presidential candidates trudged through the snow with the media traipsing behind them. New Hampshire has had a primary since the 1920s, but people started taking notice in 1968, when Eugene McCarthy nearly defeated President Lyndon Johnson in the New Hampshire Democratic primary. After the Democratic Party's reforms of 1972, primaries became far more popular, and the New Hampshire primary became even more so. New Hampshire, a state very unrepresentative of the rest of the nation (small, Whiter, and more rural), even passed a law saying that it would always hold the first primary, no matter what other states wanted to do.

But then came Iowa. Democrats in Iowa pitched the idea this way: Let us go first, and we won't hold a primary, only caucuses. And because the caucus process is so time-consuming, we'll have to start earlier. Nothing for New Hampshire to worry about. New Hampshire acceded, and Iowa became the first state where citizens cast votes. But really, who cared whether it was a caucus or a primary? Iowa became the place where the action was. The first time a presidential candidate would face voters in Iowa was in 1972. Jimmy Carter, the former governor of Georgia, understood the importance of Iowa. As he prepared for the 1976 presidential nomination, he practically lived in the state, showing up at coffee klatches, in church basements, and at individual homes to press his case. He barely won, but the next morning he was in New York doing the network television shows, which were suddenly proclaiming him the front runner among the Democrats. Iowa was now the big news, not New Hampshire.

Iowa Democrats bungled the 2020 caucus, delaying key results as the nation looked on. This was the latest in a series of difficulties with Iowa, and Democratic Party leaders seriously considered moving to have another state as the first nomination event—a state more diverse than Iowa (83 percent White), and thus more reflective of Democratic constituencies. Joe Biden (who did miserably each of the three times he ran in Iowa), former Democratic National Committee chairman Tom Perez, and other party leaders were considering moving on. Nevada (46 percent White) and South Carolina (62 percent White) were being considered. New Hampshire, traditionally the first primary in the nation, has a population that is 87 percent White, making it quite unrepresentative of the current Democratic Party.[3]

How do you become a party delegate? What's a "superdelegate"?

Party delegates choose the party's presidential candidate. The honor of becoming a delegate usually goes to the dyed-in-the-wool party faithful, the leaders of the party, those who have worked long and hard to help candidates, as well as individuals who have given money to the party. Typically, the

Democrats have more delegates than the Republicans. In 2016, for example, Democrats had 4,763 delegates. Most of them (4,056) were pledged delegates—that is, they were chosen in their respective states and pledged to vote for whoever won, whether it was Clinton or Sanders. In addition, there were 714 superdelegates, who were not bound by the votes in individual states. Superdelegates—who are members of Congress or high-ranking state party officials—are free to vote for whomever they wish. And in 2016, they overwhelmingly voted for Hillary Clinton. Superdelegates—who accounted for 15 percent of all delegates—played a much more important, and controversial, role for Democrats than Republicans. Many in the Bernie Sanders camp complained that the superdelegates overloaded Clinton with support, and that they did not represent the actual intent of the voters.

By contrast, the Republican Party in 2016 had 2,472 delegates, and about 95 percent of them were bound (that is, compelled to vote during the first round of voting at the convention for the candidate who had won their state); the remaining 5 percent were under no obligation to vote for any one candidate.

During its 2018 summer convention, the Democratic National Committee decided to cut way back on the influence of superdelegates for the 2020 presidential elections. The decision was applauded by Bernie Sanders and his followers but bemoaned by some party leaders who feared that the role of party regulars would forever be diminished. At the 2020 Democratic virtual convention, there were 775 "automatic delegates" or superdelegates.

What is the Electoral College and how does it work?

Our system of electing the president is antiquated and often confusing. About 159 million Americans cast their votes during the 2020 presidential election; but they don't directly vote for the president. When we go to the polls on Election Day, or when we sign our absentee or mail-in ballots, we are technically voting for the electors who are pledged to our candidate; we are not voting directly for the candidate. In many states, the official presidential ballot specifies, usually in smaller print, that voters are choosing electors who are pledged to the actual candidates. The Ohio ballot, for example, noted, "A vote for any candidates for President and Vice President shall be a vote for the electors of those candidates whose names have been certified to the Secretary of State." These electors, along with those from all the other states and the District of Columbia, make up the Electoral College.

Altogether, there are 538 electors, and they are divided among the states and the District of Columbia according to the number of members of Congress and senators the states have. Note that 3.2 million American citizens (more than live in Utah and twenty other states) have no representation in the Electoral College: they live in Puerto Rico. Table 5.1 shows the number of Electoral College votes allocated to each state, following the 2020 reapportionment.

Looking at the 2020 presidential election as an example, Tennessee had nine members of Congress and two senators, giving it a total of eleven electors. New York had twenty-seven members of Congress and two senators, giving it a total of twenty-nine electors. In Tennessee and New York, and throughout the states, both the Democratic and Republican parties selected a full slate of electors pledged to support Biden or Trump. When Trump won Tennessee, he received all eleven of its Republican electors; when Biden won New York, he received all twenty-nine of its Democratic electors.

The electors for each state and the District of Columbia meet in their state capitals six weeks after Election Day to cast their votes for president. (Six weeks were needed in 1789 to get everyone in the same place, because you just couldn't hop on an airplane or travel the interstate back then.)

Once the electors have completed their work, the results are sent to Washington, DC, and opened in the House of Representatives on the first day of the new Congress. Congress

Table 5.1 Electoral College Votes of the States

54	California (losing 1 from 2010)
40	Texas (gaining 2)
30	Florida (gaining 1)
28	New York (losing 1)
19	Illinois (losing 1), Pennsylvania (losing 1)
17	Ohio (losing 1)
15	Michigan (losing 1)
16	Georgia, North Carolina (gaining 1)
14	New Jersey
13	Virginia
12	Washington
11	Arizona, Indiana, Massachusetts, Tennessee
10	Maryland, Minnesota, Missouri, Wisconsin, Colorado (gaining 1)
9	Alabama, South Carolina
8	Kentucky, Louisiana, Oregon (gaining 1)
7	Connecticut, Oklahoma
6	Arkansas, Iowa, Kansas, Mississippi, Nevada, Utah
5	Nebraska, New Mexico
4	Hawaii, Idaho, Maine, New Hampshire, Rhode Island, Montana (gaining 1), West Virginia (losing 1)
3	Alaska, Delaware, District of Columbia, North Dakota, South Dakota, Vermont, Wyoming

then certifies the results, and the new president and vice president are sworn into office at noon on January 20.

Of course, we usually know who the next president will be around eleven o'clock on election night, and everything else becomes a mere ceremonial footnote. We might see a short news item in mid-December saying that the Electoral College has met and the official vote has been cast, but by then it's just a ho-hum bit of news. It is ho-hum, however, only if everything works right and there are no disputes about ballots and election procedures. And it certainly wasn't ho-hum in 2020, either on election night or throughout the transition period, and certainly not on January 6, 2021, when the electoral votes were to be certified by Congress (more on this in chapter 7).

Why did the Founding Fathers decide that we needed the Electoral College to determine presidential elections?

The US Constitution does not mention the "Electoral College" (for that matter, there is no mention of political parties in the Constitution either). However, both Article II (the executive branch) and the Twelfth Amendment (which clarifies that the president and vice president will run as a team) mention "electors." The Twelfth Amendment, ratified in 1804, spells out how the electoral system works and acknowledges the role that newly formed political parties play. In fact, the Twelfth Amendment spells out the Electoral College and the selection of the president, more so than the original Constitution. The Electoral College mechanisms and presidential selection process were written into federal law in 1845.

One central argument for having the elector system was that at the beginning of the nation's history, individuals in the new far-flung country had little understanding of the candidates and issues, hence the need for a well-informed gentry (all men, of course) who could be electors and make reasoned decisions about who should be president. The idea of a nationwide vote, and no electors, was floated at the Constitutional Convention by Pennsylvania's James Wilson, but Virginia's James Madison and other southerners quickly scotched it in favor of an electoral system that favored the South.

One of the controversial sections in the Constitution is what's known as "the three-fifths clause," the stipulation that slaves would be counted as three-fifths of a person for the purpose of apportioning congressional seats and electoral votes. This gave the slave states a decided advantage in the Electoral College. In 1803, a Massachusetts congressman calculated that the three-fifths clause added thirteen members of Congress to the southern states and eighteen electors for the next presidential contest.

Yale University constitutional law professor Akhil Reed Amar has argued that, though it has been little discussed, the fundamental rationale for keeping the Electoral College system during its earlier days was not a struggle between big states and small states, but the struggle between the North and the South, especially over slavery.[4] Without the additional electoral votes Virginia gained from the three-fifths clause, Thomas Jefferson would not have defeated incumbent president John Adams (from Massachusetts) in 1801, for example. As Amar observed, Thomas Jefferson "metaphorically rode into the executive mansion on the backs of slaves."

The Electoral College became a part of our presidential election system, and until the Civil War, the southern states had more electors than their numbers would justify, thanks to the three-fifths clause.

But over the course of American history, the Electoral College system has worked without controversy, except for the five times in history when the winner of the popular vote did not become president. In 1824, Andrew Jackson had more popular votes but not enough electoral votes to win in a four-way race, and the House chose John Q. Adams instead. In a contentious election in 1876, Republican Rutherford B. Hayes was chosen by a specially appointed election commission, though Democrat Samuel J. Tilden had more popular votes. In 1888, incumbent president Grover Cleveland had more popular votes than his opponent, Republican Benjamin Harrison, but lost in the Electoral College. In 2000, Democrat Al Gore had more popular votes but lost to Republican George W. Bush when the Supreme Court halted the recount of the Florida votes. Then, of course, in 2016, Trump handily won the electoral vote while losing the popular vote to Hillary Clinton. In the following chapter, we see how a 7 million vote advantage for Biden could have meant defeat if just a small fraction of those votes, in the right states, had gone to Trump.

Who are the electors, and how do you get to be one?

Here's a question to ask at your next dinner party: can anyone name one or two electors who cast votes for your state during the last presidential election? You'll probably get a blank stare. I know I can't name any of the nine electors from my state of Colorado. Each state political party chooses its own slate of electors, and they are usually party bigwigs, state or local party officials, big-time donors, and others who are deeply involved in their political party. So, if you want to become a presidential elector, you'd better be tight with one of the political parties.

What if "faithless" electors refuse to vote for the winner of the popular ballot?

A "faithless" elector is one of those rare electors who decides not to follow the popular election returns or the wishes of the party and votes for someone else. That happened a record seven times in 2016. One Democratic elector in Hawaii voted for Bernie Sanders instead of Hillary Clinton. Three Washington state Democratic electors cast their votes for former secretary of state Colin Powell, a Republican, while a fourth Democratic elector cast a vote for Native American activist Faith Spotted Eagle. Instead of supporting Donald Trump, one Republican elector from Texas voted for former congressman Ron Paul; another Texas Republican voted for Ohio governor John Kasich.

The votes against their parties' candidates were unusual, but they did not affect the election results. How can an elector, who is supposed to be a true party faithful, do this? Isn't it illegal? There is no federal law or anything in the Constitution that binds the electors to the will of the voters. By 2016, twenty-six states and the District of Columbia had laws that required electors to follow the election results. The curious thing, however, is that Hawaii has such a binding law, but there is no penalty for breaking it, and the faithless Democratic elector could not be punished. Two Colorado Democratic electors wanted to break their pledge to vote for Hillary Clinton but backed her after being threatened with criminal charges.

By 2018, thirty-two states had enacted some kind of "faithless electors" laws, but only fifteen states penalized or canceled the vote of the faithless electors. Then in July 2020, the Supreme Court unanimously upheld state laws that penalized electors who refused to support the presidential candidate they were pledged to support.

As noted above, during the 2016 election, voters in Washington state chose Hillary Clinton. But three Clinton electors defied the popular vote and voted instead for Colin Powell. These faithless electors were hoping that other electors around the country would also defy the popular vote and somehow deny Donald Trump the presidency. That ploy didn't work. The faithless electors in Washington state were fined $1,000 each for breaking their pledges to support Clinton.

Writing for a unanimous court in *Chiafalo v. Washington*, Justice Elena Kagan stated that Electoral College delegates have "no ground for reversing the vote of millions of its citizens." That "accords with the Constitution—as well as with the trust of the Nation that here, We the People rule."[5]

In the 2020 presidential election, there were no "faithless" electors, but, as seen below, one of the schemes cooked up by Trump supporters was to come up with alternative lists of electors, hoping to negate Biden's victory.

What if the president-elect dies before the Electoral College meets?

What happens if the presidential winner dies, say, of a heart attack, before the Electoral College meets in December? Does the winning vice presidential running mate then become the new president-elect? Or does the winning political party meet in an emergency session and possibly choose someone else (such as the runner-up nominee at the party's national convention)? That's never happened, but we can see how volatile the situation could become. Many commentators argue that it is the right (and duty) of the winning political party to choose a replacement (and for political reasons, it may not be the vice presidential running mate). Then the electors would vote the substitute into office. But we can imagine all kinds of crazy infighting: suppose the vice presidential winner is not chosen, and there's a big fight internally among the Electoral College members. Considering that this scenario is entirely unprecedented, election law expert Thomas H. Neale has predicted that there would be "confusion, controversy, and a breakdown of party discipline among the members of the Electoral College might also arise."[6] Or the public at large would be angered, rightly claiming that voters had no voice in choosing the substitute president. Such a scenario could greatly strain our already fragile election system.

What happens if no candidate receives 270 votes when the Electoral College tallies the votes?

This has happened once, in 1824, when John Q. Adams won the presidency (but not the popular vote) after a four-way race. Adams didn't have a majority in the Electoral College but was elected through a vote in the House of Representatives. Could this happen again? Indeed, it could, if there is a tight race between a Republican and Democrat and a third-party candidate who is able to win a modest number of electoral votes. Here's how it might play out: Candidate A gets 265 electoral votes, Candidate B gets 264 votes, and the third-party Candidate C gets 11 votes. When no candidate receives a majority (270 votes) in the Electoral College, then the House of Representatives must make the decision. As a practical matter, everyone will know immediately that a 270 majority hasn't been raised. But officially, the results of the Electoral College cannot be revealed until they are opened by the vice president in a special session of Congress in early January.

Here's where it gets trickier. The members of the newly elected House vote by state for the new president, and each state (no matter how big or small) gets one vote. So, the candidate who gets a majority of states, twenty-six, will win the presidency. What happens when a state congressional delegation is evenly divided, say, it has four Democrats and four Republicans? Will these lawmakers play hardball and only vote for their party candidate? Will they refuse to vote for the opposing party's presidential candidate who won their state? What happens if lawmakers in six or seven states with evenly divided delegations refuse to compromise, and no presidential candidate receives the required twenty-six state votes? And to throw a further monkey wrench, what happens if there are competing electoral results in a state—Republicans and Democrats both claiming victory in a razor-thin election with charges of fraud? All of this is uncharted and dangerous waters—politically and constitutionally. Throw in outright lies and conspiracies, fomented by the losing candidate, and it becomes a fundamental threat to democracy.

This was the scenario hatched by conservative legal scholar John Eastman, who was working for Trump. Eastman suggested that on January 6, when Vice President Pence was announcing the Electoral College results, he should declare that there were ongoing disputes in seven states. Those seven states would be discounted, and then the number of electors needed would be reduced to 228 (from 270). Of those states left, Trump would have 232 votes, while Biden would have 222. And voila, Pence would declare Trump the winner. As reporters Bob Woodward and Robert Costa observed, "No such procedure existed in the Constitution, any law or past practice. Eastman apparently had drawn it out of thin air."[7] If Democrats were too outraged by this (you think?), then Pence would throw it open to states voting; there were twenty-six congressional delegations controlled by Republicans, and thus a victory for Trump. Ultimately, nothing came of this scheme.

Donald Trump, desperate to reverse the official electoral vote, resorted to pressure on state elected officials, on US senators, and particularly on Vice President Pence, who was the presiding officer of the Senate to negate the electoral certification (more on this in chapter 7).

Meanwhile, the US Senate determines who the vice president will be. Senators vote as individuals, not by states, and if the House is deadlocked on a president, the Senate might be able to decide on a vice president much sooner.

What happens if the House is hopelessly deadlocked, split right down the middle? Then the House appoints a temporary president, who presumably would have all the powers of president until the House can figure out the mess. And what a mess it would be! Such uncertainty and partisan bickering would pose an unprecedented threat to our already fragile democratic system. But it would also reflect a political reality: the country is so deeply and evenly divided that any decision would be denounced by a sizeable minority. Lawmakers of both parties would have to display enormous courage to resolve the crisis, considering that no matter what they decide, many of their constituents would be furious.

What's the "winner-take-all" system?

"Winner-take-all" is one of the unique features of the Electoral College system. In 2020, Donald Trump received 49.93 percent of the popular vote in North Carolina; Joe Biden received 48.59 percent. But under the winner-take-all system, all fifteen electoral votes went to Trump and Biden received none. Winner-take-all is used in every state except Nebraska and Maine. In those states, the winner receives two votes for the entire state and one electoral vote for each congressional district won. In 2020, for example, the state of Maine went for Biden, but in one of Maine's two congressional districts, Trump had prevailed. Trump thus received one elector, while Biden received three.

The winner-take-all provision can easily distort the reality of the popular vote. Theoretically, a presidential candidate could lose each of the fifty states and the District of Columbia by a mere one vote (for, say, a total vote count of 74,950,051 to 74,950,000) and end up losing 538 to 0 in the Electoral College.

This scenario, of course, is far-fetched, but we saw during the 2016 election how the winner-take-all system distorted the results. Clinton won nearly 3 million more popular votes than Trump but lost in the Electoral College by 304 votes to 227.

What is a "battleground" state?

Winner-take-all also means that campaigners may bypass many "safe" states to focus on states that are considered "battlegrounds." The battleground states—those eight, ten, or perhaps twelve states—are typically toss-ups. Why, for example, would a Republican pour major resources into California, knowing that it is solidly Democratic; or why would a Democratic candidate even bother campaigning in Alabama or Nebraska, which are Republican strongholds? Democratic strategist Peter Fenn in 2012 noted that some 80 percent of the nation's voters are ignored during campaigns, whereas those living in heavily contested battleground states receive all the media attention and ground activity.[8] If you live in battleground Pennsylvania, you know all about the barrage of presidential advertising. If you live in Alabama or Massachusetts, you rarely see commercials for the presidential candidates, because those states are pretty much locked up: Alabama is reliably Republican; Massachusetts is reliably Democratic.

What states have had the most consistent record in voting on the winning side of presidential elections?

"As Maine goes, so goes the nation." That old saw was true for many election cycles, but with Franklin Roosevelt's landslide in 1936, that slogan was modified: as FDR's campaign manager snickered, "As Maine goes, so goes Vermont" (the only two states that voted for FDR's opponent, Alf Landon). Well, if not Maine, then which are the states that most consistently vote for the winner, and which consistently pick the loser? Ohio has been the true bellwether state. Since 1900, Ohio has voted for the presidential winner in twenty-eight out of thirty-one contests, or 90.3 percent.

Here are the best and worst states in voting for the winner, from 1900 to 2020 (thirty-one elections):

Best	Correct	Percentage
Ohio	28	90.3
New Mexico	25 (out of 28)	89.2
Nevada	27	87.2
Missouri	26	83.8
Illinois	26	83.8
Worst	Correct	Percentage
Washington, DC	7 (out of 15)	46.7
Mississippi	14	45.2
Alabama	15 (out of 30)	50.0
South Carolina	16	51.6
Georgia	17	54.8

Source: "Presidential Election Accuracy Data," Ballotpedia, https://ballotpedia.org/Presidential_election_accuracy_data; updated with 2020 figures.

In 2020, Ohio went decidedly for Trump, putting a dent in the state's bellwether status.

How close have recent presidential contests been?

Surprisingly, in the past seven presidential elections, only four times did the winning candidate receive more than 50 percent of the vote. As Table 5.2 shows, only George W. Bush, in 2004; Barack Obama, in 2008 and 2012; and Joe Biden, in 2020, received more than 50 percent of the popular vote.

What about third-party candidates, with no chance of winning, acting as spoilers?

A major reason winning candidates have not reached 50 percent of the popular vote is the presence of third-party candidates on

Table 5.2 How Recent Presidential Candidates Have Fared

Year	Winner (Percentage of Popular Vote) and Electoral College Vote	Loser (Percentage of Popular Vote) and Electoral College Vote
1992	Bill Clinton (43.0%), 370	George H. W. Bush (37.4%), 168; Ross Perot (18.9%), 0
1996	Bill Clinton (49.2%), 379	Bob Dole (40.7%), 159; Ross Perot (8.4%), 0
2000	George W. Bush (47.9%), 271	Al Gore (48.4%), 266
2004	George W. Bush (50.7%), 286	John Kerry (48.3%), 251
2008	Barack Obama (52.9%), 365	John McCain (45.7%), 173
2012	Barack Obama (51.1%), 332	Mitt Romney (47.2%), 206
2016	Donald Trump (46.1%), 304	Hillary Clinton (48.2%), 227
2020	Joe Biden (51.3%), 306	Donald Trump (46.9%), 232

Source: "Historical Presidential Elections," 270toWin.com, https://www.270towin.com/historical-presidential-elections/

the ballot. Table 5.3 shows the percentage of popular votes that third-party candidates have received in recent elections.

In recent years, there have been candidates for the Libertarian Party, US Taxpayers Party, Green Party, New Alliance Party, Reform Party, and many others from the fringes. Note that no candidates from these third parties have ever won an electoral vote. Nevertheless, they were able to siphon off popular votes that would have otherwise gone to a Republican or a Democrat. In earlier races, third-party candidates did gain electoral votes—George Wallace (American Independent Party, 1968), forty-six votes; Strom Thurmond (Dixiecrat Party, 1948), thirty-nine votes; Robert LaFollette (Progressive Party, 1924), thirteen votes; and Theodore Roosevelt (Progressive Party, 1912), eighty-eight votes.

Republicans have long complained that Ross Perot's 1992 showing robbed George H. W. Bush of a re-election victory; Democrats grumbled that Ralph Nader's campaign in 2000, especially in Florida, cost Al Gore the victory; Democrats also

Table 5.3 Third-Party Presidential Candidates, 1992 to 2020

Year	Candidate, Party, Percentage of Popular Vote
1992	H. Ross Perot, independent, 18.9%
1996	H. Ross Perot, Reform, 8.4%
2000	Ralph Nader, Green, 2.7%
2004	Several third-party candidates, totalling 1.0%
2008	Several third-party candidates, totalling 1.4%
2012	Several third-party candidates, totalling 1.74%
2016	Gary Johnson, Libertarian, 3.28%
	Jill Stein, Green, 1.10%
	Several others, 1.30%
2020	Jo Jorgenson, Libertarian, 1.18%

Source: "Historical Presidential Elections," 270toWin.com, https:// www.270towin.com/historical-presidential-elections/

complained that in 2016, Green Party candidate Jill Stein, who came in fourth, got more votes than the difference between Clinton and Trump in the key states of Wisconsin, Michigan, and Pennsylvania. But supporters of third-party candidates argue that it is their right to vote for whomever they wish, and that the choices offered by the two major parties aren't acceptable. There's more on 2020 Libertarian candidate Jo Jorgenson in chapter 6.

How much money is spent in presidential elections?
Do the candidates (and their allies) who spend the most money always win?

Modern presidential campaigns are multi-billion-dollar contests. For the 2016 run, the Clinton campaign and its allies spent $1.4 billion, and the Trump campaign and its allies spent $957.6 million. It certainly didn't hurt Trump's cause that he received at least $2 billion in free advertising as the media followed his every move and reported his every outrageous statement.

The 2016 figures were quickly surpassed in 2020 when the Biden campaign and its allies spent $1.6 billion and the Trump forces spent $1.06 billion. Biden was the first presidential candidate to raise over $1 billion ($1.01 billion) for his own campaign; by contrast, Trump was able to raise $785 million. (Just one month after his defeat, Trump had raised another $207 million, under the guise of using that money to help fund legal challenges to the election results.) Outside groups spent $1.02 billion during the general election, with $668 million going to help Biden and $349 million for Trump.

Another $2.1 billion was spent by the candidates running for the Democratic Party nomination. About two-thirds of that money was spent by two billionaires, Tom Steyer ($237 million) and Michael Bloomberg ($1.03 billion). Steyer received no Democratic delegates; Bloomberg won a grand total of four delegates.[9]

Thus, counting all the primaries and the general election, some $4.9 billion was spent altogether by the candidates and outside groups to persuade and motivate America's electorate.

The campaign that spends the most money isn't always the winner. We saw that in 2016, when Clinton's side spent more than Trump's side. In 2012, Mitt Romney and his allies spent more than Barack Obama and his allies, but the Obama campaign spent the money more wisely and strategically.

What kinds of reforms have been suggested for our lengthy primary and caucus season?

For years, political party officials, good-government groups, and political scientists have been writing about reforming the primary and caucus system.[10] There are many things to complain about: there is a lengthy preprimary stage, sometimes a year long, when candidates traipse around the country and participate in contrived televised debates. The system is not uniform throughout the states: it involves very few voters, and the nominating process can be over before most states have participated. In sum, the primary and caucus system is complicated, undemocratic, expensive, and exhausting.

Some have suggested *regional primaries*. For example, let all the New England and Northeastern states have their primaries on the same day, then two weeks later, all the southern states, then two weeks after that, all the Western states, then the Midwestern states, and then the Mountain states. In the next presidential cycle, rotate the regional primaries. Over the past several cycles, some southern states have held their primaries on the same day, called Super Tuesday. They have done this hoping to draw more attention to their region of the country.

Why not hold a *national primary*? For example, on a given day, all Republicans throughout the country would have a chance to choose from among the five candidates running for president from their party. Democratic hopefuls and those from smaller parties would do the same: conduct national primaries for their candidates. If no Republican (or Democrat) receives the majority of votes, a runoff election could be held the following week.

How about *rotating* the primary calendar? Let California, or Texas, or New York go first instead of Iowa, New Hampshire, and South Carolina. After all, those three big states represent 122 electoral votes, whereas the current first three states represent just 19 votes.

With every suggested reform come objections. For example, a national primary would favor the well-known candidates, who usually have amassed large amounts of money. Well-qualified but not very well-known candidates would be swept aside. A national primary would also mean a campaign based on expensive television ads and consultants. It's a lot better, some would say, to have the candidates conduct *retail* campaigning—that is, show up at people's homes, coffee shops, and local gatherings to give voters a real chance to take their measure. You simply can't do all that with a national, or even regional, campaign calendar.

People and politicians complain, but there doesn't seem to be any groundswell of support for making fundamental changes. Nor does there seem to be any major reforms coming in the foreseeable future, not from within the national and state parties or from federal or state law. So what the Democratic Party put in place in the early 1970s—an expansion of primary and caucus states—seems to be the new normal, for both major political parties. Like it or not, our presidential campaign calendar will remain eighteen months to two years long!

Why don't we just have a nationwide election where whoever gets the most votes wins, and not worry about the Electoral College vote?

If we haven't done something about the Electoral College, it's not for a lack of trying. The US National Archives and Records Administration noted that there have been more than seven hundred attempts in Congress to change or abolish the Electoral College system, and none of them have gone anywhere.[11] These are the biggest stumbling blocks: how difficult it is to amend the federal Constitution and the rising popular resistance to reform. For nearly fifty years of polling, the Gallup Poll found that well over half the population wanted to get rid of the Electoral College. But after the 2016 election, that number sharply constricted, and just 49 percent of respondents said they want to get rid of the current system. Not surprisingly, given the results, far more Democrats (81 percent) than Republicans (19 percent) want to do away with the Electoral College system.[12]

How about a straight popular vote? It sounds so simple: forget state boundaries, forget the Electoral College, don't worry about faithless electors, no need to focus on battleground states. Just let people vote: whichever candidate gets the highest number of votes wins. If, in the future, we are so splintered that there are five or six viable candidates, then require that the winner receive 50 percent of the vote. And if that candidate can't reach 50 percent, then have a runoff the next week between the top two candidates.

You'd think that Republicans would like this idea: the 6,006,429 Republican votes in the 2020 California presidential race would have all counted, and those votes wouldn't have been wasted under the winner-take-all system. Same thing for Democrats: their 5,259,126 votes in Texas would have counted, not been nullified, by the winner-take-all system.

But you can see the opposition. California Democrats would say, why give Republicans these votes? Texas Republicans would say the same thing: why reward Democrats in our state? (How undemocratic is that sentiment—don't count the other guy's vote!) In the current system, the losing side gets zero electoral votes. Small states would probably complain the most. Wyoming, Alaska, Delaware, North Dakota, South Dakota, and Montana—all have just one US representative, but add to that their two US senators each, and these small-population states now have a little bit more than they should. The smaller, rural states would complain that the densely populated big cities would have an advantage over them.

Moving to a national popular vote (as originally suggested by James Wilson in 1787) would require an amendment to the Constitution. It's possible, but enough political interests that have some sort of leverage in our current system would fight it tooth and nail.

What is the idea of a national popular-vote compact?

One recent idea, the National Popular Vote Interstate Compact, has been considered in several states. It would fix the Electoral College problem without requiring a constitutional amendment. It would make electors pledge to support the winner of the national popular vote, regardless of how the state they live in voted. For example, suppose that in 2024, a Democrat wins the popular vote nationwide, but the Republican candidate wins in Florida, and Republican electors are chosen. If Florida had joined the compact, those Republican electors would be obligated to vote for the Democrat who won the nation- wide vote, even if that meant going against all their partisan instincts. As of 2021, the compact has been endorsed by fifteen states and the District of Columbia (with 195 electoral votes) and is being considered in several state legislatures. It won't be an easy task. The compact would still need 75 electoral votes in order to reach the majority, 270.

Even if the compact were put into place, we can easily im- agine the intense partisan pressure—especially in our deeply divided times—for those electors to refuse to abide by its terms. Using our Florida example, suppose that the Republican electors from Florida refuse to go along and do not vote for the nationwide winner. This would be a new version of the "faith- less elector."

Support has come mostly from Democratic-controlled states, but there is also some Republican support. But legislatures in Florida (thirty electoral votes) and Texas (forty) haven't even considered the measure. Thus, it may have a chance, or it could die on the vine like so many other attempts to change our method of electing a president.

6

THE 2020
PRESIDENTIAL ELECTION

The 2020 presidential election was unusual, controversial, and significant. Thanks to the Covid pandemic, many of the usual trappings of campaigning had to be halted, and when votes were cast, an unusually high number were done through mail-in ballots. The popular vote clearly indicated a victory for Joe Biden, but fewer than fifty thousand votes would have tipped the election to Trump. Such are the quirks of the Electoral College system. It was the first time since 1992 that a sitting president was defeated for re-election.

How did Joe Biden win the crowded Democratic primaries?

Donald Trump, as sitting president, was unopposed in his re-election bid in 2020. All the nomination action took place on the Democratic side, with over two dozen candidates vying for the attention of voters. During the early 2020 Democratic primaries and caucuses, Joe Biden was looking pretty anemic. In Iowa, he came in fourth (with 13.7 percent of the vote); in New Hampshire, he came in fifth (8.4 percent); in Nevada, he came in second (18.9 percent), but far behind Bernie Sanders.

Then came probably his last chance: South Carolina. Win in South Carolina or go home. With the critical support of influential South Carolina congressman James E. Clyburn and thousands of African American voters, Biden won the primary with 48.7 percent of the vote, and with that win, everything turned around for him. Clyburn's endorsement of Biden was considered crucial: some 67 percent of Democratic voters said his endorsement was important in their decision.[1]

After South Carolina, Biden was on a roll, and except for coming in second in several states, Biden was the winner in forty-five more primaries and caucuses. Quickly, other Democratic candidates dropped out and endorsed him. In the general election, African American voters rewarded Biden and running mate Kamala Harris with crucial support, particularly in the battleground states of Michigan, Pennsylvania, and Georgia.[2]

"If at first you don't succeed, try, try again." Biden had run for president twice before, in 1988 and 2008. Both times he barely made any impact and was forced to drop out quickly. In 1988, he withdrew before the first primary; in 2008, he dropped out after the first contest, the Iowa caucuses, receiving just 4 percent of the vote. Amazingly, his strong win in the 2020 South Carolina primary was his first presidential primary victory ever.

How many people voted, and how many, thanks to Covid-19, voted early or used mail-in ballots?

An extraordinary number of citizens voted in 2020, more than 158 million; and it was a record high percentage, 66.8 percent of eligible voters. One of the unusual features in the 2020 election was the high number of mail-in or early voters, topping 100 million.

Before 2020, seven states—Vermont, Colorado, Utah, Nevada, Washington, Oregon, and Hawaii—had automatic mail-in balloting for their state and local elections. These states had put into place guarantees and protections to ensure that voting irregularities would be kept to a minimum, and any fraud would be subject to criminal conviction. In 2020, many states decided to move to mail-in balloting, primarily because of the fears of Covid and the impact in-person voting might have on citizens' health and safety. However, some state election systems were far less prepared than the original seven, often making it difficult for their citizens to use mail-in balloting. The Brookings Institution developed a scorecard for state vote-by-mail preparedness, with "A" meaning the best and "F" the worst, or failing. The seven states listed above joined by California and New Jersey were given an "A" for their preparedness; most of the states in the South were in the "C" (Texas, Arkansas, Georgia, Florida), "D" (South Carolina, Mississippi, Louisiana, Virginia), and even "F" (Alabama) categories.[3]

Without any justification and no evidence, Trump pounced on mail-in voting. He repeatedly insisted that mail-in voting was fraudulent: "This is going to be a fraud like you've never seen." On June 22, he tweeted: "MILLIONS OF MAIL-IN BALLOTS WILL BE PRINTED BY FOREIGN COUNTRIES, AND OTHERS. AND IT WILL BE THE SCANDAL OF OUR TIMES."[4] And it went without saying that all the alleged fraud would be perpetrated by Democrats against the president and his allies. For Trump, making it easier for people to vote meant more voters, and more voters surely would mean more who opposed him.

For many, mail-in voting broadened the number of people who would vote and provided safe and secure ways of casting a ballot. On the campaign trail, Joe Biden was asked whether he (and Trump) would accept the final judgment of the voters. "I will accept it, and he will, too. You know why?" Biden said. "Because once the winner is declared once all the ballots are counted, that'll be the end of it. And that's fine."[5]

How wrong Biden was!

How close was the election? Didn't Biden win by over 7 million votes?

Indeed, Joe Biden and Kamala Harris won by over 7 million votes. It was the largest number of citizens ever to vote in an

American presidential election, over 158 million, and Biden-Harris received 81,268,924 votes, or 51.3 percent of the popular vote. Donald Trump and Mike Pence received 74,216,154 votes, or 46.9 percent of the popular vote.

Looking at it from another perspective, 67 million more people lived in counties that Biden won. Biden won counties in which 197.9 million people lived; Trump won counties in which 130.3 million people lived. Demographer William H. Frey noted that this was the largest difference in county populations since Bill Clinton beat Bob Dole in 1996. Sixty percent of Americans lived in Biden counties.[6] Biden was able to retake the suburbs, key factors in his wins in the critical battleground states of Wisconsin, Michigan, and Pennsylvania. As we'll see below, Trump strengthened his hold on rural counties and nonurban voters.

Weren't many states heavily for Trump and others heavily for Biden?

In some states, the vote was heavily one-sided. Wyoming, with three electoral votes, was the most pro-Trump, with 69.9 percent voting for him; next came West Virginia, with five electoral votes, giving Trump 68.6 percent of the vote. By contrast, the District of Columbia, with three electoral votes, gave Biden overwhelming support, with 92.1 percent; the highest state percentage came from Vermont, with three electoral votes, which gave Biden 66.1 percent.

Notice in Table 6.1 that Democrats gained the most in lopsided states, that is, states where the winning candidate received at least 62 percent of the vote. Democrats locked up eighty-two electoral votes; Republicans gained forty-five votes.

Another way of looking at the strength of Democrats and Republicans is to look at the number of counties won by presidential candidates during the past several cycles. Altogether, there are 3,243 counties (including county equivalents, like Louisiana parishes) in the United States. They range in size from Los Angeles

Table 6.1 States Giving 2020 Presidential Candidates More Than 62 Percent of the Vote

State	Electoral Votes	Percentage of Vote to Winner
Wyoming	3	69.9% (Trump)
West Virginia	5	68.6% (Trump)
Oklahoma	7	65.4% (Trump)
North Dakota	3	65.1% (Trump)
Idaho	4	63.8% (Trump)
Arkansas	6	62.4% (Trump)
Kentucky	8	62.1% (Trump)
Alabama	9	62.0% (Trump)
District of Columbia	3	92.1% (Biden)
Vermont	3	66.1% (Biden)
Massachusetts	11	65.6% (Biden)
Maryland	10	65.3% (Biden)
California	55	63.4% (Biden)

County (over 10 million residents) to the more familiar smaller rural counties, many of which have fewer than 1,000 residents. Democrats have been winning many urban counties but have been losing the fight to gain voters in rural counties. Researcher Louis Jacobsen notes that in 2000, Al Gore won 672 counties; in 2008, Barack Obama won 876; in 2016, Hillary Clinton won 490; and in 2020, Joe Biden won 538. Jacobsen wrote that in 2020, in two states—Oklahoma and West Virginia—Donald Trump won every county. "Biden won just 2 of 120 counties in Kentucky, 5 of 92 in Indiana, and 3 of 95 counties in Tennessee." Biden won in Michigan but only carried 11 out of 83 counties; he won in Wisconsin but carried just 14 out of 72 counties; and he won in Pennsylvania, carrying only 13 out of 67 counties.[7]

The Democratic strength is increasingly in metropolitan areas. Philadelphia had its highest turnout in decades and went 81 percent to 18 percent for Biden; Denver went 80 percent to 18 percent for Biden; Chicago went 82 percent to 17 percent for Biden. Fulton County (Atlanta) went 72 percent to 26 percent for Biden, while nearby DeKalb County went 83 percent to 16 percent for Biden.

But what about the razor-thin results in some of the states?

Indeed, in several states, the margins between Biden and Trump were extremely close. Biden won three states by less than 1 percent. Here are those results:

- In Arizona, a total of 3,387,326 votes were cast. Biden received 1,672,143 votes (49.36 percent), while Trump received 1,661,686 votes (49.06 percent). For the first time since 1996, Arizona, with its 11 electoral votes, went to a Democrat, with Biden winning by just 10,457 votes.
- In Georgia, a total of 4,999,960 votes were cast. Biden received 2,473,633 votes (49.47 percent), while Trump received 2,461,854 votes (49.24 percent). For the first time since 1992, Georgia, with its 16 electoral votes, went to a Democrat, with Biden winning by just 11,779 votes.
- In Wisconsin, a total of 3,298,041 votes were cast. Biden received 1,630,866 votes (49.45 percent), while Trump received 1,610,184 votes (48.82 percent). Wisconsin, with its 10 electoral votes, usually a blue state in recent elections, went back to the Democrats, with Biden winning by just 20,682 votes.

Altogether, Biden won three critical states, and 37 electoral votes, by just 42,818 combined votes. Without these states, Biden would have only had 269 electoral votes—not enough to win.

This points out the craziness of the current Electoral College, winner-take-all system: Biden won by 7 million votes, but a turnaround of just 43,000 votes would have left him short of victory.

How about the battleground states? How did Trump and Biden fare?

Here are the results in the battleground states in 2020 and 2016. *Italics* denote a flip in votes from one party to another.

State (electoral votes)	Winner	Percentage of win	2016 winner
Arizona (11)	Biden	0.3%	Trump
Florida (29)	Trump	3.3%	Trump
Georgia (16)	Biden	0.2%	Trump
Iowa (6)	Trump	8.2%	Trump
Maine, 2nd (1)	Trump	9.1%	Trump
Michigan (16)	Biden	2.8%	Trump
Minnesota (10)	Biden	7.2%	Clinton
North Carolina (15)	Trump	1.4%	Trump
New Hampshire (4)	Biden	7.4%	Clinton
Nebraska, 2nd (1)	Biden	6.8%	Clinton
Nevada (6)	Biden	2.4%	Clinton
Ohio (18)	Trump	8.0%	Trump
Pennsylvania (20)	Biden	1.2%	Trump
Texas (38)	Trump	5.6%	Trump
Wisconsin (10)	Biden	0.7%	Trump

Were third-party candidates a factor in 2020? Ever heard of Jo Jorgenson?

There were no well-known third-party candidates this time around, no Ralph Nader (2000), Ross Perot (1992, 1996), or even Gary Johnson or Jill Stein (2016). But there was Jo Jorgenson, a lecturer at Clemson University and the presidential candidate for the Libertarian Party, who had more votes than the difference between Trump and Biden in three crucial states.

In Arizona, Georgia, and Wisconsin, Jorgenson was definitely the spoiler. In Arizona, Jorgenson received 54,465 votes (Trump lost by 11,779); in Georgia, she received 62,229 votes (Trump lost by 10,457); and in Wisconsin, she received 38,491 votes (Trump lost by 20,682).

If she were not on the ballot, would Jorgenson supporters have gone more to Trump than Biden? Might they have voted for another third-party candidate? Or might they have just stayed at home? We don't know, but as in 2016, third-party candidates have made the difference in these highly competitive races, and in the total outcome.

Although she was on the ballot in all fifty-one jurisdictions, few people could tell you who Jo Jorgenson was, what she looked like, or what she stood for. Nevertheless, she received 1.86 million votes (1.18 percent) nationwide, enough to potentially throw the election into turmoil. But next time around there might be another Jorgenson—unknown to virtually the whole electorate, who pops up in one or two highly competitive states and makes a difference.

How was Biden able to win Georgia, which almost always goes Republican?

Much of Biden and the Democrats' success in Georgia came through the long slog and dogged dedication of Stacey Abrams in getting more African Americans registered and out to vote. Abrams had served as minority leader in the Georgia House of Representatives and in 2018 ran against Republican Brian Kemp for governor. While running in the governor's race, Kemp held the job of state secretary of state, in charge of the election process. In a controversial move in 2017, Kemp purged some seven hundred thousand names from the voting rolls, and, just before the election, some fifty-three thousand voting records were put on hold; more than 75 percent of those records belonged to minority voters. Abrams, an African American, lost to Kemp by some fifty thousand votes; she refused to concede defeat and vowed to fight on.

Energized by her loss, Abrams continued her fight, establishing Fair Fight Action, a group to fight against voter suppression, concentrating its efforts in Georgia and Texas. The efforts of Abrams and her allies were instrumental in giving Biden the win in Georgia, the first time in twenty-eight years that a Democrat had won that state. Her get-out-the-vote efforts were equally important in flipping Georgia's two

US Senate seats, giving Democrats the slimmest of majorities in 2021.

In an October 2021 rally in Georgia, Donald Trump, still smarting from the Georgia loss and for what he considered a betrayal by Governor Kemp, said, "And Stacey Abrams, who still has not conceded, that's OK. Stacey, would you like to take his place? It's OK with me." Then Trump said, "Of course having her, I think, might be better than having your existing governor, if you want to know what I think. Might very well be better."[8]

What about the recounts and audits in Georgia, Arizona, and other places?

There was incredible pressure from Republicans in Georgia: how could the dominant party, their party, lose this election? Secretary of State Brad Raffensperger, a Republican, and his office were bombarded with threats from party officials and state office holders demanding recounts. As seen in the next chapter, President Trump weighed in, trying to cajole Raffensperger into finding "11,778 votes." Georgia conducted three separate recounts concluding that there was no fraud or wrongdoing. Gabriel Sterling, the Republican chief financial officer for Raffensperger's office, stated: "Our law enforcement officers and secretary of state's office spent literally thousands of hours examining ballots in Fulton County and other counties trying to track these kinds of claims [of fraud] down, and so far we've seen nothing to give any merit to it."[9] In addition, lawsuits challenging the Georgia outcome had also failed.

In Arizona, state senate Republicans insisted on an audit of votes in Maricopa County (Phoenix metropolitan area). A Florida firm called Cyber Ninjas, with no experience in election audits, was hired to conduct the investigation. The head of this firm was an avowed Trump supporter and conspiracy theorist. Prior to this, Maricopa County results had been audited several times, including two federally certified auditing firms; no irregularities were found. Governor Doug

Ducey, a Republican, defended the integrity of the election system and its outcome. Furthermore, the Trump campaign lost at least eight Arizona lawsuits prior to the Cyber Ninjas audit. Some $6.7 million of dark money from individuals and groups supported this audit, along with $150,000 that was appropriated by the Arizona Senate.[10]

The Cyber Ninja audit dragged on for months. Finally, in late September 2021, the audit was made public: Trump did not win Arizona; in fact, Biden gained more votes. Immediately, Trump blamed the media for distorting the audit findings and called for more "forensic audits" in Arizona and in other states.

A nonpartisan audit completed in Wisconsin in October 2021 found no evidence to overturn Biden's narrow victory; and a senior Republican legislative leader called the state's elections "safe and secure."[11] Pennsylvania and Texas are among the states where Republicans control the legislature and are demanding further election audits.

How did voter turnout in 2020 compare to recent presidential elections?

The voter turnout in 2020 broke election records, with 66.8 percent of eligible voters participating. Forty-two states achieved all-time-high participation rates. It brought out a raft of Trump supporters, but, even more importantly, a surge of voters choosing Biden.

Here are the turnout percentages for recent presidential contests:

2020 (Biden-Trump)	66.8%
2016 (Trump-H. Clinton)	55.7%
2012 (Obama-Romney)	54.9%
2008 (Obama-McCain)	58.2%
2004 (Bush II-Kerrey)	56.7%

2000 (Bush II-Gore)   51.2%

1996 (B. Clinton-Dole)   49.0%

1992 (B. Clinton-Bush I)   55.2%

If every eligible adult had voted, how many more people would that be?

While a record number of citizens voted, still there were 70 million eligible American adults who did not vote. In a way, we could characterize the national vote this way:

Biden: 81 million

Trump: 74 million

Did not vote: 70 million

Despite the huge amount of time, resources, and effort by both the Biden and Trump campaigns to get more people to vote, still a substantial number sat on the sidelines. It is interesting to speculate: What would happen if 75 percent, or 85 percent, of the electorate voted, rather than 67 percent? How would that impact presidential voting? If a group could be energized and boost its percentage to exceptionally high levels, how would that affect the election? Registration of voters and turnout, then, became absolutely crucial; and the party or group that can raise its voter participation rate will be able to capture more of the total. This becomes especially critical when such a group strongly favors one party over the other.

How secure was the presidential election from Russian interference and cyberattacks?

At a September 24, 2020, Senate hearing, the Trump-appointed FBI director Christopher Wray stated, "We have not seen, historically, any kind of coordinated national voter fraud effort in a major election, whether it's by mail or otherwise."[12]

The US Department of Homeland Security set up its own cybersecurity division, led by Trump appointee Christopher C. Krebs. In charge of rooting out election disinformation, Krebs determined that 2020 was the "most secure in American history,"[13] and that false information wasn't coming from Russia or other foreign actors, but from the White House.

This was too much for Trump. "The recent statement by Chris Krebs on the security of the 2020 Election was highly inaccurate," Trump wrote on Twitter, "in that there were massive improprieties and fraud—including dead people voting, Poll Watchers not allowed into polling locations, 'glitches' in the voting machines which changes voters from Trump to Biden, late voting, and many more." Krebs was promptly "terminated" as director of the Cybersecurity and Infrastructure Security Agency. After being fired, Krebs later elaborated: "[Election] Day was quiet. There was no indication or evidence that there was any evidence of hacking or compromise of election systems on, before, or after November 3. . . . We did a good job. I would do it one thousand times over."

The reaction against Trump's firing of Krebs was swift. "Of all the things this president has done, this is the worst," said Senator Angus S. King Jr. (Independent-Maine). "To strike at the heart of the democratic system is beyond anything we have seen from any politician."[14] (No, senator, the worst was yet to come.)

The Brennan Center for Justice noted, "By all measures, the 2020 general election was one of the most secure elections in our history. Voters turned out in record numbers to cast their ballots by mail and in person, and the votes were counted in a timely manner."[15]

Attorney General William Barr broke with Trump on December 1, 2020, telling reporters that "to date, we have not seen fraud on a scale that could have effected a different outcome in the election." To reporter Jonathan D. Karl, Barr said, "My attitude was: It was put-up or shut-up time. If there was evidence of fraud, I had no motive to suppress it. But my suspicion all the way along was that there was nothing there. It was all bullshit."[16] Senate Majority Leader Mitch McConnell had been urging Barr to speak out, but McConnell himself was reluctant to do so, afraid that alienating Trump might jeopardize Republican turnout in the crucial two upcoming special elections in Georgia (which Republicans subsequently lost, and thus lost control of the majority).

Later investigative reporting and memos made public clearly indicated that senior members of the Trump campaign staff knew that the claims of massive voter fraud were not true and had no basis in fact. Still, they were peddled by the president, his loyal supporters, and elements of the conservative media.[17]

In March 2021, the US National Intelligence Council, through its chief, Avril Haines, released its assessment of foreign involvement in the 2020 elections. The report stated that there was "no indication that any foreign actor attempted to alter any technical aspect of the voting process in the 2020 US elections, including voter registration, casting ballots, vote tabulation, or reporting results." However, "some foreign actors, such as Iran and Russia, spread false or inflated claims about alleged compromises of voting systems to undermine public confidence in the election processes and results."[18] The report also concluded that Russian president Vladimir Putin and a number of Russian government organizations had tried to undermine confidence in the election, to support Trump, and to denigrate Biden's candidacy. Further, the Intelligence Council had "high confidence" that China did not interfere with or try to influence the outcome of the presidential election. Some others—Lebanon's Hezbollah, Cuba, Venezuela, and cyber criminals—also tried to influence the elections, but to a far lesser scale than Russia.

While there were some foreign attempts to influence the election, the biggest threat came on the domestic front, as we'll see in the following chapter.

7

THE BIG LIE AND
ITS AFTERMATH

We have never seen anything like it: the president of the United States defeated in his bid for re-election, lashing out at his detractors, refusing to concede, refusing to congratulate his successor, trying to use the power and authority of the White House to threaten, plead, even beg for state election results to be overturned. Conservative television and social media and state and national Republican lawmakers stood behind the president or, even worse, lacked the courage to speak out against the blanket of false accusations. Quickly, it became known as the "Big Lie." It nearly succeeded but was stopped only by the courage of state and local election officials and federal and state judges. An unprecedented attack on the Capitol building by Trump stalwarts showed the world the level of disruption and disbelief stirred up by the president. Still, two years after the election, Donald Trump has doubled down, insisting that the election was stolen and he was robbed of a second term.

What was the "Big Lie"?

Journalists quickly labeled the Trump falsehoods and mistruths about the 2020 presidential election the "Big Lie." But this term has historical antecedents. Adolph Hitler first used the term "Big Lie" when blaming Viennese Jews for attempting to discredit Germany during the First World War. Then, in the 1930s and 1940s, Hitler struck. Historian Zachary Jonathan Jacobson observed that "Jews, Hitler contended, were the weak underbelly of the Weimar state that exposed the loyal and true German population to catastrophic collapse. To sell this narrative, Joseph Goebbels, the Reich Minister of Propaganda, insisted 'all effective propaganda must be limited to a very few points and must harp on these in slogans until the last member of the public understands.' "[1]

On the 2020 election, historian Timothy Snyder, who wrote the prescient book *On Tyranny*, wrote: "The idea that Mr. Biden didn't win the election is a big lie. It's a big lie because you have to disbelieve all kinds of evidence to believe in it. It's a big lie because you have to believe in a huge conspiracy in order to believe it. And it's a big lie because, if you believe it, it demands you take radical action. So this is one way we have really moved forwards towards authoritarianism and away from democracy. It's coming to a peak right now."[2]

Journalist Zachary B. Wolf outlined the basic elements of the Big Lie:

> First, "the election was stolen because it's not possible Trump didn't win."
> Second, "there was a massive technological conspiracy to rig the election."
> Third, "theories and wild claims pushed on the Internet find their way into lawsuits and are then pushed by Trump."
> Fourth, "investigators are biased, too."
> Fifth, "Trump supporters questioning the results are just good citizens."[3]

Did the "stop the steal" movement occur before Trump came along?

Columnist Jamelle Bouie points out that the "stop the steal" movement didn't begin with Trump; it has been longstanding in Republican conservative circles. The central conceit of "stop

the steal" is that Democrats can't win outright and must re-
sort to stealing the election from Republicans. The modern version, according to Bouie, dates from 2000 when Republicans
claimed voter fraud in their narrow defeats in New Mexico
and Missouri. In Missouri, the incumbent senator John
Ashcroft was defeated by Jean Carnahan, the wife of Governor
Mel Carnahan. The governor had been the candidate, but he
died just three weeks earlier in an airplane crash. After his defeat, Ashcroft became the US attorney general under the new
president, George W. Bush, and he announced a crackdown
on alleged voter fraud. In making the announcement of the
crackdown, Ashcroft stated: "Votes have been bought, voters
intimidated, and ballot boxes stuffed. The polling process has
been disrupted or not completed. Voters have been duped into
signing absentee ballots believing they were applications for
public relief. And the residents of cemeteries have infamously
shown up at the polls on Election Day."

John McCain and the Republican Party also slammed the
2008 Obama campaign, contending rampant voter fraud. Bouie
has argued that "as an accusation, 'voter fraud' has been used
historically to disparage the participation of Black voters and
immigrants—to cast their votes as illegitimate. And Obama
came to office on the strength of historic turnout among Black
Americans and other nonwhite groups. To the conservative
grass roots, Obama's very presence in the White House was, on
its face, evidence that fraud had overtaken American elections."[4]

The nonpartisan think tank Atlantic Council stated that
"stop the steal" had been evident throughout Donald Trump's
campaigns and elections. Its Digital Forensic Research Lab reported that "stop the steal" had been "a hallmark of nearly
every election throughout Trump's political career." Trump
political associate Roger Stone used it first to help Trump
during his 2016 primaries and then to discredit Hillary Clinton
during the 2016 general election.[5] With just three weeks to go
before Election Day, Trump claimed that the results would be
"a big ugly lie." During the third debate between Clinton and
Trump, moderator Chris Wallace repeatedly asked Trump to

affirmatively state that he would abide by the election results. "I will tell you at the time," Trump responded. "I will keep you in suspense." Clinton responded that her opponent's comments were "horrifying." Then at a rally the next day Trump said, "I will totally accept the results of this great and historic presidential election, if I win." *If I win.*[6]

What groups were pushing the "stop the steal" and Big Lie efforts?

A little-known group, Women for America First, hired red buses with the words "Stop the Steal" emblazoned on them. They went from town to town, holding rallies and drumming up support from the grassroots enthusiasts, local officials, and an array of conspiracy theorists. The leader, Amy Kremer, had been a fervent supporter of Trump and a leader in the Tea Party movement. Trump adviser Stephen Bannon and entrepreneur Mike Lindell helped fund the bus tour. The Women for America First were the original planners for the January 6 event, but once Trump got involved in it, it became a White House production.[7]

The biggest, loudest, and most persuasive voice, of course, was Trump's. Months before the general election, he was claiming massive fraud in the mail-in voting processes, and after the election, and ever since, Trump has persistently claimed that the election was stolen from him. Trump had help from allies and supporters. From September 1, 2020, to February 2, 2021, there were 8,200 online news articles containing the words "Stop the Steal" or #StoptheSteal," with 70 million engagements; some 43.5 million social media engagements were registered in December 2020 alone, mostly on YouTube, Facebook, Twitter, Pinterest, and Reddit.[8]

Right after the election, Trump sympathizer Sean Hannity of Fox News set the tone: "While the very frail, the very weak, cognitively struggling Joe Biden is probably fast asleep in his basement bunker, dreaming of picking out drapes for the Oval Office, well, investigations continue in multiple key states—where hundreds now of sworn affidavits are being filed, lawsuits are being filed, alleging serious election mis-conduct."[9] Fox News, OAN (One America News), and other pro-Trump media outlets kept up the drumbeat of voter fraud accusations. A liberal media watchdog organization, Media Matters for America, tallied 774 times that Fox reporters and their guests stated that the election was rigged or cast doubt on it—even after Fox had called the election for Biden.[10]

On the more provocative side, militant, far right groups like the Three Percenters, the Boogaloo Boys, Proud Boys, QAnon, and others stoked the falsehood: the election was stolen from Donald Trump.

Why did so many Republicans believe the Big Lie?

Most Americans didn't buy the Big Lie, but most Republicans did. In a March 2021 poll conducted by the Public Religion Research Institute (PRRI), for example, fewer than three out of ten Americans (29%) agreed that "the 2020 election was stolen from Donald Trump." But two-thirds of Republicans (66%) believed that the election was stolen. (Some 72% of independents and 95% of Democrats disagreed that the election was stolen.) And the more people got their news from Trump-friendly right-wing sources, the more they believed the Big Lie. For "Fox News Republicans" 86% "completely agreed" or "somewhat agreed" that the election was stolen; 96% of "Far-right news Republicans" agreed that the election was stolen.[11] For them, the election of Joe Biden was calamitous, unacceptable news; many Trump supporters were unable to move past reality and their doubts were energized by conservative mainstream and ultra-right social media, conspiracy peddlers, and, most of all, Trump himself.

How did Trump's fervent base come to believe this fabrication? First, Trump pushed the false narrative to his ardent supporters. Advisers and friends told him to move on, but Trump continued to push the Big Lie and to punish any Republicans who questioned his falsehoods.

Second, on election night, Trump was indeed ahead of Biden in several critical states; then, once mail-in and absentee ballots were counted, the tide turned. This was most noticeable in Pennsylvania, where Trump held a 700,000-vote lead by midnight on Election Day. But more than 3 million mail-in ballots had to be processed, and thanks to a decision by the Republican-dominated state legislature, those ballots could not be opened before 7:00 a.m. on Election Day. By one o'clock in the morning following Election Day, some 467,000 ballots from Democratic-heavy Philadelphia and Pittsburgh still waited to be counted; thousands more had not yet been counted in Democratic-friendly Montgomery County. Republicans tend to vote at the polls on Election Day, but Democrats preferred to vote by mail-in or absentee ballots. Certainly, many Trump supporters would go to bed on election night thinking that Pennsylvania and the election itself had gone their way.

Third, Republican voters were convinced of voter fraud by the constant barrage of doubt and outrage coming from Fox News and other conservative media outlets, Trump's personal lawyer Rudy Giuliani, and a gaggle of other supporters.

Why did so many Republican members of Congress go along with the Big Lie?

Some Republican lawmakers publicly cast doubt on the Big Lie; few, however, had the courage to directly oppose Trump. One Republican lawmaker who did stand up to the president was the member of Congress from Wyoming, Liz Cheney. She was outraged by the January 6 insurrection, squarely blamed President Trump for the incitement, voted for his impeachment, and later joined the House committee investigating the insurrection. "I think what Donald Trump did is the most dangerous thing, the most egregious violation of an oath of office of any president in our history," Cheney said of Trump's incitement and attempts to interfere with the Electoral College certification. She also compared Trump's rhetoric to that of the Chinese

Communist Party, with Trump trying to discredit the federal election system. "When you listen to Donald Trump talk now, when you hear the language he's using now, it is essentially the same things that the Chinese Communist Party, for example, says about the United States and our democracy," she said.[12]

Cheney was kicked out of the leadership of the Republican House caucus and soon had a Trump-endorsed Republican ready to take her on in Wyoming's 2022 primaries. Trump trashed Cheney, calling her "warmongering and very low polling." One of the most conservative of Republican lawmakers, Cheney was chastised by Trump but has received help from former president George W. Bush and a host of moderate Republican leaders and their money. Cheney and Republican Adam Kinzinger of Illinois had joined the House January 6 committee, and for that action, they were both censured by the Republican National Committee. The resolution accused them of "participating in a Democrat-led persecution of ordinary citizens engaged in political discourse."[13]

Trump was losing case after case in state and federal courts, but in one last desperate move, 126 Republican members of Congress joined a lawsuit brought by the attorney general of Texas and seventeen other Republican state attorneys general. This case went directly to the Supreme Court but was much more of a publicity stunt (and a gesture of loyalty to Trump) than an actual case. As seen below, the Supreme Court summarily dismissed the case, noting in just a few words that Texas had lacked standing to sue.

On the night of the insurrection, Senator Mitt Romney (Republican-Utah), no friend of Trump's, lashed out at Trump to sustained applause from lawmakers: "We gather due to a selfish man's injured pride and the outrage of supporters who he has deliberately misinformed for the past two months and stirred to action this very morning. What happened here today was an insurrection incited by the president of the United States."

Senate Majority Leader Mitch McConnell had declared Biden the winner in December but didn't want to jeopardize the two Georgia runoff primaries, so he publicly kept quiet about Trump's lies. But on Trump's last day in office, McConnell issued a stinging rebuke. "The mob was fed lies," McConnell charged. "They were provoked by the president and other powerful people, and they tried to use fear and violence to stop a specific proceeding of the first branch of the federal government which they did not like."[14]

Altogether, 147 Republican members of Congress refused to certify Biden's victory. In the Senate, Ted Cruz (Republican-Texas) and Josh Hawley (Republican-Missouri) were the ring leaders (along with six other senators) protesting Biden's victory. Finally, at 4:00 a.m. on January 7, Biden's victory was certified.

Why did so many Republicans go along? One answer that kept coming up was that since so many Republicans believed the Big Lie, their elected officials had to agree too, or at least not confront Trump and their constituents with the truth. In an interview on *60 Minutes*, Liz Cheney was asked if a lot of Republican colleagues came up to her quietly and admitted that they agreed with her. Cheney's response: "Yes. Both in the House and Senate." Cheney continued, "The argument that, that you often hear is that if you do something that is perceived as against Trump that, you know, you'll put yourself in political peril. And that's a self-fulfilling prophesy because if Republican leaders don't stand up and condemn what happened, then the voices in the party that are so dangerous will only get louder and stronger."[15]

In 2021, Donald Trump hit the campaign trail and doubled down on his claim of a stolen election. In the meantime, Republican lawmakers, at all levels of government, remained silent and thus complicit.

To what lengths did Trump go to challenge and refute the election results?

Jeffrey Rosen, William Barr's successor at the Department of Justice (DOJ), told Trump that the DOJ couldn't change the outcome of the election. According to notes taken by Justice Department official Richard Donoghue, Trump replied, "just say the election was corrupt + leave the rest to me and the R. Congressmen."[16]

Trump strongly hinted that he could replace Rosen with Jeffrey B. Clark, a DOJ official sympathetic to Trump's views. Rosen refused to go along and told the president that if his plan went through, there would be a mass resignation of DOJ officials (and White House lawyers as well, it turned out). Indeed, as the New York Times reported, Clark sought to involve the DOJ in an effort to overturn the election results and plotted with Trump to oust Rosen.[17]

Two weeks after the election, Trump summoned Michigan Republican officials to the White House to try to convince them to overturn the results, particularly in Wayne County (Detroit), where Biden won overwhelmingly. Days later, Michigan Republican legislative leaders stated that there was no evidence of wrongdoing that would change the results: Joe Biden won. In normal times, this would be considered an extraordinary breach of election law and ethics—one party in the race (Trump) attempting to persuade state lawmakers to reverse the outcome. Nearly a year later, at a rally in Ohio, Trump gave out the names and phone numbers of the two Michigan officials he met with in November: "Call those two senators now and get them to do the right thing, or vote them the hell out of office!"[18]

An hour-long telephone call between Trump and Brad Raffensperger, the Georgia official in charge of election administration, gave the world a glimpse of the president's attempt to overturn the results. The telephone call was recorded and someone in the White House leaked it to the press.[19] All the world learned of Trump's plea to Raffensperger: "find 11,780 votes, which is one more than we have." Raffensperger stuck to his guns, pushed back against the president's begging, and would not decertify the results or steal away votes from Georgia citizens. Yet even in September 2021, Trump sent a letter to Raffensperger charging, with no credible evidence, that the election results had to be decertified: "Large scale

Voter Fraud continues to be reported in Georgia," read the first line of the letter.[20]

Arizona. Georgia. Pennsylvania. Michigan. Wisconsin. Texas. And the list goes on of states where Trump has claimed, without a shred of credible evidence, that voter fraud had taken place.

Did Vice President Mike Pence have the authority to overturn the election?

No, he did not. Donald Trump repeatedly urged Mike Pence to block the certification of Joe Biden's victory. Pence would not go along. But Trump continued to assert that Pence had the authority to overturn the election results. "Mike Pence did have the right to change the outcome. . . . Unfortunately, he didn't exercise that power—he could have overturned the election!" Trump claimed in late January 2022. But just a week later, Pence rebuked the president's assertions: "This week our former president said I had the right to 'overturn the election.' . . . Donald Trump is wrong. I had no right to overturn the election." He continued, "Frankly, there is no idea more un-American than the notion that any one person could choose the American president. Under the Constitution, I had no right to change the outcome of the election."

The vice president's role at the joint session of Congress is only ceremonial: he opens up the electoral-vote counts from each state alphabetically, reads them aloud, and calls for any objections. If only one member of the House and one member of the Senate objects to a particular state's electoral-vote count, the issue must be debated. Republican Congressman Paul Gosar (Arizona) and Senator Ted Cruz (Texas) led off the challenges by objecting to Biden's victory in Arizona. Then came the rioters who attacked the Capitol.

The procedures for certifying the electoral vote rely on an 1887 law, the Electoral Count Act (ECA). It was adopted in response to the controversial 1876 presidential election, where a clear winner was not chosen until just days before the Inauguration in March. But the ECA language is confusing and sorely needs modern language and clarification. Its ambiguity permitted Trump and his supporters to claim that whole slates of voter-chosen electors should be replaced by competing slates chosen by Republican-dominated state legislatures.

For years, scholars and election experts have warned about the ambiguities and potential for mischief in a hotly contested election. There is some hope that bipartisan legislative reform of the ECA might be able to clarify the weaknesses of this law.[21]

How did state election officials react?

The American system of administering elections is highly decentralized. Most of the attention is given to local officials at the county level, followed by a more centralized office at the state level. This state level is usually handled by an elected official, often called the secretary of state or the chief election officer. In twenty-four states, the secretary of state is elected by the people; in five states, this individual is appointed by the governor; and in nine states, there is a commission (often bipartisan) to administer elections.[22]

The secretary of state's office is responsible for ensuring that election laws are being followed throughout the state, maintaining a statewide voter registration database, and having a system to certify voting equipment used in the state. The 2000 presidential election in Florida, with its "hanging chads" and faulty ballot design, highlighted some of the difficulties found in local jurisdictions. Then came 2020 and the charges hurled at state and local election officials by Trump and his supporters. Raffensperger and his staff were subjected to verbal abuse and threats, calls for their resignation, and attacks on their professionalism when they refused to overturn the results. The Georgia election officials were not alone: election officials, especially Republicans, who have defied the Big Lie have been treated as villains or traitors and have endured death threats.

In a June 2021 report entitled "Election Officials under Attack," the Brennan Center for Justice noted the "unprecedented" pressure that state and local officials had come under.[23] They had become scapegoats for election results that Trump and his allies simply would not accept. For example, Al Schmidt, one of three Republican election commissioners in Philadelphia, defended the integrity of the vote, which went for Joe Biden. Then Trump called him out: stalkers grabbed his cell phone number, death threats followed, and his wife and family had to leave town. Schmidt was not alone; election officials in other states have been harassed and threatened; fortunately, no one has been killed.

The Brennan Center reports that political party leaders have censured or replaced election officials and lawmakers have introduced bills making it a crime to proactively send mail-in ballots or purchase advertisements for upcoming elections on social media platforms. "Most troubling," the report states, "state legislatures across the nation have taken steps to strip election officials of the power to run, count, and certify elections, consolidating power in their own hands over processes intended to be free of partisan or political interference."

How successful were Trump and his supporters in the courts?

Funny thing about the legal system: when arguing a claim in court, lawyers must have evidence, not speculation; they must point to solid, factual materials, not rumor, innuendo, and conspiracy theories. Public figures, like politicians, often brag, exaggerate, use colorful language, and step over the line between truth and untruth. Certainly the all-time champion has to be Donald Trump. The *Washington Post*'s tally on Trump lies, mistruths, distortions, and falsehoods reached 30,573, an average of 21 erroneous claims a day during his presidency.[24] This is a far cry from Jimmy Carter, who, on the 1976 campaign trail, pledged to the American public, "I'll never tell a lie. I'll never make a misleading statement."

Trump's election lawyers, within ten days of the election, knew that the allegation of election fraud couldn't be proved. There was no substantial evidence, no glaring irregularities, and certainly no "wholesale fraud." On November 12, when the Arizona results showed an irreversible lead of more than 10,000 votes, Trump's election lawyers were pitted against the president's personal lawyer, Rudy Giuliani, who wanted to pursue conspiracy theories and questionable practices. Trump decided to go with Giuliani, making him the point man for the legal fight ahead. Thus, November 12, 2020, was the day when Trump's effort to reverse his loss in the courts became an "all-out, extralegal campaign to disenfranchise millions of voters based on the false notion of pervasive fraud."[25]

But in the courts, the Big Lie had become the Big Loser. By the time the Electoral College officially voted, in mid-December, Trump and his allies had lost fifty-nine lawsuits, in state courts, federal district courts, federal appeals courts, and the Supreme Court. A federal appeals court judge, Stephanos Bibas, a Trump appointee, put it in a nutshell: "Free, fair elections are the lifeblood of our democracy. Charges of unfairness are serious. But calling an election unfair does not make it so. Charges require specific allegations and then proof. We have neither here."[26]

A tally late in December 2020 found that eighty-six judges—from state court level to the US Supreme Court, both Democrats and Republicans—had rejected at least one postelection lawsuit coming from Trump and his allies. This indicated a "remarkable show of near unanimity across the nation's judiciary."[27]

Probably the most embarrassing lawsuit was the one filed by the attorney general of Texas, joined by seventeen other Republican attorneys general as friends of the court. The lawsuit attempted to overturn 20 million votes in four battleground states that went to Biden. The *New York Times* found that most of the suit was drafted by lawyers close to the White House. Legal red flags were popping up all over. "It is most likely the court will deny this in one sentence," wrote James E. Nicolai, deputy solicitor general of North Dakota.[28] The Supreme Court did just that (in three sentences): "The State of Texas's motion for leave to file a bill of complaint is denied for lack of standing under Article III of the Constitution. Texas has not demonstrated a judicially cognizable interest in the manner in which another State conducts its elections. All other pending motions are dismissed as moot."[29]

Didn't Trump's lawyers and allies get into trouble with the courts and the legal profession?

In June 2021, the New York State Appellate Court temporarily suspended Rudy Giuliani's law license, stating that there had been "uncontroverted evidence" that he had made "demonstrably false and misleading statements" defending Trump and the Big Lie. In its thirty-three-page statement, the court said that Giuliani's conduct "immediately threatens the public interest and warrants interim suspension from the practice of law." Further, the court stated that he "directly inflamed" the tensions that led to the January 6 insurrection. Giuliani, who made his name as a law-and-order federal prosecutor, had been mayor of New York City ("America's Mayor") and had been Trump's personal lawyer.[30] Trump immediately sent out a tweet: "Can you believe that New York wants to strip Rudy Giuliani, a great American Patriot, of his law license because he has been fighting what has already been proven to be a Fraudulent Election?"[31]

Sidney Powell, a lawyer from Texas and, for a while, a Trump favorite, went on Fox Business Network and claimed that Trump had won the election by a landslide. She then filed multiple lawsuits in Arizona, Georgia, Michigan, and Wisconsin. But Powell failed miserably; her cases were lacking in solid evidence, clients did not have standing to sue, and issues became moot. In dismissing Powell's case in Wisconsin, US District Court chief judge Pamela Pepper wrote, "Federal judges do not appoint the president in this country. One wonders why the plaintiffs came to federal court and asked a federal judge to do so. . . . After a week of sometimes odd and often harried litigation, the court is no closer to answering the 'why.' "[32]

Powell, Lin Wood, and several other lawyers were sanctioned by a federal judge in Michigan. The lawyers filed a suit in December 2020, but it was summarily dismissed by the federal judge Linda Parker, who called it "frivolous." The Powell voter fraud claims, Parker wrote, were "nothing but speculation and conjecture." "This lawsuit represents a historic and profound abuse of the judicial process," and the case "was never about fraud—it was about undermining the people's faith in our democracy and debasing the judicial process to do so." Michigan attorney general Dana Nessel and other state government officials asked that the lawyers be disciplined for filing a frivolous claim, sloppily written with typos and factual errors. Judge Parker asked that formal disbarment proceedings begin against the lawyers and that they be required to attend classes on the ethical and legal requirements for filing lawsuits.[33]

What about the defamation suit brought by Dominion Voting Systems?

Dominion Voting Systems, the firm that supplied voting services in a number of states, filed a $3 billion defamation suit against Trump lawyers Sidney Powell, Rudy Giuliani, and MyPillow CEO Mike Lindell. A federal judge in Washington, DC, let the lawsuit proceed, stating that Dominion had "adequately alleged" that Powell and Lindell made their claims "knowing that they were false or with reckless disregard for the truth." The judge wrote that "a reasonable juror" could conclude that Sidney Powell did not have a video of Dominion's founder saying that "he can change a million votes, no problem at all." Further, a sensible juror could conclude that Lindell's charge that there was a "vast international conspiracy that is ignored by the government but proven by a spreadsheet on an Internet blog is so inherently improbable that only a reckless man would believe it." Lindell had declared that Dominion had the "biggest crime ever committed in election history against our country and the world" and that Dominion had created an algorithm to flip votes away from Trump.[34]

On its website, Dominion Voting System stated that it was filing these suits to "defend our good name and reputation."[35] Dominion also filed lawsuits against Fox News, NewsMax Media, and the OAN Network, media outlets that pushed the Big Lie.

In the end, has there been any proof of "massive voter fraud" and a "stolen election" as repeatedly charged by Trump and his supporters?

The answer quite simply and unequivocally is no. There was no proof or even suggestion of any "massive voter fraud." It was (and continues to be) all a lie, a lie of extraordinary proportions, fed by the ego and determination of the defeated president, supported by the silence of Republican lawmakers and officials who know better, whipped up by conservative and far right media outlets, and taken as gospel by millions of supporters willing to believe what they want to hear.

As we've seen in chapter 1, over the years there had been claims of massive voter fraud but simply no proof. With the 2020 election, senior Trump administration officials have rejected any notion of massive voter fraud. The Department of Homeland Security head of cybersecurity, Christopher Krebs, called the 2020 election "the most secure in American history." FBI director Christopher Wray stated that his agency had not seen any coordinated efforts at voter fraud. Attorney General William Barr echoed that assessment: no massive voter fraud. The Brennan Center called the 2020 election "one of the most secure in our history." Federal and state judges routinely threw out unsubstantiated allegations of "massive voter fraud."

States conducted their own investigations. The Ohio secretary of state found 27 possible illegally cast ballots—out of 5,883,999 (or 0.00046 percent). In Georgia, investigators found 4 ballots were cast by dead people—out of 4,999,716 (or 0.00008 percent). Audits in Nevada, Texas, and Arizona all came to the same conclusion—no evidence of widespread voter fraud.[36]

The guardrails, however tenuous, held for the moment: state and local elections officials (Republicans as well as Democrats) risked their careers and reputations by refusing to bend to Trump's will. Judges rejected the claims of fraud and dismissed conspiracies, warning lawyers that lawsuits require evidence and legitimate claims, not posturing, hyperbole, and falsehoods. Still, the Big Lie persists, with former president Trump doubling down, declaring that the number one issue in years to come will be the exposure of the massive fraud of 2020. Trump has also done some rebranding: he has flipped the Big Lie on its head. Now, he tells audiences, the Big Lie comes from the mainstream media, Democrats, and other conspirators who are telling voters that Biden won.

Social scientists for decades will study how this Big Lie, spun by a masterful pitchman, became ingrained in the suspicions and worldviews of so many people.

Have we ever seen a president or major candidate promote this kind of falsehood?

No, the Big Lie pushed by Trump is unprecedented. Sure, other candidates over the years have groused about the outcome of elections, but no candidate, especially a sitting president, has gone to the lengths that Trump did. No presidential candidate has disparaged the election process, cast confusion and discord on the integrity of voting, refused to accept the results unless he wins, and continued to do so months after the election determined to claim, brazenly and openly, that he had won. The falsehood is historic; the damage to the American election process is immeasurable.

In really tight past presidential elections, how did the losing candidate react?

In 1960, Richard Nixon lost to John F. Kennedy by one-tenth of a percentage point—49.7 percent to 49.6 percent—losing the popular vote by 112,827, or just 0.12 percent out of more than 68 million votes cast. Altogether, Kennedy won 303 electoral votes, while Nixon won 219. In 1960, 269 electoral votes were needed. Some Republican leaders and Nixon campaign staffers cried foul, claiming that there was widespread voter fraud in Texas (24 electoral votes) and Illinois (27). Senator Barry Goldwater of Arizona focused on Chicago and Kennedy ally Mayor Richard J. Daley: Chicago, Goldwater declared, was "the rottenest election machinery in the United States."

Had Republicans been able to overturn the results in Texas and Illinois, Nixon would have had 270 electoral votes, one more than necessary to win. (To add to the confusion, there were fourteen unpledged electors from Mississippi [eight] and Alabama [six] and a "faithless" elector in Oklahoma—all of whom went for a protest candidate, the segregationist senator from Virginia, Harry F. Byrd.) Nixon was urged to challenge the results in Illinois, Missouri, New Jersey, and big cities with heavy Catholic populations. But the day after the election, Nixon delivered three speeches, acknowledging Kennedy's victory. In private, Nixon was angry, firmly believing the election was stolen; but in public, he was more statesman-like: conceding defeat and wishing the new president well. Nixon later wrote in his autobiography that he did not contest the election because "charges of 'sore loser' would follow me through history and remove any possibility of a further political career."[37] Nevertheless, the GOP pushed ahead with attempted investigations and lawsuits in eleven states, none of which showed conclusively that Nixon had been robbed. (One state, Hawaii, with three electoral votes, even shifted from Nixon to Kennedy after an audit.) Looking deeply into the election, Professor Edmund Kallina Jr. argued that there was voter fraud in Chicago (helping Democrats) and the rest of Illinois (helping Republicans), but not enough to change the outcome.[38]

In 2000, Al Gore, who had a half-million more popular votes than George W. Bush, lost by a whisker in Florida when a controversial 5-to-4 decision of the Supreme Court stopped ballot counting. The legal wrangling went on for weeks and the political tension was high. But in the end, soon after the Supreme Court made its decision, Gore spoke from his ceremonial office in the Eisenhower Executive Office Building: while he was deeply disappointed and sharply disagreed with the court's decision, "partisan rancor must now be put aside. I accept the finality of the outcome . . . and tonight, for the sake of our unity as a people and the strength of our democracy, I offer my concession."[39] Gore displayed the dignity of the office and the strength of democratic values, and later, as outgoing vice president, presided over the official counting of the electoral vote, then joined the inaugural ceremony on January 20 as Bush II was sworn into office.

Hillary Clinton called Trump the night of the election to congratulate him, but she waited until the next day to give a concession speech. As journalist Jena McGregor wrote, "This was not just a concession speech, even if it had the gracious calls to her supporters to give Trump 'an open mind and a chance to lead.' It was also an inspiring message aimed directly at young people, particularly young women and young girls, who Clinton seemed to feel a responsibility to address in the wake of her historic campaign—and ultimate loss."[40]

Trump apparently never got the Nixon "sore loser" memo. Trump never made a concession speech, never congratulated Biden, never wished him well, balked for weeks before letting the transition process go forward, and aggressively sought to perpetuate the Big Lie, even to the point of fomenting discord and refusing to quash the January 6 insurrection. Like much of what Trump did in office, these actions (and failures to act) were unprecedented.

8

MONEY, MEGA-DONORS, AND WIDE-OPEN SPENDING

"Money is the mother's milk of politics." That old saying seemed quaint in 1971 when Congress enacted the first important campaign-finance laws that regulated and limited how much could be contributed and spent in elections. But so much has changed since then. In recent years, our federal campaign laws have been eviscerated by court decisions, and federal elections have been flooded with money coming from outside interests. Much of the money spent in our federal campaigns is not reported and not regulated, coming from tax-free groups with feel-good, misleading names. How did we get here? How much difference does a lot of money really make in a campaign? Who are some of the big spenders in national politics?

What federal rules and regulations controlled campaign financing before 1971?

For much of the twentieth century, federal campaign financing operated on a cash-and-carry basis. No contribution records had to be kept, no checks had to be written and recorded, and there were no limits on how much money could be raised or spent. Furthermore, the two major political parties and their candidates relied on big donations from wealthy contributors.

Historian Robert Caro wrote about how Senate Majority Leader Lyndon Johnson helped his fellow Senate Democrats in the 1950s. Johnson's aides and cronies would fly down to Texas and then back to Washington with their suit coats and pockets stuffed with cash from oil barons, ready to be distributed to Johnson's favorite Senate allies. There was no federal oversight, no campaign law to stop them, just grateful senators ready to accept the money and to thank their leader and his generous (and anonymous) supporters.[1]

But the really big money came in the 1972 presidential race, when the incumbent Richard Nixon was battling against George McGovern. Insurance magnate W. Clement Stone donated $2.1 million, nearly all of it to the Nixon campaign; likewise, Richard Mellon Scaife, heir to the Mellon oil and banking empire, gave $1 million to the Nixon campaign. Not to be outdone, Stewart R. Mott, heir to a General Motors fortune, gave $400,000 to the McGovern campaign and another $422,000 to other Democrats. Headlines screamed in protest at these outrageous amounts of money. Today, that money, even adjusted for inflation, would be small potatoes.

What also captured the attention of lawmakers were the shady campaign financing practices evident during the Nixon campaign, when unreported, "laundered" money was coming in from unknown national and international sources. It was time for effective federal election laws.

What did the Federal Election Campaign Act of 1971 do?

In 1971, Congress enacted the Federal Election Campaign Act (FECA) and then in 1974 substantially bolstered it with amendments during the Watergate scandal. The campaign-finance law had three main objectives: first, to curb the influence of wealthy donors; second, to require that donations be reported; and third, to put a ceiling on how much money could be raised and spent for federal campaigns. It also created the Federal Election Commission (FEC) to monitor campaign monies and impose penalties on violators when necessary. The law only applies to federal elections, such as elections for

Congress, the US Senate, and the presidency; it does not apply to state or local elections.

The law set limits on how much individual donors could give to a candidate ($1,000 per election), to a political action committee ($5,000), and to a political party ($20,000) and established a total allowed per year ($25,000). It also set limits on how much money could be spent on a campaign. In general elections, amounts were established for presidential candidates ($20 million each), US Senate candidates ($150,000), and House candidates ($70,000).[2] The FECA banned contributions from foreign sources, created a public financing system for presidential elections, and set reporting requirements for contributions of $200 or more.

Can individual candidates spend as much as they want on their own campaigns?

Soon after the FECA became law, the Supreme Court made a major decision on campaign finance, establishing the principle that individuals running for office and independent expenditure organizations (such as the Sierra Club or the National Rifle Association) could spend as much of their own money as they wanted.

In 1976, in the case *Buckley v. Valeo*,[3] the Supreme Court ruled that the FECA limits on campaign expenditures impaired candidates' ability to get their messages out to voters and represented "substantial, rather than merely theoretical, restraints on the quantity and diversity of political speech." From now on, the court ruled, those restraints would not apply, and individual candidates would be free to spend as much of their own money as they wanted. Likewise, the court ruled that independent expenditure organizations were free to spend as much money as they wanted on what was called "issue advocacy." Independent organizations could now advocate their positions (keep our children safe, keep guns away). To avoid having to declare the independent spending provision unconstitutional because of vagueness or being overly broad, the court suggested the terms "vote for," "support," "elect," "cast your ballot for," "defeat," and "reject" as examples of independent spending that still could be regulated. Thus, an advertisement saying "fight hard to defeat Senator Early" could still be subject to spending limits.

The ruling had a major impact on federal campaign-finance law. From that point on, candidates for federal office could spend as much of their own money as they wanted on their campaigns (and as we'll see, many of those wealthy candidates spent a lot of their own money). It also permitted independent groups (or individuals) to spend as much money as they wanted to advocate issues. We'll see later how even that provision was loosened in the *Citizens United v. Federal Election Commission* case.

What's the difference between "hard" money and "soft" money?

In the 1980s, journalists began making a distinction between "hard" money (which is regulated and must be reported under the FECA) and "soft" money (which is not covered by federal laws). In 1978, the FEC changed its regulations to permit corporations and labor unions (which were barred from giving hard money) to give money to state and local party units to fund voter registration drives. Journalists quickly labeled these donations "soft money." How much could corporations and unions give? The FEC regulation did not specify and set no limits. Then, in the following year, the FECA was amended to allow the national political parties to spend money on what were called "party-building activities" by state and local party affiliates, which wouldn't count against the hard-money ceiling established by federal law. These activities went beyond giving money just for voter registration drives. It meant that the Democrats, Republicans, and any other political parties could put money into their state and local organizations to pay for computers, bumper stickers, registration activities, get-out-the-vote drives, and other functions to help build up their parties.

It took a couple of election cycles before the ramifications of soft money sank in, but soon, the political parties were seeking out and aggressively recruiting wealthy individuals, unions, and corporations to give them soft money. A wealthy individual could give only $25,000 per year under the hard-money restrictions, and unions and corporations could give nothing. But after the creation of soft money, the sky was the limit. Soon corporations, unions, and wealthy individuals, both Democrats and Republicans, were giving hundreds of thousands of dollars.[4]

But some corporate leaders and wealthy donors balked at being constantly hit up to give money, crying "donor fatigue." Soft money came to an end with the enactment of the Bipartisan Campaign Reform Act of 2002. But, as we'll see, when one source of campaign funds shut down, others quickly opened up.

What are political action committees (PACs)?

Labor unions and corporations were forbidden to give money directly to candidates. But labor unions, beginning in the 1940s, created separate organizations they called political action committees (PACs), collected money from their members, and gave it to the candidates they favored. Business was slow to catch on to the practice, but, by the 1970s, business PACs were also growing rapidly. By 2010, there were 4,859 PACs, and the number jumped dramatically, to 7,223, in 2015 with the emergence of super PACs.[5]

There are several different kinds of PACs. First, there is the *connected* PAC, affiliated with a labor union, corporation, or membership organization. Most PACs fall into this category. Corporate PACs generally divide their donations evenly or at most 40-60, between Republicans and Democrats. Labor unions almost always heavily contribute to Democrats, with only a small percentage going to Republicans. Corporate and trade association PAC money almost always goes to incumbents who are up for re-election. A subset of connected PACs is known as *foreign-connected* PACs—that is, formed by the American divisions of foreign-owned companies (such as the Toyota Motor North America PAC).

The second category of PAC consists of those that are *nonconnected*. Nonconnected PACs often focus on a specific public policy or an ideology; they are called "nonconnected" because they have no parent organization, unlike a political party, business enterprise, or membership organization. Nonconnected PACs are independent of other organizations and must raise money to support their administration and the solicitation of funds. Examples of nonconnected PACs include the National Rifle Association Political Victory Fund, Constitutional Rights PACs, and EMILY's List.

A third category, the *leadership* PAC, was created in the 1980s. Leadership PACs became vehicles for the leaders in the House and Senate to create another source of PAC money, independent of their own campaign war chests, so that they could distribute that money to candidates in their own party, party committees, or those in their sphere of political influence. Leadership PACs have mushroomed; there are now 542 such PACs, so that everybody in Congress (and several retired members) can be considered a "leader." With money to throw around that is not very carefully monitored, members of Congress can try to gain influence through the money they have to give out. A member of Congress may be in trouble and badly in need of extra campaign funds for the next election. Another lawmaker's leadership PAC can come to the rescue— and put that member in political debt.

Back in 1991, the House and the Senate passed rules banning federal lawmakers from receiving honoraria for speeches. It was the right thing to do: inflated honoraria could be used to pad a lawmaker's income and was nothing more than a form of soft bribery. But now, with leadership PACs, lawmakers are finding numerous, and legal, ways to enhance their well-being. Instead of going to fellow lawmakers or to political campaigns, leadership PAC money can be spent on more personal considerations. Need extra tickets to the big football game? (Representative Gregory Meeks, a New York Democrat, paid $35,000 for National Football League tickets out of his leadership PAC funds.) Want to spend more time on the golf course? (Senator Saxby Chambliss, a Georgia Republican, spent over $100,000.) Need to find a job for your ne'er-do-well nephew? (Over seventy-five political congressional campaigns had relatives on the payroll.) In 2013, a 60 Minutes investigation reported that leadership PACs serve as "slush funds"; they are a way for members to enjoy an inflated lifestyle and provide themselves with an annuity for when they leave office.[6] And lawmakers appear to have little incentive to reform or tighten up on PAC rules when they themselves are the beneficiaries. PACs are still important sources of campaign funds, but they are restricted by hard-money limits; super PACs and dark money, with unlimited spending and often no need to disclose the source of funds, are where the real action is.

What did the McCain-Feingold Act do to fix campaign-finance problems?

But some reform-minded lawmakers have tried for years to update the 1971 FECA, as amended in 1974. There have been plenty of hearings, speeches, and reports, but nothing of substance from Congress. Many lawmakers, particularly Republicans, balk at campaign-finance reform, knowing that cutting off supplies of money can only hurt their re-election chances. Senator Mitch McConnell (Republican-Kentucky) was candid when he spoke in 1999: "Take away soft money and we [Republicans] wouldn't be in the majority in the House and the majority in the Senate and couldn't win back the White House. . . . Hell is going to freeze over first before we get rid of soft money."[7]

But the reform-minded lawmakers persisted. In 2002, under the leadership of John McCain (Republican-Arizona) and Russ Feingold (Democrat-Wisconsin), Congress enacted the Bipartisan Campaign Reform Act (BCRA), often referred to as the McCain-Feingold Act. McConnell's hell did freeze over. Soft money was banned: it could not be raised for national political parties, its use by state parties was restricted, and federal candidates and officeholders were restricted in how they could raise or spend soft money. Right away, millions of dollars of campaign funds were made unavailable, and labor unions, corporations, advocacy groups, and wealthy individuals lost a critical tool for influencing elections.

A second BCRA reform prohibited issue-advocacy "electioneering" expenditures by corporations and labor unions in the sixty days before a general election or within thirty days of a primary. This meant that labor unions, corporations, and other groups couldn't run issue-advocacy advertisements during that window of time. But there were problems with this reform. First, "electioneering communication" was a fuzzy term; it wasn't clear exactly what it meant. Second, the prohibited communication was limited to cable and broadcast television advertising; it did not include newspapers or the expanding world of online communication. We were just in the early stages of using websites, text messaging, and blogs— and members of Congress didn't consider these communication vehicles important enough to include (or more likely, they didn't understand the potential of online communication).

A third reform was to increase the amount of hard (regulated) money that individuals could give to candidates, political parties, and PACs. Inflation had eaten away at the $1,000 limit for individual contributions to candidates set in 1971. A $1,000 donation in 1976 was worth just $318 in 2002. Now the BCRA allowed an individual to give $2,000 per candidate over a two-year election cycle, and for a total of $95,000 over the same two-year cycle to individuals, PACs, and political parties. These limits would also be indexed, so that in 2008, for example, the individual limit would be $2,300, not $2,000.

Immediately after the BCRA was passed, Mitch McConnell, the National Rifle Association, the California Democratic Party, and others sued in federal court to try to overturn it, arguing that the ban on soft money was a restriction of freedom of speech as protected by the First Amendment. In a deeply divided decision, the Supreme Court, in *McConnell et al. v. FEC* (2003), upheld most of the BCRA provisions. The court found that the restrictions on soft money were minimal restrictions of free speech, and that the government had the authority to prevent both actual corruption and the appearance of corruption from unfettered campaign monies.

What do organizations do to get around campaign funding restrictions?

"Money, like water, will always find an outlet," wrote Justice John Paul Stevens in the majority opinion in *McConnell v. FEC*. By that, he meant that Congress was justified in making rules to prevent shady campaign practices. But with soft money banned, it looked like candidates in federal campaigns would have to rely solely on hard (or regulated) money—which to many was just pocket change. How could a candidate for the US Senate, for example, run a decent $10 million campaign when all he could get was a measly $2,000 as a maximum contribution from an individual?

It took maybe a nanosecond for campaign-finance lawyers to figure out ways to get around BCRA restrictions. Most of the focus in campaign-finance laws had, understandably, been on the FECA and its amendments, FEC advisory opinions and regulations, and then on the BCRA. But there was another important regulator: the Internal Revenue Service (IRS). This became plainly evident as campaign-finance lawyers realized that political organizations, which are established under IRS rules, had an opportunity to expand the reach of their financial influence in federal campaigns.

Enter the 527 organizations. Section 527 of the IRS code (26 U.S.C. §527) has been around since 1975. It stipulates that partisan political organizations—such as the Republican and Democratic National Committees, state political parties, or PACs—can be considered "political organizations" for the purposes of the tax code but are not under the jurisdiction of the federal campaign law. The 527 groups were active during the 1990s, but after the passage of the BCRA and the ban on soft money, they became increasingly popular. Contributions to a 527 group are tax-exempt, and they can be of any amount. There are some restrictions: 527s must report the names of their donors and their funding and expenditures to the IRS. Another fundamental restriction: 527s cannot directly advocate the defeat or the election of specific candidates. Still, a 527 is a great vehicle for raising huge amounts of money for the purpose of expressing views on campaign issues. Mitch McConnell's hell may have frozen over when soft money was banished, but soft money has been resurrected, disguised as a 527 group.

Here are some of the most active 527 federally focused organizations and the money they have spent (in millions): NextGen Climate Action (liberal, Democratic: $23.5); Service Employees International Union (liberal, Democratic: $19.6); EMILY's List (Democratic, pro-choice: $19.4); and College Republicans (conservative, Republican: $15.8).[8]

How did the Supreme Court undo campaign-finance reform in Citizens United and subsequent cases?

A conservative advocacy group called Citizens United was established in 1998 as a specific type of nonprofit known as a 501(c)(4) "social welfare" organization. One of its founders, David Bossie, later became deputy campaign manager for Donald Trump during the 2016 presidential campaign. In 2008, Citizens United produced *Hillary: The Movie*, a ninety-minute documentary that was highly critical of Clinton. It wanted to make *Hillary* available on cable television via video-on-demand during the thirty days leading up to the 2008 presidential primaries, and it wanted to run ten- and thirty-second advertisements for the film on broadcast and cable TV.

The FEC, citing the McCain-Feingold Act, barred Citizens United from broadcasting the advertisements during the thirty-day window before the primaries. A federal district court agreed with the FEC and ruled that *Hillary: The Movie* was in fact a campaign ad, not a documentary or a movie as the title wanted us to believe. Sure, *Hillary* could be sold on DVD, shown in movie theaters, or posted on YouTube. But Citizens United would not be permitted to advertise it during the period of the ban. Citizens United sought relief by appealing to the Supreme Court.

At issue before the Supreme Court was this question: is it a violation of free speech for the McCain-Feingold law to prohibit Citizens United from advertising or showing *Hillary: The Movie* during the sixty or thirty days before a general or a primary election? The court heard arguments in *Citizens United v. Federal Election Commission* in March 2009 (well after the 2008 primaries had ended) and in January 2010 delivered its opinion.

The court ruled that the federal government could not ban political spending by corporations (such as Citizens United) during elections. Such bans, according to Justice Anthony Kennedy, were "classic examples of censorship." Kennedy, writing for the majority, didn't see corruption as a problem when big money is involved in elections: "Independent expenditures, including those made by corporations, do not give rise to corruption or the appearance of corruption."[9]

Others sharply disagreed. Senator John McCain was forthright in his anger toward the court: "What the Supreme Court did was a combination of arrogance, naiveté, and stupidity, the likes of which I've never seen." In an unusual gesture, President Obama, in his 2010 State of the Union address, delivered just days after the court decision, declared that *Citizens United* "reversed a century of law that I believe will open the floodgates for special interests—including foreign corporations—to spend without limit in our elections."[10] Seated in the front rows of the House chamber were the Supreme Court justices. When Obama said the above, the cameras covering the speech swung around to Justice Samuel Alito, who, in a break with decorum, mouthed the words "not true," reacting perhaps to Obama's whole statement or his exaggeration of the impact the court's decision would have on foreign companies.

Another 2010 court decision made a dent in our federal campaign law. Just two months later, the Washington, DC Circuit Court of Appeals, in *SpeechNow.org v. Federal Election Commission*, ruled that the $5,000 contribution limit imposed on individuals who want to give to a third party such as a super PAC was unconstitutional. The Supreme Court let the Court of Appeals decision stand.

Here was the one-two punch: the *Citizens United* decision said that corporations, unions, and other entities could spend as much money as they wished on independent expenditures. The *SpeechNow.org* decision permitted independent expenditure organizations to raise as much money as they could. After the *SpeechNow.org* decision, hundreds of new organizations were created, called "super PACs."

One more court decision affected the McCain-Feingold Act (BCRA). Shaun McCutcheon, a wealthy conservative businessman from Alabama, was frustrated that he could only spend so much money to help federal candidates and causes that he favored. He had "maxed out" on sixteen candidates and wanted to spend more, and he considered the ceiling found in the law to be both an impediment to and a violation of the First Amendment. He was joined in his suit by the Republican National Committee (RNC). The Supreme Court agreed with McCutcheon and the RNC. In 2014, it ruled in *McCutcheon v. Federal Election Commission* that the ceilings imposed on individual giving to candidates ($48,600) and to PACs and political parties ($74,600) were unconstitutional. Over a two-year cycle, the maximum that could be donated under the BCRA was $123,200 (for the 2013–2014 election cycle); after the *McCutcheon* ruling, the sky was the limit, and individuals could spend as much as they wanted.

Chief Justice John Roberts, writing the majority opinion, said, "Money in politics may seem repugnant at times to some, but so too does much of what the First Amendment vigorously protects. If the First Amendment protects flag burning, funeral protests, and Nazi parades—despite the profound offense such spectacles cause—it surely protects political campaign speech despite popular opposition."

Dissenting, Justice Stephen Breyer saw it differently: "Taken together with *Citizens United v. Federal Election Commission*, today's decision eviscerates our Nation's campaign-finance laws, leaving a remnant incapable of dealing with the grave problems of democratic legitimacy that those laws were intended to resolve."[11]

With the federal campaign law in tatters and spending limits removed, wealthy individuals, corporations, labor unions, and other interested parties were able to flex their campaign muscle through the Internal Revenue Code.

What are 501(c) groups, and how do they impact campaign spending?

Section 501(c) of the IRS code (26 U.S.C. §501) regulates a wide variety of nonprofit organizations. You may be familiar with 501(c)(3) groups, such as churches and cultural institutions. These 501(c)(3) organizations are "absolutely forbidden" from giving money to or advocating for a candidate, but they can raise awareness of issues. Otherwise, they could be denied tax-exempt status.

In 1954, Congress passed the Johnson Amendment (authored by Senator Lyndon Johnson) prohibiting religious leaders from giving sermons endorsing specific candidates before elections. Churches, synagogues, mosques, and other religious organizations were also prohibited from raising money for candidates. Although the provision was rarely enforced, Donald Trump promised to "totally destroy" it. The repeal showed up in the 2017 tax bill but was ruled nongermane and was dropped.

But three other 501(c) categories have found ways to be involved in campaign financing, and some such organizations have contributed heavily to candidates and causes. The 501(c)(4) organizations are designated "social welfare" groups. *Citizens United* gave 501(c)(4) organizations the green light to participate in campaigns and elections. Soon, the IRS was flooded with applications for new 501(c)(4) organizations. Such organizations must be nonprofit, and their mission must exclusively be to promote "social welfare." The IRS definition of a "social welfare organization" is one "that may be performing some type of public or community benefit but whose principal feature is lack of private benefit or profit." Just about any organization could wiggle its way into that definition.

These organizations can engage in election activity, usually by running television ads and other forms of communication, but they cannot spend more than 49.9 percent of their income on political activities. Here is the real benefit: they do not have to report who their donors are or the amount they contributed, and such donations can be tax-exempt. The original understanding of 501(c)(4) groups was that they would be local civic leagues or volunteer fire departments, not thinly disguised political operations.

Conservative activists and organizations were quick to jump on the 501(c)(4) bandwagon. One of the best known was Crossroads GPS, established by conservative activist Karl Rove. On the progressive side, Organizing for Action was created after Barack Obama's successful 2008 presidential campaign. And of course, one 501(c)(4) group now has a permanent place in campaign law history: Citizens United.

Beyond 501(c)(4) groups, there are two other categories: 501(c)(5) and 501(c)(6) organizations. The (c)(5)s are tax-exempt labor or agricultural groups; the (c)(6)s are chambers of commerce and business leagues. They may also engage in political campaigns on behalf of or in opposition to candidates, provided this does not constitute the organization's primary activity.[12]

How do super PACs differ from ordinary PACs?

The term "super PAC" was coined to reflect this new set of money-generating organizations. We might think that a super PAC is a PAC on steroids. But despite the name, a super PAC is technically not a PAC (and thus is not regulated by the FECA). Legally, super PACs are "independent-expenditure-only committees." That is, super PACs cannot give money to a candidate or a political party, and they can only run political ads independently of a candidate.

That last requirement—that super PACs operate independently of the candidates—sometimes flunks the laugh test. Mitt Romney, in 2012, referred to "my super PAC," and long-time Bush family aide Mike Murphy took over the pro–Jeb Bush super PAC Right to Rise. Right to Rise will probably go down in history as the most ineffective of all super PACs. It raised a ton of money ($121 million), but the former Florida governor was incapable of connecting with voters, and he ended up dropping out of the race early, after the South Carolina primary. This experience also taught us a valuable lesson: money can't always buy votes. Do we know for sure that super PACs are in fact independent and are not coordinating message, strategy, or operations with candidates' campaigns? Not really. If asked, these groups mostly answer that question with winks and nods, vigorously maintaining the campaign fiction that the organizations do not work together. This is possible because of the FEC's failure to do any real enforcement with these so-called independent organizations.

A new set of PACs is now showing up, the *scam* PACs. A super PAC might bring in $1 million, but $995,000 of it is spent on consultant and fundraising fees; just $5,000 goes to the intended candidates. It's an old con, separating money from gullible people, but apparently, it's working in the new world of super PACs. The FEC is aware of many of these problems but has failed to take any action against them.

Candidate Donald Trump in 2015 blasted super PACs, calling them nothing more than scams, and vowed not to seek their help. He soon changed his tune. The Center for Public Integrity noted that by the end of his presidential campaign in 2016, more than one hundred super PACs had worked on his behalf, spending more than $72 million. Trump was aided during his campaigns and during his presidency by groups called America First PAC, America First Policies, Committee to Defend the President, Great America PAC, Future45, Rebuilding America Now, National Rifle Association Super PAC, and many others.[13] Altogether, in 2016, super PACs spent $1.34 billion for all candidates and causes.

During the 2020 presidential election, super PACs spent an enormous amount of money, skyrocketing past the 2016 figure and reaching $2 billion for the first time. But most of the super PAC money was aimed directly at Trump or in favor of Biden. An analysis by the Center for Responsive Politics noted that there was $275 million worth of super PAC advertising against Trump, $250 million of pro-Biden advertising by super PACs, $227 million of anti-Biden spending, and just $42 million of pro-Trump spending.[14]

What is "dark money" and how important has it been in recent elections?

As the name suggests, *dark money* refers to campaign funds whose sources or amounts don't have to be revealed. Thanks to a flood of dark money in recent elections, we have lost one of the core principles of the original federal campaign

Table 8.1 Largest Dark-Money Contributors, 2008–2014, in Millions of Dollars

Group Name	Ideological Leaning	Amount
Freedom Partners Chamber of Commerce	Conservative	$323.9
Center for the Protection of Patient Rights	Conservative	$169.1
Crossroads GPS	Conservative	$64.2
Sea Change Foundation	Conservative	$62.2
Climate Works	Liberal	$51.5
TC4 Trust	Conservative	$47.5

Source: Adapted from "Who Are the Top Dark Money Donors?," OpenSecrets.org, https://www.opensecrets.org/dark-money/top-donors (accessed September 23, 2021).

law—transparency. This wasn't always the case. In 2004, well over 95 percent of all federal donations were made with full disclosure—names of donors, where they worked, and how much they gave. But by the 2012 election, full disclosures had fallen precipitously. This is thanks to *Citizens United* and the more active role played by 501(c) organizations that do not have to reveal their donors.[15]

Which dark money organizations hide the names of their donors? The investigative team at Open Secrets (the Center for Responsive Politics) looked through thousands of 990 tax forms (Organization Exempt from Income Tax) to find the top donors to politically active 501(c) nonprofits. Table 8.1 shows the biggest dark-money contributors from the 2008 through the 2014 election cycles (the latest figures available).

Who are the top individual mega-donors, how much have they spent, and where do they stand politically?

At the top of the list of mega-donors are the Koch brothers, David and Charles. They have been giving money to and setting up conservative operations since the mid-1980s. In 2012, the Koch brothers spent over $400 million in an attempt to defeat Barack Obama. Before the 2016 presidential elections, they announced their goal of raising $889 million. But when

Donald Trump became the Republican candidate, the Kochs backed off their pledge to donate that massive sum of money. By mid-2015, some one thousand employees were working for Koch-sponsored political organizations, such as Americans for Progress, Concerned Veterans for America, and the Libre Initiative (meant to attract Hispanic voters). Journalist Kenneth Vogel described the Koch political operation as "among the most dominant forces in American politics, rivaling even the official Republican Party in its ability to shape policy debates and elections."[16]

Casino magnate Sheldon Adelson reportedly gave over $150 million during the 2012 presidential campaign, first to Newt Gingrich, then to Mitt Romney's campaign. Adelson's money (and accompanying influence) became so seductive that reporters dubbed the early stages of the race the "Sheldon Primary," because Republican candidates were showing up in Las Vegas to curry favor with the billionaire. Fairly new on the mega-donor scene in 2016 was hedge-fund billionaire Robert Mercer, who supported Ted Cruz before turning his support to Trump. Mercer and his daughter Rebekah were allies of Stephen Bannon and helped to steer the big-data firm Cambridge Analytica to the Trump campaign.

On the progressive side, George Soros was at one time the go-to mega-donor, but he has since been eclipsed by others, especially Tom Steyer, who spent nearly $100 million during the 2016 election cycle and in 2018 poured money into television ads urging the impeachment of President Trump. Former New York City mayor Michael Bloomberg, now a Democrat, played a leading role in the 2018 elections, donating over $100 million of his own money to support Democratic candidates, then spent over $1 billion on his own presidential nomination campaign in 2020.

Table 8.2 shows the top ten donors to federal campaigns during the 2020 cycle.

Casino magnate Sheldon Adelson, who died in early 2021, and his wife, Miriam, were by far the biggest donors to federal

Table 8.2 Top Individual Contributors to Federal Campaigns, 2020, in Millions

Name	Total	Hard Money	Outside Money	Recipients
1. Sheldon and Miriam Adelson	$218.2	$3.0	$215.2	Rep., 100%
2. Michael Bloomberg	$152.5	$0.9	$151.6	Dem., 100%
3. Mike and Taylor Steyer	$72.1	$2.1	$70.0	Dem., 100%
4. Richard and Elizabeth Uihlein	$68.3	$3.3	$65.0	Rep., 100%
5. Ken Griffin	$67.4	$1.1	$66.3	Rep., 100%
6. Timothy Mellon	$60.1	$0.1	$60.0	Rep., 100%
7. Dustin and Carl Moskovitz	$50.6	$1.0	$49.5	Dem., 100%

Source: "Who Are the Biggest Donors?," Opensecrets.org, https://www.opensecrets.org/elections-overview/biggest-donors?cycle=2020&view=fc (accessed September 23, 2021).

campaigns. In addition, the Adelsons also donated more than $82 million in the 2016 election cycle as well as $150 million in 2012.

Notice one important thing in Table 8.2: just a small percentage of the money these wealthy donors spent went to FEC-regulated hard money. The rest was channeled through super PACs or other vehicles set up to circumvent hard-money restrictions. After all, if you plan to donate $50 million, it's difficult to give it away in $2,700 or $5,000 chunks, as required by the FECA. The table also doesn't give the full measure of giving.

What about regular people? Do they give money to political candidates?

For all the focus on mega-donations from wealthy donors, the question remains, what about money given by average people, say, those who can contribute $50, $100, or perhaps $200 to a candidate? When he was running for the Democratic presidential nomination in 2016, Vermont senator Bernie Sanders liked to boast that he had received millions from everyday donors, and that the average donation was just $27. He made it a point of pride to say that he didn't take any money from any kind of PAC. Sanders's online fundraising was unparalleled in modern presidential-election history: during the primaries he was able to gather a total of $226.1 million. Nearly half of that sum, $99.6 million, came from 221,382 donors who gave him less than $200 each.[17] In September 2016, well after Sanders had quit the race, his campaign announced that he had collected over a million donations online.

Getting a lot of people to donate small amounts, say, an average of $25, is certainly possible, especially because online donating is easy, convenient, and inexpensive. It is a healthy sign that there is a groundswell of support from thousands, maybe hundreds of thousands, of voters who wish their candidate well. It also communicates the underlying message that the candidate isn't relying on a handful of very wealthy people, who undoubtedly will come back for a favor or two.

But let's do the math. One anonymous donor can set up a super PAC to help elect a candidate, spending $25 million to finance that effort. It would take a million donors, giving $25 each, to match that rich guy. For candidates and causes, it's just so much simpler and easier to tap into the pockets of wealthy individuals. Of course, candidates will swear that they are not being bought by deep-pocket donors, but we can just about guarantee that the next time the rich guy calls the senator's office, he gets immediate attention.

Here's another stark reality. Despite what the Bernie Sanders campaign showed us, very few people give money to political candidates. The Center for Responsive Politics noted that in 2016, out of a total US adult population of 245.2 million, just 0.68 percent (1,672,050 individuals) donated more than $200, and only 0.10 percent (253,352 individuals) gave the maximum of $2,700.[18] Let's do a few other estimates. Suppose that 1 million individuals give small amounts to federal candidates or give through their union or their company's PAC and that another million give money to state and local candidates. This adds up, generously, to around 4 million out of 245.2 million adults giving money to candidates, or about 1.6 percent of the total adult population. But in the 2020 elections, there was a remarkable outburst from people giving small amounts to candidates. Some 22.9 percent of donations to federal candidates in 2020 came from individuals who gave $200 or less. This is a far greater percentage than four years earlier.[19]

But there was also a level of small-donation campaign shenanigans in 2020. People giving money to the Trump campaign were not fully aware that their one-time donations were being repeated, without their knowledge or consent. FEC records indicated that more than $135 million had been refunded to donors by Trump, the RNC, and associated accounts. Peter Loge of the Project on Ethics in Political Communication at the George Washington University concluded that it was "pretty clear that the Trump campaign was engaging in deceptive tactics. If you have to return that much money you are doing something either very wrong or very unethical."[20]

How well has the FEC performed its job of enforcing campaign-finance rules?

The FEC has had many critics over the years, and deservedly so. It has been called a "toothless tiger," a "watchdog without a bite," "borderline useless," and "completely useless." Two critics, Fred Wertheimer and Don Simon, dubbed it the "Failure to Enforce Commission," noting that in recent years, the FEC has been "completely dysfunctional."[21] The FEC's investigations of campaign wrongdoing are time-consuming; it has no real power of enforcement; it cannot go into court to enjoin illegal activities; and its Republican members, especially, have balked at enforcing campaign-finance laws. Wertheimer and Simon see the FEC as the kind of agency many in Congress would like to create: it has few powers, does little with those powers, and lets campaign-finance abuse go on without penalty.[22]

Didn't the IRS get in trouble for trying to oversee these organizations?

Shortly after the *Citizens United* decision, in January 2010, the IRS started seeing a great number of applications from newly formed 501(c)(4) groups, mostly from conservative organizations. The IRS, concerned about possibly fraudulent groups, flagged organizations whose names included the words "patriot," "Tea Party," or "9/12 Project" (a group created by conservative activist Glenn Beck). This raised a firestorm of protest, particularly from conservative members of Congress and other activists. President Obama demanded the resignation of the IRS director, Steven T. Miller, calling the agency's actions "inexcusable." The Treasury Department's inspector general delivered an exhaustive report on what the IRS had done. The report found that the IRS had taken a shortcut when it targeted conservative groups, but that it had done the same thing with progressive organizations, flagging those that had the words "progressive," "occupy," and "green energy" in their names. Unquestionably, the IRS had crossed the line, with predictable accusations of targeting groups based on ideology and partisanship.[23]

Where does all that campaign money go?

When a candidate spends millions on an election, where does all the money go?

Looking just at House and Senate candidates, the FEC recorded over 16.9 million receipts from January 1, 2017, through April 4, 2018, going toward everything from fundraising costs, meals, staff payroll, office expenses, political consultants, postage, database management, Internet advertising, website design and services, travel, gasoline, and a wide variety of other essential expenditures. But the biggest expense of all, in most campaigns, is the cost of creating and broadcasting television commercials. The big beneficiaries? Local television stations and media consultants.

What are the most expensive campaigns at the federal (but not presidential) level?

The first $100 million Senate race came in 2014; the first $200 million race came in 2018. Since then, the lid on spending has been blown off. The 2020 Senate races produced nine out of the top ten most expensive races in American history, topped by the two most expensive races, the Georgia special elections, both won by Democrats. A staggering $510 million was spent in one of the Georgia runoffs and $363 million was spent on the other. It wasn't too many presidential election cycles ago when $510 million would fund an entire national campaign.

Not making this list was the most expensive contest, measured by cost per vote: the 2020 Maine Senate election, pitting incumbent Susan Collins against Sara Gideon. The total cost was $207 million and cost over $268 per vote. At one time, $5 per vote was considered a really expensive race; but then again, at one time, just a couple of decades ago, a $5 million Senate race was considered exorbitant. To give a further reality check on the exorbitant campaign expenses, Governor Edmund Muskie, running for the US Senate seat from Maine in 1958, spent $37,350 ($353,554 in 2021 dollars) to defeat incumbent Fred Payne.

The principal factor here is not the population of the state or the number of expensive media markets. From Table 8.3, we would expect Florida, with the largest population of the states listed and the greatest number of media markets, to be the most expensive. We certainly wouldn't expect small-population states like South Carolina or Iowa to be on the list. But the real key is partisan competitiveness: the desperate attempt by both Republicans and Democrats and their allies to hold on to, or gain, a Senate seat.

Table 8.3 Most Expensive US Senate Races, in Millions of Dollars

Year	State, Candidates	Total $ Spent (in Millions)	$ Per Vote
2021	Georgia (runoff)	$510.0	$114.09
	Jon Ossoff-D (50.6% of votes); *David Perdue-R (49.39%)		
2021	Georgia (runoff)	$363.0	$80.95
	Raphael Warnock-D (51.0%); *Kelly Loeffler-R (48.9%)		
2020	North Carolina	$298.9	$57.09
	*Thom Tillis-R (48.7%); Cal Cunningham (46.9%)		
2020	South Carolina	$276.9	$111.70
	*Lindsey Graham-R (54.4%); Jaime Harrison-D (44.2%)-D		
2020	Iowa	$261.6	$161.58
	*Joni Ernest-R (51.8%); Theresa Greenfield-D (45.2%)		
2018	Florida	$213.4	$26.06
	Rick Scott-R (50.05%); *Bill Nelson (49.93%)		
	* Denotes incumbent.		

Source: "Nine of the Most Expensive Senate Races of All Time Happened in 2020," Opensecrets.org, https://www.opensecrets.org/news/2020/12/most-expensive-races-of-all-time-senate2020/. Accessed September 24, 2021.

We also saw some very expensive Senate races in 2018. Florida topped the list with $213 million spent, followed by Missouri ($107.8 million), Texas ($101.6 million), Nevada ($89.2 million), Arizona ($85 million), and Indiana ($83.8 million). Again, the main factor was partisan competitiveness: incumbent Democratic senators lost in Florida (Bill Nelson), Missouri (Claire McCaskill), Nevada (Dean Heller), and Indiana (Joe Donnelly). Arizona was an open seat, and in Texas the Republican incumbent (Ted Cruz) managed to hang on against a vigorous challenger (Beto O'Rourke).

About twenty years ago, it was highly unusual to see a House election campaign costing more than $1 million. As time went on, $1 million became the average spent for contested House elections. More recently, we have seen House races that cost far more, and much more outside money being thrown into the contests. The most expensive race of all time occurred in 2018, when $42.4 million was poured into California's Thirty-Ninth District, won by Democrat Gil Cisneros. In 2018 and 2020, nine

House campaigns each totaled more than $30 million when counting candidate funds and outside money. The key reason they cost so much is because outside groups are eager to try to capitalize on a weak incumbent or see an opportunity to capture an open seat.[24]

With the margin between Democrats and Republicans so small in 2020—just a three-seat majority for Democrats—many congressional elections in 2022 will be fiercely fought and, guaranteed, very costly.

Do candidates who amass the most money always win?

The answer is generally yes, but only when the candidate is up for re-election or is well known. This is most evident in the House of Representatives. Each election cycle, incumbent members of Congress, from either party, will win re-election 95 percent to 97 percent of the time. A lot of that has to do with gerrymandered districts, which heavily favor one party over the other. Another factor is that a member of Congress with a constituency of 250,000 or so voters can fairly easily connect with those voters while in office. A good office staff and good communications operation go a long way to reaching those voters. But money is also a big factor. Many members of Congress have amassed considerable war chests, either through their own campaign efforts or through their own leadership PACs. For example, during the 2016, 2014, and 2012 congressional races, incumbents running for re-election gathered about six times the amount of funds gathered by their opponents.

What about self-funded candidates?

Wealthy candidates are a different story. Candidates with lots of money but no experience in government or politics usually aren't very successful. (Donald Trump, of course, is the exception here.) Looking at the self-funded candidates (that is, candidates who put in at least $500,000 of their own money) in House and Senate races since 2000, we find that the track record for self-funders is abysmal. Altogether, 343 campaigns for the House and Senate were self-funded. In only 50 of those campaigns did the self-funder win; and the higher the percentage of the self-funding, the greater the chance that the candidate would lose. Many of the 50 winners were either incumbents or well known and didn't rely on their own funds exclusively to finance their campaigns.

Let's look at some of the high rollers. Table 8.4 is a list of the most expensive federal, state, and local campaigns in recent years into which wealthy candidates put their own money. As we see, spending a lot of money doesn't always ensure success.

Table 8.4 How Did They Do? Wealthy Candidates Who Spent Their Own Money

Candidate	Office (Year)	Own Money Spent	Won or Lost
Michael Bloomberg	Dem. Nom. Pres. (2020)	$1.09 billion	Lost
Tom Steyer	Dem. Nom. Pres. (2020)	$338 million	Lost
J. B. Pritzker	Illinois Governor (2018)	$171.5 million	Won
Meg Whitman	Calif. Governor (2010)	$144 million	Lost
Michael Bloomberg	NYC Mayor (2009)	$102 million	Won
Michael Bloomberg	NYC Mayor (2005)	$85 million	Won
Michael Bloomberg	NYC Mayor (2001)	$74 million	Won
Tom Golisano	NY Governor (2002)	$74 million	Lost
Rick Scott	Florida Governor (2010)	$73 million	Won
Donald Trump	President (2016)	$66 million	Won
Ross Perot	President (1992)	$63 million	Lost
Jon Corzine	NJ Senate (2000)	$60 million	Won
Linda McMahon	Conn. Senate (2010)	$50 million	Lost
Linda McMahon	Conn. Senate (2012)	$49 million	Lost
Mitt Romney	Rep. Nom. Pres. (2008)	$45 million	Lost

Source: Adapted from "Top Self-Funding Candidates," Opensecrets.org, https://www.opensecrets.org/elections-overview/top-self-funders (accessed September 26, 2021).

Where are we now with federal campaign laws?

Let's look back at the goals of the landmark FECA of 1971 and its amendments and see where we are. One of the basic goals of the act was to create transparency: if you give more than $200 to a federal candidate, political party, or PAC, it must be reported and made public. That is still the law. But if you want to spend a couple million dollars, you can easily hide it.

Here's another thing you can do to keep your donations anonymous: create a 501(c)(4) group late in the campaign season, say, in September before a November election. Dump millions of dollars into it, which can have a major impact on an election. Disband the group a couple weeks after the election. No one will be the wiser. The IRS, understaffed and overwhelmed by its monitoring task, won't get around to looking at the purpose and spending of your now-disbanded 501(c)(4) until well after the fact.

A second FECA goal was to set limits on how much individuals could contribute. That idea has been blown out of the water. Sure, there is a $2,700 maximum for an individual contribution to a primary, runoff, or a general election. But look again at Table 8.2: just a small fraction of the spending by the biggest spenders went through "hard" money of the FEC, and tens of millions went to outside groups trying to influence the elections. As we've seen, there's no longer a ceiling on total hard-money expenditures, thanks to the *McCutcheon* decision. Anyone with a lot of money to burn can easily spend it (and easily hide it).

Earlier campaign laws forbade unions and corporations from directly donating to campaigns. That's still the law. But thanks to the *Citizens United* and *SpeechNow.org* Supreme Court decisions, unions, corporations, and other groups can spend as much as they want in independent spending. These recent Supreme Court and federal court rulings have basically nullified McCain-Feingold, the BCRA of 2002.

Here is the bottom line on federal campaign money. Small-amount donors now have very easy access to candidates: pull out your smartphone, click an app, and donate to a candidate or cause. It couldn't be easier. Yet despite the ease and simplicity of donating, few people do contribute.

But if you've got a lot of money and you don't want reporters or others knowing where the money came from or how much you've spent, it couldn't be a better time for you. If you want everyone to know how much money you have lavished on candidates or causes, it's also a great time for you.

Much more money is being poured into federal (and many state and local) campaigns. That may be good for local television stations and political consultants, but it should be troubling for the rest of us.

Despite these efforts by the Open Secrets team, the full extent of dark money remains unknown to the public.

9

INNER WORKINGS
OF MODERN CAMPAIGNS

Major political campaigns, everything from big-city mayoral contests to presidential campaigns, rely on a battery of professional campaign consultants and operatives. Without these professionals, candidates would have a very difficult time navigating through the landmines and pitfalls of campaigns.

Why can't candidates just run on their own, without the need for consultants and handlers?

It sounds like a simple idea: candidates running on their own ideas, without the need for speechwriters, pollsters, media people, and political pros telling them what to say, where to go, and how to conduct a campaign. But given the reality of modern campaigns, the unassisted candidate could be a recipe for disaster.

For a first-time candidate, there's no steeper learning curve than that found in a political campaign. The novice politician who has decided to run for mayor or city council or even Congress is immediately faced with the big questions: What's my message? Who can help me raise money? How much money do I need to run a campaign? How do I contact voters? What do I say about my opponent? Do voters know anything about me and what office I'm running for? The list goes on, and the candidate is faced with plenty of challenges: a well-funded opponent who is gearing up for a campaign against her; an on-line media campaign mounted by an outside, unknown group criticizing her at every turn; and, most troubling, an indifferent public that, no matter how many times our candidate repeats her story and makes her pitch, still doesn't know who she is, what office she's seeking, and what she stands for.

Friends, family, and coworkers can help and offer her support and encouragement. But what can also help is the advice and counseling of seasoned political veterans, political consultants, and operatives who've done this before, know all the tricks of the trade, and can help the candidate maneuver through political minefields and avoid rookie mistakes.

Most campaigns are local, funded out of the candidate's pocket or through friends and family, and are carried out with the help of dedicated volunteers. But when we get to more expensive contests, professional campaign consultants are more and more likely to be called upon. As we saw in chapter 6, the average congressional seat costs more than $1 million today, and many other local contests cost hundreds of thousands of dollars.[1]

What are the key elements of any successful political campaign?

The campaign team must focus on three crucial things. First, it must develop a clear, consistent, easily understood, and winning message. Second, it must identify voters friendly to the campaign (and those who might be persuaded) and convey that message to them. Finally, it must get them out to vote. Of course, none of this can happen unless the campaign (and its allies) raises enough money to keep everything afloat.

Sometimes the message is simple and aspirational: "Yes, We Can" (Obama) or "Bridge to the Twenty-First Century" (Bill Clinton) or "It's Morning Again in America" (Reagan). Trump's "Make America Great Again" sounded suspiciously like Reagan's "Let's Make America Great Again," but, nonetheless, it worked. But sometimes those slogans just don't resonate with voters: "Nixon's the One" or "Kinder, Gentler Nation" (George H. W. Bush) or "I'm with Her" (Hillary Clinton). The jury is still out on Biden's 2020 "Build Back Better" slogan.

Creating a slogan, and developing a consistent message behind it, often takes months of preparation: thousands of voters surveyed, focus groups probed, and hundreds of hours of data analysis and creative marketing.

Where are the voters who will support the candidate, and how should the campaign appeal to them? Beginning in the early 2000s, and especially with Barack Obama in 2008 and 2012, campaigns ramped up the use of technology to analyze and probe the millions of bits of data they have on voters. Some political consulting firms specialize in voter mapping and data and can tell campaigns—whether presidential or local mayoral—where the voters are, their voting histories, what their interests and habits are, and even their hopes and fears. Do you like anchovies? Chances are you're not a Republican. Campaigns can microtarget their audiences with far greater precision than ever before. At one time, the best consultants could do was to identify "soccer Moms" or "NASCAR Dads." Now, thanks to all the digital information we leave on social media sites and the cookies we build on commercial sites, campaigns can know whom to reach and what specific messages to convey. The effort is costly and time-consuming, but campaigns are investing heavily in this kind of information.

The third element harkens back to the old days of shoe-leather politics: getting out the vote. This means knowing who your voting base is, getting them registered to vote, and energizing them. Getting dedicated supporters to vote usually isn't a problem, but getting soft supporters or fence-sitters to participate could mean the difference between winning and losing. It means sending out a barrage of emails, making social media pleas and telephone calls, offering free rides to the precincts—doing anything it takes to get lingering supporters to vote. This also can take an extraordinary amount of staff resources and last-minute financial and physical resources.

What do you mean by political consultants, and what kinds of services do they provide?

The principal role of the strategists in any campaign is to control the chaos: to bring their skills, past campaign experience, and discipline to an often-unruly business. Campaign or political consultants are individuals and firms that provide key services to candidates, political parties, and interest groups. For big-money campaigns, such as a $50 million race for the US Senate, a campaign will hire a variety of skilled and experienced consultants. A candidate will hire *strategists* (for example, a general consultant to oversee the whole operation, a campaign manager, media experts, pollsters, and direct-mail specialists). The campaign will also hire *specialists* (candidate and opposition researchers, speech writers, lawyers and accountants familiar with campaign law, television-time buyers, telemarketers, microtargeting specialists, web designers, social media coordinators, and more). The campaign will also buy the services of *vendors*, firms that supply voter files, yard signs, campaign software, and the like.[2]

Most political campaigns don't spend $50 million or anything close to it. The great majority of our half-million campaigns are low-key and inexpensive and don't have the funds to hire experienced campaigners. If a campaign has less than $50,000 to spend, chances are there will be no professionals involved; or if there are, it will be just a campaign manager plus a lot of volunteers. But surprisingly, as we saw in chapter 8, plenty of local races—from school board to local sheriff—have budgets greater than $50,000.

What do media consultants provide?

Since the beginning of the television age in the 1950s, candidates for office, especially for statewide offices and for president, have relied on television advertising to introduce themselves to voters. They try, in fifteen- or thirty-second ads, to sell their campaign message. For many decades, political media consultants have been the darlings of the campaign world. They are the ones who craft and mold the television image of their candidates and present them to the viewing public. The best of these consultants, who rake in lucrative percentages of each television buy, along with their own production fees, can make handsome livings from their work with candidates and causes.

There have been profound changes in the media landscape over the past thirty or so years: the once-dominant networks now compete with a proliferation of cable channels and start-up networks, and television competes with streaming services and a variety of social media sources. Television viewers can block advertisements, watch their favorite shows at times of their own choosing, and often focus their eyes on two or more screens at once. Television viewing as a percentage of the average adult's viewing behavior has gone down steadily. Nevertheless, television is still a dominant force in political campaigns.

Video techniques have changed as well. Instead of a well-lighted, well-choreographed thirty-second advertisement, candidates may prefer a cinéma vérité approach: handheld camera, poor lighting, and herky-jerky movements, making their professionally produced advertisements look amateur (and thus more authentic). Such campaign videos are more likely to show up on YouTube, as web advertisements, on reality television, and on a variety of social media sites.

What do pollsters do for a campaign?

Pollsters have sometimes been called the "radar system" of a political campaign. There are two basic types of pollsters—public and private. When we encounter a news story about public opinion, the research has come from a public pollster, such as Gallup, Harris Interactive, and other firms. That information is meant to be shared with the public. By contrast, private polling is conducted by candidates, political parties, and others who use the findings to mold strategy, test ideas, and determine what is and is not working in a campaign. This information is not normally shared with the public, and it becomes an important tool for a campaign.

A private polling firm hired by a campaign will try to determine several things, at different points in a campaign. At the very beginning of a campaign, a pollster can tell a candidate what issues resonate with voters, how many people recognize the candidate's and potential opponents' names, and a variety of other matters. During the campaign, pollsters will take snapshots of public opinion, through separate surveys of 500 to 1,500 people, and through focus groups of 8 to 15 carefully selected individuals, who can give the campaign a different sense of public opinion. Pollsters can help a candidate to frame issues, tailor speeches to fit audiences, and, through daily tracking polls, see how the campaign is progressing. Because fewer people today answer their phones, relying on caller ID to screen unwanted calls, and because many people have abandoned landlines altogether, pollsters have more and more turned to online polling.

How much information do political campaigns have on the average voter?

Plenty. In fact, some data firms boast of having nine hundred or so data points on the average individual. They know, for example, where you live, the last time you voted, your political party affiliation, and how much money you have given to campaigns. But they also know far more: what kind of car you drive, what your salary range is, where you buy your groceries or clothes, and where you go online and in the physical world. Where do researchers get this information? From public records at state election boards, data vendors who scan through warranty information, the data kept by grocery store chains and other retail establishments, social media companies, and many, many other sources.

The digital world has opened up so much more information about our preferences. All that stuff we buy online and information we post on Facebook and other platforms—it all becomes a part of our digital profile, ready for campaigns to analyze and exploit.

If a campaign wants to reach voters who have hunting and fishing licenses, consulting firms can identify them. Need to know which families send their kids to private schools or usually vote Republican but turned against Trump in 2016? Need to know where to find that 12 percent of voters who are Democratic in a deeply Republican district? Data management firms can tell you all that.

The newest wrinkle is psychographic targeting: tailoring a message to trigger an individual's fears or hopes. Donald Nix, the CEO of Cambridge Analytica, the marketing firm that worked for Ted Cruz and Donald Trump, explained, "If you know the personality of the people you're targeting, you can nuance your messaging to resonate more effectively with those key audience groups."[3] Cambridge Analytica got into deep trouble for improperly obtaining personal data from over 50 million Facebook users. The idea behind psychographic targeting is to go directly to a person's emotions, perhaps bypassing their brains, and convince them through the clever use of words, symbols, and text. Commercial advertisers and media specialists have been doing this for a very long time, going after the heart rather than the brain (think of all those cute puppies and sunsets), but it remains to be seen if psychographic targeting, with its massive amounts of data and tailored algorithms, can add one further persuasive tool to those of campaign managers.

Who have been some of the most important political consultants over the years, and where are they now?

Political consultants generally work in the background. After all, it is the candidate who is most important, not the consultants or the campaign team. On election night, it is the candidate up at the podium, smiling and waving, surrounded by family and friends; the consultants are over in the corner enjoying the victory. Even when we think of high-stakes presidential politics, most people will draw a blank when they are asked who managed Mitt Romney's or Barack Obama's 2012 campaigns or Hillary Clinton's 2016 campaign.[4] Okay, who managed Trump's campaign (Bill Stepien) and Joe Biden's campaign (Jen O'Malley Dillon) in 2020?

We know more about Donald Trump's 2016 campaign because of the legal troubles of Paul Manafort (his one-time campaign manager) and the media attention given to Corey Lewandowski, Roger Stone, and Kellyanne Conway. Other political consultants become known because after working on presidential contests, they became media figures, appearing regularly on television and writing books. Years ago, it was Lee Atwater (working for George H. W. Bush), Roger Ailes (working for Nixon and, later, becoming president of Fox News), James Carville (working for Bill Clinton), and Karl Rove (working for George W. Bush). More recently, David Axelrod (working for Barack Obama) has become a regular on television, along with Paul Begala (who worked for Bill Clinton). These are just the tip of the iceberg, the celebrities, among thousands of other consultants working for candidates up and down the electoral ladder.

In 2016, it was Hillary Clinton's race to lose. How did her consultants and strategists get it wrong, and did Trump show that consultants aren't all that necessary or smart in getting a candidate elected?

There's no question that the Clinton team miscalculated and flubbed the campaign. The campaign leadership was made up of bright, talented, and experienced political operatives who had worked on presidential elections before, been involved in Democratic administrations, and had plenty of experience with the vagaries of campaign life.[5] The strategic team was supported by hundreds of campaign staffers, both in the campaign's Brooklyn headquarters and in field offices throughout the country.

By contrast, the Trump campaign was a revolving door of consultants and newbies. Many of the best Republican consultants refused to get involved with the Trump campaign, and those who did were sometimes second or third tier.

The race was Clinton's to lose. Few election prognosticators, including this author, gave Trump much of a chance. So what happened? Several things to note: First, the public just didn't like Hillary Clinton. She had historically low approval ratings; only Donald Trump had lower numbers. Second, she'd had a very tough primary contest against an outsider, Bernie Sanders. There were hard feelings among his followers and many were reluctant to join forces with the Clinton campaign during the general election. Third, perhaps lulled by the predictions by many public and private pollsters of a Clinton landslide victory, the campaign went after states it thought it might capture from Republicans, rather than manning the barricades in states where Clinton might be vulnerable. For example, Clinton never visited Wisconsin, a state that had gone Democratic in six straight presidential elections, only to lose it (and the election) by a whisker. Fourth, the campaign relied too much on its voter data-mining effort, assuming that Clinton was winning but failing to understand the intensity of the support that Trump was getting. Naysayers on CNN scoffed at the predictions of Trump loyalist Jeffrey Lord, who predicted that Trump would win Pennsylvania. Just look at the size and intensity of the crowds that flock to see Trump, Lord said. He was right: the intensity at the campaign rallies was palpable. Fifth, the disclosure by FBI director James Comey of another round of Clinton emails came at the worst possible time and slowed her last-minute momentum. Finally, the presence of two third-party candidates, Gary Johnson and Jill Stein, meant the difference in the votes in those crucial states. Stein was ideologically closer to Clinton than to Trump, and had those Stein voters chosen Clinton, she would have won Pennsylvania, Michigan, and Wisconsin.

Filmmaker and liberal activist Michael Moore predicted, five months before the election, that Trump would concentrate on four Rust Belt states—Ohio, Michigan, Pennsylvania, and Wisconsin. These states had recently elected Republican governors and were ripe for Trump's tough message and bluster. Moore, who grew up in this blue-collar heartland, described Trump as a "human Molotov cocktail" and said that's why "every beaten down, nameless forgotten working stiff who used to be part of what was called the middle class loves Trump."[6]

The Trump campaign also received considerable help in targeting and get-out-the-vote efforts, especially in Wisconsin, from the Republican National Committee.

How could a well-oiled consulting and campaign team— far more experienced, richer, and larger than Trump's—fail to win? Perhaps this tells us something about the limitations of political consultants and strategy—they can only do so much. It also tells us that money, even strategically spent, certainly cannot guarantee an election victory. Forget Trump's bombast, his boasting, and his outright lying. His supporters were fervent in their support: he was going to tear down the walls of privilege and Washington elites; he was going to "drain the swamp" and turn the mess around from day one of his presidency. He was defiantly against political correctness, unafraid to ban Muslims, and going to build a wall that Mexico would pay for, and he would make America great again.

Enough voters (46.1 percent) bought into that angry and defiant message, and he squeaked through. White rural voters, especially those without a college education, overwhelmingly and enthusiastically supported him. Minority voters, especially African Americans, who had vigorously supported Barack Obama, were not as enthusiastic about a Hillary Clinton presidency.

What about Trump versus Biden in 2020? How did the campaign strategies fare?

As outlined in chapter 6, the 2020 presidential campaign was an exceptional race. Joe Biden, the epitome of the Washington insider, had served in the Senate from 1973 until 2009, when he became vice president for eight years. Twice before, in 1988 and 2008, he ran for the Democratic presidential nomination. And both times he failed miserably. In 2020, he got in the crowded Democratic primary field but continued losing through the first crucial primaries: he came in fourth in Iowa and fifth in New Hampshire. For Biden's campaign, dysfunctional, running out of money, and dispirited, it was a near-death experience. It seemed like Biden's last chance would be the South Carolina primary, where, thanks to the strong support from African American Democrats, he was able to pull off a stunning victory. Anita Dunn, a veteran Biden ally, urged Jen O'Malley Dillon, a longtime Democratic operative, to come onboard as campaign manager. O'Malley Dillon, one of the best Democratic field operators, brought campaign experience and savvy to the sagging campaign. She quickly brought order to the chaotic campaign and was a steady hand who brought harmony and coordination to the competing interests of the campaign, the state parties, interest groups, and the national party apparatus. Much of this was done through telephone calls, Zoom meetings, and text messages. Much of it was accomplished in O'Malley Dillon's personal headquarters, the third floor of her family's home in suburban Maryland. Often her Zoom meetings were late at night, with O'Malley Dillon conducting the meetings from the seat of her Peloton bike.

The Trump re-election effort, first led by Brad Parscale, was much more of a traditional campaign, with Trump continuing to travel around the country. Huge rallies were Trump's signature event during the 2016 campaign; he held some big rallies in 2020, but Covid inevitably curtailed them. Trump's poll numbers sagged, primarily because of the pandemic but also voters' weariness of the tempestuous previous four years. The campaign also employed a serious digital operation and, together with the Republican National Committee, had a significant get-out-the-vote effort, knocking on 1 million doors a week. The Trump team was highly successful in motivating its base, particularly the evangelical Christian vote, which turned out in higher-than-expected numbers. Parscale lost favor with Trump, and during the summer of 2020, Bill Stepien became the campaign manager. Stepien, a veteran of New Jersey campaigns, had earlier served as a top campaign operative for the 2016 Trump campaign and had been in charge of the White House political office under Trump. After the Trump loss, Stepien and two top campaign operatives reopened a political consulting firm, hoping to aid Republican candidates, and especially Donald Trump, in the upcoming years.

10

DIRECT DEMOCRACY— BALLOT CAMPAIGNS

Many campaigns have no candidates involved, just issues. Ballot campaigns have become an integral part of American policymaking, and immigration reform, tax increases, marijuana legalization, and other hot-button issues are decided directly by the citizenry. Running a ballot issue campaign involves petition gatherers, legal teams, and often a different approach to convincing the electorate than seen in traditional candidate-focused campaigns.

When and why did ballot campaigns become a part of American politics?

Our form of government is, for the most part, representative. We choose lawmakers who then make laws and policy decisions on our behalf. At times, citizens rise up against what they perceive as unfair treatment or neglect on the part of their representative leaders. This happened near the beginning of the twentieth century, when progressive reform movements in several states pushed for greater citizen participation in the making of laws. Farmers and rural folks were irritated: they argued that their elected officials weren't paying attention to them. In 1897, Nebraska became the first state to permit local ballot initiatives; the next year, South Dakota became the first state to have ballot initiatives on state issues. Utah, Oregon, and California soon joined these pioneering states. Currently, twenty-six states and the District of Columbia provide some form of direct democracy. It's mostly a western state phenomenon; more than 60 percent of all ballot initiatives come out of California, Colorado, Oregon, North Dakota, Arizona, and Washington. And thousands of counties, cities, and towns throughout the United States use ballot initiatives to determine local policies.

The point of direct democracy is that voters get to make the decision on a policy instead of relying on appointed representatives. Even today, small towns in New England hold annual town meetings at which budgets and local matters are discussed and voted on. But the much larger venue for direct democracy is the states that give voters the tools of initiatives, referendums, and recalls.

What's the difference between initiatives, referendums, and recalls?

The *initiative* is the most common form of ballot issue, and it is available in twenty-four states and the District of Columbia. An initiative is crafted by an interest group that has gathered the minimum number of signatures needed to place the measure on the ballot. It is then voted on by the people. If it passes, it becomes the law of the state or locality. For example, if activists want to have recreational marijuana legalized in a state, they gather enough signatures to make the measure a ballot initiative, and it is then voted up or down by the people during the next general election. If the initiative passes, the measure becomes law and has the same force as a bill passed by the legislature.

Eighteen states permit *initiated constitutional amendments* to be proposed by the initiative process. For example, South Dakota voters in 2020 passed a constitutional amendment permitting sport wagering in Deadwood. However, the barriers are higher: some states require petitions signed by up to 15 percent of eligible voters, and some states require passage by super majorities (60 percent or more of voters) before such a measure is approved.

There are plenty of variations and exceptions to this model. Often, a ballot initiative is created by a group of citizens, but in many cases, an initiative is created and funded by business interests (insurance firms, tobacco companies, Indian casinos) or membership groups (auto-dealer associations or healthcare organizations), by wealthy individuals, or even by political consultants who are intent on gaining business. The original idea, that concerned citizens will revolt against a nonresponsive legislature, has in many instances been replaced by high-powered and well-financed organizations and individuals hoping to circumvent legislative scrutiny.

A *referendum* is a ballot issue that begins in the state legislature and ends with the vote of the people. There are three basic types of referendums. First is the *legislative referendum*, which gives voters the opportunity to say yes or no on a bill the state legislature has proposed. The issues most typically sent to the voters for approval or disapproval are changes in the state constitution or tax and bond revenue changes. All fifty states have this kind of referendum mechanism. The second type is the *popular referendum*, which gives voters the chance to approve or repeal an act that was passed by the state legislature. Twenty-four states have this provision. The third type is the *advisory referendum*, which is rarely used. Lawmakers may pose a question to the public, seeking advice on a policy issue, but the results of the referendum are not binding on the state government. For example, on the Maine 2018 ballot, citizens were asked to give their opinion on bond issues for improving water quality and supplementing state university and community college budgets. Here is Question 5: "Do you favor a $15,000,000 bond issue to improve educational programs by upgrading facilities at all 7 of Maine's community colleges in order to provide Maine people with access to high-skill, low-cost technical and career education?"[1]

A *recall* is the vote of the people to remove an elected official from office. Nineteen states and the District of Columbia permit the recall of elected state officials.[2] A recall starts with a petition requiring a certain number of signatures of voters, and then the fate of the elected official is decided by the voters in an election.

California is one of the easiest states in which to launch a recall of an elected official, and since 1960, every governor— liberal, conservative, outstanding, or mediocre—has been the subject of a recall. Just one such effort, however, succeeded, when Governor Gray Davis was removed from office in 2003. On the ballot to succeed him were 135 candidates, and the one with the most name recognition, movie star and body builder Arnold Schwarzenegger, became the new governor.

In 2021, Governor Gavin Newsom was also on the recall ballot. Fed up with his overtly liberal policies and his handling of the pandemic, enough Californians signed a petition to recall him. In California, a recall petition must be signed by valid registered voters, enough to match 12 percent of those who voted in the last election; that meant that 1,495,709 valid signatures had to be on the petitions; Newsom's opponents, mostly Republicans and conservatives, gathered 1.7 million signatures.

In the Newsom recall effort, voters faced two questions on the ballot: Should the governor be recalled? Then, who should be the next governor? If voters say no to the first question, then the second is moot. If they say yes to the first question, then they have to select from among the seventy-four candidates on the ballot.[3] This time around, there was no Arnold Schwarzenegger on the ballot, but there were a few retired Republican politicians on the ballot. Probably the best-known challenger was Caitlyn Jenner, once an Olympic decathlon champion, now a reality television star, and talk show host Larry Elder, who became the leading opponent. Taking a page out of the Trump playbook, Elder charged, weeks before voting began, that the election was riddled with fraud. Newsom easily won and thus the second part of the recall effort was moot.

The hotbed of recall activity in recent years has been Wisconsin. In 2011, seven Wisconsin state senators survived recalls, but two did not. The next year, one state senator was recalled, two others survived, and a fourth resigned amid the recall efforts. Also in 2012, the Republican governor Scott Walker withstood a recall attempt. Thirty-four states permit the recall of local officials, and that's where most recalls have occurred. Such recalls have usually come because of failure of the elected official to perform duties, a felony conviction, gross incompetency, drunkenness, or a violation of the oath of office.

How does a recall differ from an impeachment? A recall involves a petition for removal and then a vote by the people. An impeachment involves the state legislative bodies, which must vote on the removal of the officeholder. A recall is relatively rare, and impeachment is even rarer. In one rare instance, there were both actions: Arizona voters in 1988 had enough signatures to start a recall of Governor Evan Mecham, but the legislature intervened and impeached him before he faced the voters.[4]

What states have direct democracy through ballot campaigns? What about at the local level?

Thirty-three states and the District of Columbia have some provisions for direct citizen voting on initiatives, referendums, constitutional amendments, and recalls. Table 10.1 shows the direct democracy mechanisms that are available in each state.

Hundreds of local jurisdictions have ballot issues, which often include proposals to increase taxes for roads, libraries, public services, and so forth.

Table 10.1 States That Permit Ballot Campaigns

State	Type of Ballot Campaign
Alaska	Initiative, referendum, recall
Arizona	Initiative, referendum, constitutional amendment, recall
Arkansas	Initiative, referendum, constitutional amendment
California	Initiative, referendum, constitutional amendment, recall
Colorado	Initiative, referendum, constitutional amendment, recall
Florida	Constitutional amendment
Georgia	Recall
Idaho	Initiative, referendum, recall
Illinois	Constitutional amendment
Kansas	Recall
Louisiana	Recall
Maine	Initiative, referendum, constitutional amendment
Maryland	Referendum
Massachusetts	Initiative, referendum
Michigan	Initiative, referendum, constitutional amendment, recall
Minnesota	Recall
Mississippi	Constitutional amendment
Missouri	Initiative, referendum, constitutional amendment
Montana	Initiative, referendum, constitutional amendment, recall
Nebraska	Initiative, referendum, constitutional amendment
Nevada	Initiative, referendum, constitutional amendment, recall
New Jersey	Recall
New Mexico	Referendum
North Dakota	Initiative, referendum, constitutional amendment, recall
Ohio	Initiative, referendum, constitutional amendment
Oklahoma	Initiative, referendum, constitutional amendment
Oregon	Initiative, referendum, constitutional amendment, recall
Rhode Island	Recall
South Dakota	Initiative, referendum, constitutional amendment
Utah	Initiative, referendum
Washington	Initiative, referendum, recall
Wisconsin	Recall
Wyoming	Initiative, referendum
District of Columbia	Initiative, referendum, recall

Source: "States with Initiative or Referendum," Ballotpedia.org, https://ballotpedia.org/States_with_initiative_or_referendum.

How do political consultants get involved in ballot issues?

We like to think of ballot campaigns as being started by concerned citizens hoping to make a positive change. But it's often political consultants and their firms, specializing in ballot issues, who do the work. Political consultant Robert Nelson spoke candidly about why he liked initiative campaigns: "An initiative has no political party, no public record to defend or promote, no personality to charm or disgust the voters. And there are no brothers-in-law who need a job. An initiative is just waiting for you to define it and give it life."[5] And we might add, in many cases there is a lot of money to be raked in by political consultants.

In California, especially, money for ballot issues has flowed generously into the hands of political consulting firms. What services do political consultants provide in high-stakes ballot campaigns? Law firms specializing in ballot issues are hired to make sure the wording of a proposed initiative will be lawful. Political consultants are hired to get signatures on petitions, create television and social media communication advertisements, build political coalitions, conduct door-to-door campaigning, survey public opinion through polling and focus groups, pinpoint likely voters using microtargeting techniques, create positive stories in the press, conduct opposition research to try to besmirch the opponents, compose and send out millions of pieces of direct mail, raise enough money to make all of this happen, and serve as general consultants to the entire operation. All this is to get the message across to voters to vote either yes or no.[6]

Complex issues are boiled down to simple phrases and slogans, sometimes all the better to confuse or misdirect the public. As far back as the 1940s, the pioneer political consultants Clem Whitaker and Leone Baxter were working for clients who wanted to repeal California's full-crew law for railroads—that is, a law requiring a certain number of railroad workers on a train crew. Opponents thought that there were too many railroad workers, and they called the practice "feather-bedding." Whitaker and Baxter created a jingle, "I've Been Loafing on the Railroad" (sung to the popular 1940s tune "I've Been Working on the Railroad"), which they played five to ten times a day for over a month on two hundred radio stations. When they worked on a school-aid initiative, they created a catchy rhyme: "For Jimmy and me, vote 'yes' on 3."

Political consultants and public relations flacks have continued this fine tradition of obfuscation and misdirection by trying to humanize an issue, scaring people about endless red tape and growing bureaucracy, pointing out what they consider needless waste and added tax burdens, or attacking a potential regulation as an assault on individual freedom.

In a 2008 editorial, journalist John Diaz described how consultants wrapped that year's California ballot issues with warm and fuzzy messages linked

> to the issue of the ages (this is *for the children*, Prop. 3) or the cause of the day (this is about *energy independence* and *renewable resources*, Props. 7 and 10). If it's a tough sell on the facts, give it a sympathetic face and name such as "Marsy's Law" (Prop. 9, victims' rights and parole) or "Sarah's Law" (Prop. 4, parental notification on abortion). Prepare to spend a bundle on soft-focus television advertising and hope voters don't notice the fine print or the independent analyses of good-government groups or newspaper editorial boards.[7]

One interesting variation on this theme was the recent attempt by California citizens to create online privacy protections through a ballot initiative. Powerful Silicon Valley firms like Google and Facebook objected to having online privacy policy determined by a ballot initiative. But after the disclosure of the Facebook data breach by Cambridge Analytica in 2018, it looked like such an initiative might pass. The threat of a citizen-backed initiative forced the legislature to come up with compromise legislation, establishing at least some measure of online protection.[8]

What was California's Proposition 13?

California approved ballot campaigns in 1911; since then, voters have had to decide on more than 1,253 ballot issues. Most have been decided since the mid-1970s. The real spark in modern-day California ballot fights was Proposition 13, an initiative to limit state property taxes. Proposition 13 was the brainchild of two retired businessmen, Howard Jarvis and Paul Gann. In a *Time* magazine cover story, Jarvis described himself as a "pain in the ass" and a "rugged bastard who's had his head kicked in a thousand times by the government." Two political consultants, William Butcher and Arnold Forde, got involved and drummed up support from voters, who up till then hadn't been paying much attention. They mailed out an official-looking envelope with these words on it: "Your 1978 Property Tax Increase Statement Enclosed" and in big red letters, "response required." Of course, the letter wasn't official, but it got people's attention, and once voters were aware of the issue, Proposition 13 comfortably passed. Soon voters in other states were pressing for tax reduction initiatives: twenty-two states limited property taxes in 1979; eighteen reduced income taxes; fifteen reduced sales taxes; and twelve cut other taxes.[9]

Over the years, California voters have faced a bewildering set of ballot initiatives. In 2018 alone, there were twelve matters on the ballot, including expanding rent control, repealing the gas tax, considering dialysis regulations, approving children's hospital bonds, and more.

The big winners in all this are the special interests, which can bypass the deliberative process of the legislature, the political consultants, and the local television stations that rake in millions from campaign advertising.

How many people are affected by ballot initiatives?

Ballot issues can impact a great number of citizens. In fact, Ballotpedia, the online encyclopedia of ballot issues, noted that in 2016, some 250 million residents were affected by issues decided directly by the people.[10] Table 10.2 shows some of the most important issues and the number of people affected.

How much money is spent on ballot campaigns, and who spends the money?

The amount spent on ballot campaigns, of course, varies from state to state and depends a lot on how many media markets there are in the state, the cost of getting petitions signed, and other factors. The nonpartisan National Institute on Money in State Politics found that from 2005 through 2016, over $5 billion was spent on ballot issues throughout the states.

In 2016, there were a total of 216 ballot issues nationwide, and $893 million was spent to pass or defeat the issues. California, as usual, led the pack in the number of ballot issues—eighteen—and the amount of money spent on them, nearly $470 million. Colorado, which spent $74 million on its nine ballot issues, came in second. Not every ballot issue generates big-time spending. That same year, in fifteen statewide ballot issues in Alabama, just $97,000 was spent altogether. In 2020, voters in thirty-four states weighed in on 129 ballot issues: 93 of the measures passed. Some $756 million was spent on California's 13 ballot issues in 2020.[11]

Table 10.2 Number of Persons Affected by 2016 Ballot Issues

Marijuana legalization	82 million
Minimum-wage increase	26.2 million
Gun control	51 million
Tobacco-tax increase	51 million
Tax measures	123.3 million

Source: "2016 Ballot Measures," Ballotpedia.org, https://ball otpedia.org/2016_ballot_measures.

As you may suspect, money talks. Supporters of successful 2016 ballot issues raised three times the amount of funds as the losing sides. But just 13 percent of all that money came from individuals; the rest was from labor unions, business organizations, and ideological organizations. Totaling up all the contributors shows more than five thousand who gave to ballot campaigns. But the real money came from the ten contributors who gave $10 million or more (for a total of $247 million). And the biggest spenders of all were from Big Tobacco: Philip Morris ($40.2 million); Altria, the parent company of Philip Morris ($18.8 million); and Reynolds American ($39.3 million). Big Tobacco had mixed results: it lost in California but was successful in Colorado, North Dakota, and Missouri on various tobacco- and smoking-related issues.

How successful are ballot issues? What is "choice fatigue"?

What happens when voters are faced with ten or twenty candidates for office and often the same number of ballot issues? Voters frequently don't even know half the names of the candidates and may not have read anything about many of the issues. In the voting booth they are faced with often-complicated language and hard-to-understand choices. When that happens, many voters just vote no. This is called "choice fatigue."[12] The problem is compounded when scores of candidates vying for office are at the top of the ballot. (In 2010, voters in Cook County, Illinois, were faced with 93 candidates for office; California voters in 2003 had to choose from among 135 candidates for governor!)

Researchers have found that if a decision appears higher up on the ballot, there is a greater chance of voters saying yes: when the issue is farther down the ballot, there's a much greater chance that voters will say no—simply because they are tired or confused or figure that when in doubt the best thing to do is to vote against. Thus, there is a not-so-hidden bias for voting no, especially when the ballot is long and complicated.

What are the downsides of ballot initiatives and direct democracy?

We can see from the discussion so far that there are plenty of potential problems with direct democracy. The campaigns for and against a measure are often presented in simplistic, even misleading, terms. Contentious and complicated issues are reduced to yes-or-no choices, and voters, often with little knowledge of the issues, will make those choices and in many instances instinctively vote no when they do not understand an issue. The deliberative process and the tendency to compromise inherent in the decision-making of a deliberative body, such as the state legislature, are lost when a ballot issue is determined by the voters. Direct democracy bypasses the representative nature of our democracy, that is, having important and complicated issues decided by our elected officials. When state legislatures are crippled with indecision or are in the grip of partisan deadlock, direct democracy can be an attractive alternative. But we also need to recognize its drawbacks.

Is there a federal recall mechanism? Can voters recall a member of Congress, a cabinet member, or the president?

The states have the right to impose term limits on state elected officials, but they do not have the right to impose term limits on or change the qualifications or conditions of service of federal officials. Twenty-three states had imposed congressional term limits, but in 1995, the Supreme Court, in *U.S. Term Limits, Inc. v. Thornton*, ruled that states could not impose restrictions on federal officers that were stricter than those specified in the Constitution. Thus, those state term-limit restrictions were ruled invalid.[13]

Nor is there any provision in the US Constitution that allows for the recall of federal elected (or appointed) officials. The only federally elected officials are the president, vice president, and members of the House and the Senate. The only recourse in the Constitution is through the process of impeachment, as spelled out in Article II, section 4:

> The President, Vice President, and all civil Officers of the United States shall be removed from Office on Impeachment for, and conviction of, Treason, Bribery, or other High Crimes and Misdemeanors.

Note that the impeachment clause applies to "all civil officers," not members of Congress. In recent years, there have been several successful impeachments and convictions of federal judges, who were mostly charged with tax evasion, bribery, lying, and sexual misconduct. President Bill Clinton was brought up on impeachment charges in 1998–1999. He was charged with lying under oath and obstruction of justice. The House voted to impeach him, but the Senate would not convict. Richard Nixon, who was threatened with impeachment, resigned before the full House could take action. Then came Donald Trump, who was twice impeached in the House of Representatives. In December 2019, he was impeached for abuse of power and obstruction of Congress, when he was charged with unlawfully trying to use Ukrainian officials to influence the 2020 US presidential election. The second time came with just days left in his term, when Trump was charged with incitement of insurrection following the January 6, 2021, insurrection. Both times, Trump escaped conviction in the Senate as Republicans rallied behind him.

The House and the Senate both have the power to kick out fellow lawmakers or censure them. A number of southern senators were expelled at the beginning of the Civil War for backing the Confederacy. In recent times, two senators resigned rather than face expulsion. Harrison A. Williams Jr., a Democrat from New Jersey, resigned in 1982 because of his involvement in the Abscam sting (bribery, conspiracy, and conflict of interest). Robert W. Packwood, a Republican from Oregon, resigned in 1995 because of sexual misconduct and abuse of power. David Durenberger, a Republican from Minnesota, was "denounced" in 1990 for his involvement in a variety of questionable activities, including converting campaign cash into personal money.[14] The House of Representatives expelled Michael Myers, a Democrat from Pennsylvania, in 1980 (Abscam) and James Traficant, a Democrat from Ohio, in 2002 (bribery, obstruction of justice).

What about a national referendum? Is it allowed in the Constitution? What might the ramifications of a nationwide ballot initiative be?

Our federal system is a representative form of government, and there is no mechanism in the US Constitution that allows for a nationwide ballot issue or referendum. We sometimes say that voting for one candidate or another is a referendum on the political process, but that is certainly not the same thing as a national referendum. Some might argue that a national referendum may be the way to go, given the stalemate and lack of policy initiatives on the part of Congress. If lawmakers can't decide, the argument goes, let us do it for them.

But just imagine what a national ballot issue or referendum might look like. Perhaps on the ballot, along with everyone in the country voting for presidential electors, citizens would be voting on whether marijuana should be banned nationwide, or whether the death penalty should be abolished, or whether all abortions should be prohibited. A referendum might call for Obamacare to be presented to the voters for an up-or-down vote, or perhaps there would be a vote in redefining citizenship and restricting immigration.

There could be a lot of questions about such a national ballot issue. One of the biggest potential problems with a ballot initiative would be the lack of the deliberative, compromise process. (Of course, this is one of the reasons people want it in the first place.) Issues can be complex, the consequences unknown, the deliberative process and the bargaining and compromise short-circuited. In a national referendum, public policy choices could be sold to voters using hype, exaggeration, and one-sided arguments, and the process could be poisoned by the infusion of extraordinary amounts of money filling the airwaves and social media with false narratives.

A national referendum is antithetical to our long-standing representative form of government. To be sure, our national government is going through some extraordinarily difficult and polarized times. But would a system of national referenda pose a better solution, or simply further exacerbate our current problems? Establishing a national referendum policy would require an amendment to the Constitution, and that is extremely unlikely.

11

HOW CAMPAIGNS
HAVE CHANGED

Although the fundamentals of modern campaigning remain intact, there have been enormous changes since the beginning of the twenty-first century. Most of those changes spring from advances in technology, the penetration of social media, and the Wild West of digital communication. Campaigns, up and down the line, have also seen a significant infusion of money as partisan battles heat up and contests become more expensive.

We discussed some of the big changes in campaigns in earlier chapters, including the dramatic rise in statewide and congressional races, as well as the increased costs of presidential elections. We saw in chapter 8 how the campaign finance laws basically have been obliterated to create a wide-open system in which money can be spent at will and in many cases does not have to be reported. We saw how campaigns use analytics and algorithms to sharpen their understanding of voters' interests, fears, and demands. These too are campaign tools unheard of only a few years ago. One of the most important changes, the intrusion of Russian and other foreign hacking into our voting systems and into social media, was discussed in chapter 7 and will be discussed later in chapter 12.

Federal candidates now say, "I'm [name] and I approve this message." When did that become a part of campaigning, and why?

North Carolina congressman David R. Price, a Democrat, introduced an amendment to the Bipartisan Campaign Reform Act (2002) called the "Stand by Your Ad" provision. It required federal candidates, starting in 2008, to acknowledge that an ad that voters are encountering in the media belongs to their campaigns and that they approve of its content. At the very beginning or at the very end of the commercials are these words: "I'm [name] and I approve of this message."

This tells voters that the radio or television ad is from the candidate and not some outside interest group. The Stand by Your Ad provision also means that candidates have to own the content of their ads: they can't claim they didn't know anything about their tone or message. The amendment didn't completely solve the problem of accountability, nor did it necessarily clean up ads or online communications that are not covered by the provision. But it helped to put federal candidates on notice: this is yours, you have approved it, and you now must take full responsibility.

How has the digital revolution changed campaigning?

Just think of the changes there have been in the way we communicate with one another. Nearly everyone has a mobile phone, probably a smartphone, attached to a belt buckle or in a back pocket or purse, always at the ready to capture phone and text messages, news feeds and updates, and loaded with apps. Our phones are becoming our primary means of communicating with others. These changes in communication have come just in the last decade or so and they have dramatically affected politics and campaigning.

Here's a short timeline of digital events and how they affected politics:

1995   Matt Drudge creates *The Drudge Report*,
a website aggregator of political news,
conservative opinion, and gossip. Drudge
claimed to attract 10.6 billion visits to his
website in 2017 and 2018.

1998   MoveOn.org is created in response to the
effort to impeach Bill Clinton. MoveOn.org
later becomes a potent force as an independent
expenditure vehicle for progressive
candidates.

2000   Presidential hopeful John McCain raises over
$2 million online in just one week. Candidates
for office start building rudimentary websites.

2003   Presidential hopeful Howard Dean launches
first presidential candidate blogsite.

2005   YouTube is created. It becomes an integral part
of presidential communications in 2008.

2006   Twitter goes public, and later serves as
important communications tool, especially for
Donald Trump in 2016.

2007   The first Apple smartphones become available.
The flip-phone becomes pretty much a relic in
your grandfather's closet.

2008   Online contributions become an integral part of
presidential campaigns.

2012   The Obama re-election campaign invests more
than $100 million in online technology.

2016   Bernie Sanders sets a record for collecting
small-amount contributions online. Russian
Internet hacking and manipulation become a
reality in the US presidential election. There is
unwarranted use of Facebook and other social
media files for fake news and manipulation.

2018–2020   There are further revelations of Russian
hacking and manipulation, as well as attempts
by state and federal authorities to address this
issue. There is stoking of the Big Lie on social
media.

Is regular television dead, or is there still room for national and
local television news coverage in our digital age?

If you remember black-and-white TV, you know that television, starting in the 1950s, became one of the key communication tools for presidential and other candidates. The three
networks—ABC, NBC, and CBS—along with their local
affiliates were the main sources of news. Big-city markets often
had no more than the three network channels along with one
or two independent stations and a public television station;
smaller markets often had no more than three stations. In the
1970s came cable television, and then premium cable, and the
explosion of choices on TV.

We may have relished the freedom of having five hundred
channels (at a hefty monthly subscription price), but in the
2000s, we are presented with many viewing options, like digital streaming and movies on demand. Have we given up on
television? Can candidates for office still rely on TV to show
their ads? Despite the explosion of available sources and
changes in viewing habits, the answer is yes, television is still
an important medium for candidates. First, we still watch a
lot of television, but not necessarily on a TV screen. Much of
that watching occurs on smartphones, tablets, and computers
rather than on flat-screen TVs, and much of that viewing is
streamed or time-shifted using video-on-demand and digital
recording devices like TiVo.[1]

Viewers are cutting the cord from pay TV subscriptions. The
research firm eMarketers estimates that 33 million adults have

cut their traditional pay-TV service. Overall, in 2018, about 186 million US adults watched traditional pay TV. Meanwhile, there is steady growth in over-the-top, Internet-delivered services, like Netflix (147.5 million viewers in July 2018), Amazon Prime Video (88.7 million), Hulu (55 million), and HBO Now (17.1 million).[2]

In fact, mobile is the busiest and most relied-upon platform. Deloitte Global recently predicted that by 2023, the typical user will interact with her smartphone fifty-two times a day, a 20 percent jump from 2018. There also has been a big growth in the adoption of smartphone apps.[3]

The bottom line for campaign communications is that there are many more opportunities to reach people, through regular, cable, and premium cable television; through specialized apps; through YouTube and other Internet services; through social media—it's an abundance of communication channels, platforms, and devices. It's not just the message senders who are operating twenty-four/seven—it's the receivers too.

That creates more opportunities but also raises problems. With all those options, how does a campaign capture people's attention? Campaigns are using social media much more and investing more heavily in Internet-based advertising, trying to grab viewers' attention. Big-budget campaigns, especially Senate, gubernatorial, and presidential races, are relying much more on data gleaned from our digital sources. The more candidates learn about voters' viewing habits, the better they can home in on what matters to them and how to reach them.

Above all, content matters. How can a candidate or a cause break through and grab the attention of a passive and oftentimes inattentive public? Clever commercials, fresh approaches, compelling arguments, likeable candidates or surrogates—all this is still important and still the main challenge to media advisers and producers.

There is more polling done today than ever before. Is it worthwhile, and is it more accurate than past polling?

Right before the 2016 presidential election, public opinion polls were telling us that Hillary Clinton had a 70 percent (or even up to 99 percent) chance of winning—and then she lost. What happened? Was this a failure of the polling industry, or was it an election that turned out to be too close to predict accurately?

At its first annual meeting after the 2016 election, the American Association of Public Opinion Research tried to come to grips with what went wrong. The group's delegates and researchers came up with three reasons: first, at the last minute (or even in the polling booth), undecided voters went over to Trump; second, the turnout of Trump supporters was higher than expected; and third, state polls in the Rust Belt did not adjust for the education levels of voters in 2016, and thus underestimated the fact that Trump support was stronger among those with lower education attainment.[4]

Pollsters have been embarrassed before in predicting presidential election outcomes. It was a disaster for the Gallup Poll and others to proclaim that Harry Truman would lose to Thomas Dewey in 1948; and it was even worse when the widely read straw poll of the *Literary Digest* boldly predicted that Franklin Roosevelt would lose in 1936 (he won every state except two). But those examples are from before modern polling techniques and today's better understanding of statistical analysis.

For decades, pollsters relied on telephone surveys conducted over landlines. But many Americans, especially those without gray hair, have switched over to mobile phones and ditched landlines. Trying to reach people on their cell phones presents problems for pollsters, however. It costs a lot more money because federal law forbids pollsters from automatically dialing cell phones. A mobile phone user may be anywhere: in a coffee shop, stuck in traffic, walking down the street, or in a classroom. It is easy to imagine a mobile phone user not responding at all or impatiently hanging up, rather than candidly and thoughtfully answering thirty or fifty questions over a twenty-minute time span. (It is hard enough getting respondents to answer those questions when they are sitting at home using a landline phone.) Because mobile phones are, well, mobile, there's no way for a pollster to know in advance if the person contacted resides in a certain geographic area. But pollsters simply can't ignore cell phone–only voters. They are including more cell phone users in their surveys but still trying to figure out how to weight the samples and adjust the polling results to accommodate their voices.

Another factor in polling is the increased use of Internet-based polling. Internet polls have some attractive features: they can involve many more respondents (ten thousand instead of a thousand telephone respondents); they have a higher response rate; and they allow individuals time to think before responding, perhaps over forty-eight hours. Online surveys can be multimedia, so that respondents have a chance to look at a variety of video images. And the answers can be tallied in real time, yielding results more quickly than can be done with phone data. But pollsters continue to worry about self-selection (respondents being eager to participate instead of chosen randomly) and other inherent flaws in Internet polling. Online polls have made great strides, however, in developing ways to pull representative samples from those who volunteer to participate.

Also on the scene are robo-polls, those automated telephone calls in which people are asked a short series of questions and instructed to "press 1" for a certain answer and to "press 2" for another answer. Critics argue that these polls aren't reliable, because you can't screen out children, and there's no chance to ask open-ended questions or for an interviewer to probe an answer further. Defenders claim that respondents are more likely to give honest answers to recorded voices than to live interviewers.[5]

In any event, we are seeing many more public polls, ranging from the scientifically valid to the spurious. Private polls (done by the campaigns themselves) generally stick to traditional methods, such as landline calls, along with selected cell phone interviews, but they are also employing Internet and robocalls.

Another development in survey research has been the rise of poll aggregators, such as HuffPost Pollster (https://elections.huffingtonpost.com/pollster) and Nate Silver's FiveThirtyEight (http://www.fivethirtyeight.com). These sites collect poll results from different sources. Multiple polls can be compared, and, particularly when the same questions are asked, they can be checked against each other.

Has early voting changed the way campaigns are run? Has early voting been good for voters and for democracy?

Many states have adopted early voting and no-fault absentee balloting. Voters are permitted to cast their ballots a week, two weeks, or even up to six weeks before the general election in November. In 2012, some 36 percent (46 million) of all voters didn't wait for Election Day; in 2016, the estimate is that 50 million voters cast their votes early. In the 2018 midterms, some 36 million voters cast early ballots—a record-breaking number for a midterm election.[6] Many of those "nontraditional" voters are in the three states that use mail-in ballots—Washington, Oregon, and Colorado. Many people understandably would want to vote earlier if they have the chance, and avoid the crowds. But if 25 percent or 35 percent of the voters cast their votes before Election Day, how does that affect the strategy and planning of the campaign teams?

It means that a campaign can't wait until the last week to drive home its message. The candidate and the campaign team must try to reach as many of those early voters as possible. It also means that campaigns that have the resources can ask their likely early deciders if they have voted and, if so, then concentrate their efforts on potential voters who are waiting for Election Day. That's an expensive thing to do, but with enough money and resources, campaigns can jump ahead and focus on those who haven't cast their ballots.

How have outside voices expanded their impact on campaigns?

Not too long ago, an election for Congress meant one candidate running against another, with perhaps the state political parties chipping in to help. But by the 1990s, congressional elections had become increasingly nationalized. Local issues, though still important, were at times brushed aside by a broad range of national matters. National organizations such as the National Rifle Association, the AFL-CIO, pro-choice and pro-life organizations, and many more groups started getting involved. A voter watching a television commercial often had to squint to read the fine print trying to find out what organization had sponsored the ad. Some of the groups sponsoring ads hid behind innocent-sounding names, like "Concerned Citizens for . . ." or the "Committee to Protect Our Children's Future." Sometimes, even the candidates and their campaigns didn't know what or who was behind the ads.

As we saw in chapter 8, big-money donors like Tom Steyer, George Soros, Sheldon Adelson, and the Koch brothers, and the political organizations they created, have poured a ton of money into elections to help or to defeat candidates. With the polarized atmosphere and sharp partisan divide, contests for Congress, governor, state legislature, and others have gone from being merely local to being of national importance, and have jumped from million-dollar contests to ones costing multimillions of dollars.

Social media also fosters national and even global discussions of state and local contests, sometimes with "money bomb" explosions of small donations ignited by news events such as scandals, upset victories, and whomever Donald Trump chooses to tweet about.

With Trump banned from Twitter and Facebook, alternative right-wing social media have gained hundreds of thousands of new users. Gab considers itself a right-wing alternative to Twitter; Rumble is the alternative to YouTube; MeWe is a conservative version of Facebook; and Signal and Telegram have attracted many followers seeking privacy, where users can send end-to-end encrypted messages.[7]

Popular social media sites, Facebook in particular, have come under increasing federal government scrutiny. It has been charged that the algorithms created by these companies foster controversy and anger, distort reality, and serve as platforms for extremist ideas and movements. The classic concept of free speech has collided with the reality of manufactured turmoil, conspiracy theories, and foreign and domestic subterfuge of American elections.

In sum, how have campaigns been transformed since the twentieth century in the first two decades of the twenty-first century?

Let's look at the difference between campaigning in the latter years of the twentieth century and campaigning today.[8]

Role of consultants. In the twentieth century, consultants were dominant in creating the message and strategy and maintaining communication discipline. The campaign manager, a general consultant, pollsters, the media team, and direct-mail specialists would join up with senior campaign staffers to guide the campaign through the many hurdles it might face. Today, consultants still dominate, and they understand that winning campaigns must integrate online communication and data analytics.

Television. Back then, television was the most important communication vehicle for most big races. Today, television is still important, but now it competes with a dizzying array of online channels and platforms.

Speed of campaign events. Back then, there was more time to create television ads, analyze upcoming issues, and respond to attacks from opponents. Today, campaigns at times run at warp speed, twenty-four/seven, giving candidates and their teams less time to adjust their strategy and message.

Figuring out campaign problems. Previously, much of the campaign relied on the experience of campaign professionals, guesswork, and what worked in the past. Today, there is a much heavier reliance on research and data and analytics and metrics that guide the campaign's decisions.

Fundraising and campaign spending. In the twentieth century, money was usually raised through big-ticket events, expensive direct-mail solicitations, and relatively few small-amount donors. Today, inexpensive online technology has allowed campaigns to efficiently and inexpensively collect small donations. Then again, as we have seen, small donations can be overshadowed by just a few well-placed mega donations.

Outside voices. We never had to worry about foreign interference in American elections a decade ago. Today, federal national security and cybersecurity agencies along with state election officials are on alert for potential intrusions from foreign bad actors. It is not only Russia that presents a threat but also China, Iran, and other governments and forces that can cause mischief through misinformation, hacking into election systems, and, most importantly, sowing seeds of doubt about the legitimacy of democratic elections.

But today, outside forces are not the most malevolent actors. What is far more troubling are the attempts within American political circles, pushed by the former president, to cast doubt on American democratic processes. Let's discuss these elements in the concluding chapter.

12

THREATS TO DEMOCRACY

Our democracy depends on honest, clean, and fair elections in which all eligible adults are free to participate. The biggest threat today is the insistence by former president Trump that the elections were stolen. That falsehood—that Big Lie—and its acceptance by such a significant portion of his followers and allies undermine democratic values. But there are plenty of other ways that our democratic systems have been undermined, from lack of citizen involvement to disparagement of government institutions and the free press, the influence of mega-donors trying to buy elections, and foreign and domestic interference.

Elections matter. For the millions of Americans who participate, voting for public officials or voting on ballot issues is their one—and often only—chance to affect public policies and to choose leaders and representatives. Trust in government and institutions matters; so too does trust in news outlets and the media. These are basic elements of a sound and thriving democracy. But as we have seen throughout this book, our democratic values are being threatened in a fundamental and profound way.

What's happened to our faith in democracy?

Today, nearly all Americans feel that democracy is being threatened. A recent public opinion poll, conducted in September 2021 for CNN, shows the depths of that concern. A full 93 percent of respondents say that democracy is either under attack (56 percent) or being tested (37 percent). Just 6 percent think that America is no longer in danger. Republicans were much more pessimistic than Democrats: some 75 percent of Republicans say democracy is under attack, compared to 46 percent of Democrats.[1]

Trump's Big Lie has thoroughly permeated his base: 78 percent of Republicans believe that the election was stolen from Trump, and 54 percent of Republicans believe there is solid evidence that proves Trump won.[2] There is no solid evidence, only the drumbeat of lies, distortions, and denials, with Trump as the biggest cheerleader. And support of the Big Lie has become a litmus test for candidates and elected Republicans. If you want Trump's loyalty, his backing, and his endorsement, you must support his falsehood that the election was stolen.

What is the global impact of the January 6 insurrection?

The whole world was watching as fervent Trump loyalists breached the fences, broke into the Capitol, ransacked offices, and threatened lawmakers and especially Vice President Pence. Americans, of all political leanings, were angered, shocked, and frankly embarrassed by this display of mob rule. Stability and order have been hallmarks of the American exchange of power from one administration to another. That image was shattered on January 6. The world saw chaos, disorder, and an attempted coup in the making. The Senate and the House were about to certify the Electoral College votes, officially giving Biden the presidency. Protestors, some draped in Trump flags, wearing MAGA hats and military gear, and brandishing clubs, created havoc, hunted down lawmakers, and tried in vain to halt the august ceremonial proceedings.

Was this some banana republic, a tin-horn dictatorship grasping to hold on to power? The visual impact, seen throughout the world, must have bemused authoritarian leaders and horrified those who looked to the United States as a beacon of stability, free choice, and democratic values. America's self-image was shaken, fundamentally and profoundly.

Yet, the majority of Republicans in the House refused to certify Biden's victory; only ten House Republicans and seven Senate Republicans later voted to impeach Trump for inciting the insurrection. And soon disinformation and partisan tap dancing emerged: the rioters were just a bunch of tourists; the rioters must have been Antifa agitators intent on planting false flags; or the disturbances following the George Floyd murder were far more serious than this.

The House special committee looking into the January 6 insurrection has been asking hard questions and digging through video, audio, emails, and written memoranda to determine who in the White House and in Congress may have conspired to bring all this about, who neglected their duties, and who ultimately was responsible for the political turmoil and damage to America's reputation.

What has happened to trust in government and institutions?

Over the decades, trust in the federal government has steadily declined. Americans have been shaken by the Vietnam War, Watergate, cultural shifts, shrinking of the middle class, rise of globalism, terrorist attacks, and prolonged military actions overseas.

Trust in American institutions has fallen, and in 2021, we reached a low point. In a Gallup Poll that year, respondents had "a great deal" or "quite a lot" of confidence in small business (70 percent) and the military (69 percent). But government institutions fared far worse, with relatively few expressing high confidence in the presidency (38 percent), the Supreme

Court (36 percent), and Congress (12 percent). Confidence in the media also received dismal scores: television news (16 percent), newspapers (21 percent), and technology companies (29 percent). For the most part, these levels of confidence fell below 2020 and 2019 levels.[3]

What doesn't help, of course, is a president who made it a blood sport to ridicule and demean institutions. Donald Trump promised to "drain the swamp" in Washington, spinning out horror stories of corruption, malfeasance, and incompetence. The mainstream media were the "enemies of the people," the intelligence community was a bungling bureaucracy, and Trump knew far more than the generals and the military. All this, coming from the bulliest of pulpits, certainly could not have elevated confidence in government and institutions.

Has any other president refused to participate in the inauguration of his successor?

The peaceful transition of power from one president to another has been a vital element in the American democratic pageant. But Donald Trump refused to participate in the 2021 inauguration ceremony that installed Joe Biden as the forty-sixth president of the United States. This was pure sour grapes, a childish display of bad conduct and bad sportsmanship. It sent the strong message to his base: Trump was cheated and Biden is not the real president.

Since the beginning of the twentieth century, there have been five presidents defeated for re-election: William Howard Taft (1912), Herbert Hoover (1932), Gerald Ford (1976), George H. W. Bush (1992), and Donald Trump (2020). On Inauguration Day, it is customary for the retiring president to greet the new president at the White House, and they ride together to the Capitol for the ceremonies. Sometimes the ride between the White House and the Capitol was frosty, but at least the losing president was gracious enough to attend, giving the country and the world the sense that, despite the political differences, American democracy was strong.

Not so with Donald Trump. He decided not to attend the Inauguration of his successor. At 8:17 in the morning on Inauguration Day, Trump entered a Marine One helicopter, which transported him and Melania Trump to Joint Base Andrews, where a sparse crowd of loyalists said their goodbyes. Neither Vice President Pence nor any Republican congressional leaders were there to bid him farewell.

It had been 152 years since another outgoing president refused to participate in his successor's swearing in. In 1869, outgoing president Andrew Johnson stayed in the White House while his successor Ulysses Grant was sworn in. John Adams in 1801 did not attend the swearing in of Thomas Jefferson. According to the White House Historical Office, Adams had not received an invitation from Jefferson and did not want to impose himself on the ceremony. His son, John Quincy Adams, did not attend the inauguration ceremony (1829) when he lost the presidential election to Andrew Jackson.[4]

Is voter suppression real?

For the most part, all adult citizens can vote. Very few adult citizens (mostly those with felony records and those who are mentally incapacitated) are lawfully denied the right to vote. All others, in theory, can participate. In practice, however, a different story emerges. One of the major concerns is voter suppression, the deliberate effort to make it more difficult for certain groups of voters to exercise their right.

Voter suppression has a long and ugly history in this country. Over the years, the political forces in power, especially in the South, have routinely tried to make it difficult or have even blatantly denied citizens the right to vote. The days of grandfather clauses, literacy tests, poll taxes, and the like are over, and were finally put to rest through the Voting Rights

Act of 1965. But there have been plenty of ingenious (and ham-handed) attempts to keep people from voting.

It should come as no surprise that those most affected are minorities and persons of color. The laws tightening up voting participation may appear to be neutral and objective on their face, and their legislative creators will say with a straight face that they are designed to clean up voter files and prevent voter fraud. Nevertheless, these laws invariably strike directly at the most vulnerable voters, making it more difficult for them to participate and inventing ways to discourage them from voting.

In a 2018 survey, the *Atlantic* magazine and the Public Religion Research Institute noted that African Americans and Hispanics are more likely than Whites to face voting barriers. They noted "deep structural barriers." The problems included having trouble finding polling places, having no polling sites in inner-city neighborhoods, missing the deadlines for voter registration, having difficulty getting off work in time to vote, and being told incorrectly that they were no longer on the voting rolls or they didn't have the proper identification. The research showed that "voter suppression is commonplace, and that voting is routinely harder for people of color than for their white counterparts."[5]

Voter suppression in particular had an impact on the 2016 election, especially the voter-identification law in Wisconsin engineered by the Republican-dominated legislature. Requiring voters to produce an ID knocked thousands of African Americans (the great majority of whom were Democrats) off the voting rolls. As Vann R. Newkirk, the author of the study, noted, "Trump's chances in 2016 may have turned not only on the approval or disapproval of white voters, but also on how effectively state laws, access issues, and social penalties conspired to keep black and Hispanic voters away from polling places."[6]

Following the 2020 presidential election and the January 6 insurrection, there was a rush in Republican-dominated state legislatures to enact restrictive voting laws; at the same time, there was a push in Democratically controlled state legislatures to make voting easier and to expand the voting rolls. Eighteen states adopted restricted voting during their 2021 sessions, all doing so under the guise of protecting against fraudulent voting—a claim shown over and over again to be spurious. In tracking this legislation, the Brennan Center for Justice stated, "This wave of restrictions on voting—the most aggressive we have seen in more than a decade of tracking state voting laws—is in large part motivated by false and often racist allegations about voter fraud."[7] During the first six months of 2021, more than four hundred pieces of legislation were introduced in forty-nine states to restrict voting.

The attempts to restrict voting fall into several categories: (a) making it harder for citizens to cast through mail-in voting; (b) making in-person voting more difficult, for example, by shortening voting hours; (c) expanding the purging of voters; and (d) increasing the barrier to voting by requiring voter IDs. Some of the laws took the final determination of a vote out of the hands of election officials and gave it to state legislatures. This seemingly mundane move means that state election officials (like Georgia secretary of state Brad Raffensperger) can now be circumvented by decidedly political state legislatures.

Two states getting the most nationwide attention because of their voting restrictions were Georgia and Texas. In reaction to the Georgia laws, a number of corporations publicly objected, and Major League Baseball decided to move its All-Star game to Denver. Colorado, ironically, has been a model state in terms of ballot security and a pioneer in mail-in voting. In Texas, Democratic legislators fled the state in order to stymie a vote on the new Texas voter restriction laws. The lawmakers fled to Washington, DC, imploring Congress to enact remedial legislation. But Texas governor Greg Abbott and the Republican-dominated Texas legislature ultimately prevailed, and the law went into effect in September 2021. It was immediately challenged by voter advocacy groups.

On the other hand, twenty-five states enacted fifty-four laws making it easier to vote. In these states, the legislatures were controlled mostly by Democratic lawmakers. Virginia, leading the way, enacted nine such new laws. These states expanded early voting, made mail-in voting easier, restored the right to vote for former felons, and gave greater accessibility to disabled voters. In all, during the first six months of 2021, more than nine hundred bills were introduced in forty-nine states to expand voting rights.

While a number of states have not finished their sessions, here is a rundown of those states that have passed restrictive and those that have passed expansive voting laws in 2021.

Restrictive laws (18 states):
Florida, Georgia, Alabama, New Hampshire, Indiana, Kentucky, Iowa, Arkansas, Louisiana, Kansas, Oklahoma, Texas, Wyoming, Montana, Idaho, Utah, Arizona, and Nevada.

Expansive laws (25 states):
Maine, New Hampshire, Vermont, Massachusetts, Connecticut, New York, New Jersey, Delaware, Maryland, Virginia, Kentucky, Indiana, Illinois, Minnesota, North Dakota, Louisiana, Oklahoma, Montana, Colorado, New Mexico, Washington, Oregon, Nevada, California, and Hawaii.

Note that several states—New Hampshire, Indiana, Kentucky, Louisiana, Nevada, Montana, and Oklahoma—have enacted both restrictive and expansive laws during their 2021 legislative sessions.

Who was paying for these efforts to restrict voting?

Investigative journalist Jane Mayer, who previously had focused on dark money in campaigns, explored the money behind the 2020 voter fraud allegations. Her article was aptly titled "The Big Money behind the Big Lie."[8] Mayer noted that most of the money came from rich individual conservatives, think tanks and organizations, and activist lawyers. Since 2012, the Bradley Foundation of Milwaukee has been challenging voting rights under the guise of combatting voter fraud. The Bradley Foundation, a conservative, private, tax-exempt organization worth $850 million, has been on the leading edge of fighting for restrictive voting.

The key actor in the Bradley Foundation's drive, according to Mayer, is Republican election lawyer Cleta Mitchell, who aggressively has charged voter irregularities during the 2020 election. On talking with Mayer, Mitchell defended herself and like-minded voting skeptics: "We are not crazy. At least not to us. We are intelligent and educated people who are very concerned about the future of America. And we are among the vast majority of Americans who support election-integrity measures."[9]

Also involved have been the Heritage Foundation and the American Legislative Exchange Council (ALEC), which have helped write model legislation for use in Republican-dominated legislatures.

Why can't we just have one federal set of laws to protect voting rights?

For over fifty years, the Voting Rights Act of 1965 provided a basic security, guaranteeing the right to vote for all Americans. The law passed with broad bipartisan support; so did its extension every five years. That was then. We have moved, unfortunately, a long way from the sentiments uttered by President Ronald Reagan when he signed the extension to the Voting Rights Act in 1981: "For this Nation to remain true to its principles, we cannot allow any American's vote to be denied, diluted, or defiled. The right to vote is the crown jewel of American liberties, and we will not see its luster diminished."[10]

The Biden administration and Democratic leaders set as a priority laws that would restore protections found in the Voting Rights Act and protect the integrity of the election system. In 2021, Republicans in the Senate already had blocked a sweeping elections bill, known as the For the People Act. This bill would have ended partisan gerrymandering, protected early voting and mail-in voting, and increased campaign financing transparency.

Another Democratic bill is the John Lewis Voting Rights Act, which its advocates say would strengthen the Voting Rights Act of 1965 in the wake of the *Shelby County* and the *Brnovich* decisions. It is named after the Georgia congressman and civil rights leader who died in 2020. Representative Terri Sewell of Alabama, who introduced the legislation, said, "Old battles have become new again. I want you to know that the modern day barriers to voting are no less pernicious than those literacy tests and those poll taxes. And what we must do, as we did back in the '60s, is when we see states running amok, we need federal oversight."[11] The House approved the measure on a straight party line vote: not a single Republican voted for the bill.

Yet, as long as there is unanimous opposition from Republicans for national election reform, it will not happen. The only short-term remedy is for Democrats to determine that the filibuster will not apply to voting rights issues. That is a tough sell, particularly when Democrats need to have every one of their caucuses on board. Democratic Senators Joe Manchin of West Virginia and Kyrsten Sinema of Arizona voiced their opposition to removing the filibuster.

Mitch McConnell, perhaps unwittingly, laid out the truth when he opposed federal law expanding and protecting voting rights: Republicans fear that when more people vote, their party will lose. McConnell stated that the voting rights legislation is a "partisan power-grab" and is not about voting rights. "It's about letting Washington Democrats control the terms of political debate and all fifty states' election laws."[12]

Why are Republican lawmakers so intent on making voting more difficult?

Behind the mask of making elections safer and rooting out fraud is the underlying fear that in the not-too-distant future, White people will be a minority in the United States. The base of the Republican Party is shrinking: older White voters are dying off, non-college-educated White voters are shrinking in number, young voters are flocking to the Democratic Party, rural areas are losing population, and Republican policies have thoroughly alienated African American voters and a substantial portion of other minority voters.

What to do?

The answer is clear: gerrymander congressional districts so that Democrats (read "minorities") will have their impact diminished, and impose restrictive voting measures to prevent fraud and promote transparency (read "put up as many barriers against minority voters as we can get away with").

But what if the political landscape were different? What if the Republican Party embraced policies that supported and defended minority groups? What if they embraced a big tent philosophy, trying to gain as much support from other groups rather than drilling down and amplifying support for its shrinking base? Let's again ask the question: if Latinos and African Americans didn't vote overwhelmingly for Democrats but voted fifty-fifty or even more in favor of Republicans, would we have these aggressive moves by conservative legislatures to suppress their right to vote and perform gerrymandering origami? It strains credulity to believe that voter suppression and gerrymandering would cease.

Which is worse: international interference in our elections or domestic attempts to undermine them?

In 2016, we became worried about foreign interference when it was revealed conclusively that Russian organizations were actively seeking to upset the election. One of the biggest challenges would be the hacking of vulnerable state electronic voting systems. As we saw in chapter 1, some states are simply not prepared to fix potential cyber problems, through investing either more money or more talent. Before the 2016 presidential election, thirty-three states and thirty-six local governments requested the Department of Homeland Security's help in protecting their systems from possible cyberattack. After the election, two more states and six localities also requested assistance. In July 2017, department officials warned that twenty-one state election systems were potentially vulnerable to attacks from Russian agents and others.[13] In March 2018, Congress approved $380 million to be divided up by the fifty states and five territories and used to improve their election security systems, but even this allocation won't solve problems immediately.

More evidence has been gathered showing Russian operatives were involved in attempts to manipulate recent American elections. The US Senate Select Committee on Intelligence probed Russia's interference and found that it "undertook a wide variety of intelligence-related activities targeting the US voting process. These activities began at least as early as 2014, continued through Election Day 2016, and included traditional information gathering efforts as well as operations likely aimed at preparing to discredit the integrity of the US voting process and election results."[14]

Another report commissioned by the Senate Select Committee outlined serious malicious activities by Russia's state-supported Internet Research Agency (IRA), the clandestine operation that actively tried to interfere with the 2016 American elections. According to New Knowledge, the research organization commissioned by the Senate committee, the IRA engaged in a "multi-year coordinated disinformation effort" campaign. The IRA used Instagram, more so than Facebook or Twitter, as its platform of choice. It explicitly targeted African American voters and engaged in voter suppression by urging voters to choose a third party or by proclaiming "stay home on Election Day, your vote doesn't matter." The messages and fake groups set up by the IRA "had a very clear bias toward Donald Trump" and an "anti-Hillary Clinton sentiment." The IRA efforts, New Knowledge concluded, were "designed to exploit societal fractures, blur the lines between reality and fiction, erode our trust in media entities and the information environment, in government, in each other, and in democracy itself. The campaign pursued all those objectives with innovative skill, scope, and precision."[15]

The two-volume report of Special Counsel Robert Mueller found "sweeping and systematic" Russian interference in the 2016 election but did not find a criminal conspiracy between the president and the Russian government. Trump continued to characterize the investigation as a "hoax" and "witch hunt." Several House and Senate committees and federal courts in Washington and New York continue the probes into election irregularities.

In 2018, the *Washington Post* asked a hundred cybersecurity experts about state election security, and 95 percent of them concluded that the systems were not sufficiently protected against a potential cyberattack. Still, millions of Americans went to the polls in 2018 and voted with old digital voting machines that are vulnerable to hacks; even more worrisome is that these machines offer no paper trail to back up and verify the votes.[16]

As outlined in chapter 6, foreign influence was present during the 2020 elections, but US national security experts were convinced that the election systems were secure.

Yet the bigger danger is not the attempts of foreign actors to interfere with our election systems, hacking of software, or even use of social media platforms to sow discontent and discord. The danger comes from within: false election narratives, pushed from the very top, that the elections were a sham, that there were massive failures in mail-in and early voting, and that such fraud happened only in big cities controlled by Democrats.

Why don't more citizens participate in voting? Is registration the barrier?

Many eligible adults aren't registered to vote, despite such efforts as the 1993 National Voter Registration Act (also known as the Motor-Voter Act), which makes it possible to register to vote at department of motor vehicle locations and other public places. Registration is conducted by states only; there is no national voter registration. And as we have seen, there have been efforts, particularly by Republican-controlled legislatures, to tighten registration and eligibility requirements, under the guise of combatting voter fraud.

All states require some form of identification (driver's license, state-issued ID card) and proof of residency. Some states, especially those active in creating restrictive voting laws in 2021, have walked a fine line between measures that clean up messy voting records and those that place a burden on potential voters, particularly minority voters.

Fifteen states and the District of Columbia offer same-day voter registration, allowing voters to register and vote on Election Day. Two other states permit same-day registration for citizens who are voting early. In most other states, voters must register between eight and thirty days before Election Day.

There is considerable evidence that same-day registration leads to an increase in voter participation, usually by 5 percentage points. But studies have not concluded that early voting and increased participation have advantaged one political party over the other or whether certain populations will be the beneficiaries.[17]

Voter registration should not be so difficult. In fact, two websites, Vote.org and Vote.gov, make it simple to determine registration deadlines and eligibility. When the singer Taylor Swift sent an Instagram message about the importance of voting to her millions of followers, voter registration spiked on Vote.org, which had 154,490 visitors during the next day alone, up from the typical 14,078 visitors.[18]

Curiously, the United States is one of the few democracies that leave voter registration in the hands of potential voters rather than employ a system of automatic registration undertaken by governmental authorities. The United States is also an outlier in electing political partisans to head our state election boards.

What about voter apathy, especially among young voters?

The 2020 election saw a large increase in voter participation. Given the tense political climate, it is not surprising that so many people were determined to cast their vote. Still, 70 million eligible voters chose not to participate. Yes, we have had a problem with voter apathy. As we've seen, in nonpresidential election years, voter participation falls way off. In chapter 1, we saw how few people voted in recent big-city mayoral races and that in typical congressional races in nonpresidential years, the percentage of eligible voters going to the polls rarely comes close to 50 percent. The result is that only those who are ideologically fired up, partisan activists, or retirees with time on their hands routinely show up in healthy numbers.

Even in today's supercharged political atmosphere, many potential voters are (a) just not interested in politics, (b) can't name even one person running for office, (c) don't think their vote will make a difference, (d) believe the whole system of government is corrupt and don't want anything to do with it, or (e) have other things to do with their time than engage in this basic civic duty.

Civic duty, as well as self-interest, should persuade voters, of all ages, to become involved in the election process. So yes, there still remains a significant problem of voter apathy, distrust, and disinterest.

Why not hold general elections on the weekend or make Election Day a national holiday?

Austria, France, Germany, New Zealand, India, Belgium, and many other countries have been able to figure this out: hold elections on the weekends or make them a national holiday so that most voters won't be working and can more easily get to the polls.[19]

In 172 countries surveyed, the United States ranks 139th in voter turnout. If it is an evident goal of democracy to increase participation, then we really should try measures that would help accomplish that. Weekend or national holiday voting, along with easier registration, might help increase participation. Even better might be to move to the mail-only ballot system found in several states. The advantages include no waiting in line, no need to take time off from work, having several weeks to study the ballot and make informed choices, lower costs because they are less expensive to run than traditional polling stations, easier access for voters with mobility issues, and, most importantly, a paper trail for every vote. A key provision of the Biden administration's voting rights legislation is to create a national holiday, along with making it easier for citizens to vote.

How confident should we be about our decentralized election system?

Our long-standing practice is that elections are controlled and implemented at the state and local levels. Given the current state of technology and our commitment to rooting out flaws in the election system, it is probably better to have a decentralized system than a centralized one. It is better to have hundreds of small mistakes than have a nationwide breakdown of voting integrity. Imagine that we have a centralized system for counting votes in presidential elections. That is, all results are sent directly to a computer system in Washington to tally the voters and verify their accuracy. Such a system would have to be very secure, as safe as bank records and financial transactions, and constantly attended to and upgraded. Otherwise, it would be a tempting target for hackers intent on falsifying and deleting records and all sorts of other mischief. Sweden and Australia, among other countries, have such a centralized system, but the United States does not.

But clearly, our state and local election systems—from the private voting-machine vendors and software programs to the training of local election officials—need further protections and upgrades. Our decentralized system has over thirteen thousand electoral jurisdictions that are operated by states, counties, and local administrations. We saw in the 2000 presidential election that Florida's system was a hodgepodge of new voting machinery and antiquated machines, faulty software, and unreliable reporting systems. In 2020, with the extremely tight elections in key battleground states, it became even clearer that state and local systems need to be protected and made secure. The multiple recounts and audits in several states, however, have given us encouragement that the decentralized system is working, without major flaws, without fundamental administrative error, and certainly without "massive voter fraud."

How can we combat "fake news" and social media lies?

Candidates for office often complain about the press: news coverage is biased, doesn't get the story right, or fails to cover an important campaign event. Many of those complaints have come from conservatives, who have adopted the term "mainstream media" to deride newspapers like the *New York Times*, *Wall Street Journal*, and *Washington Post*; television networks like CBS, CNN, and MSNBC; and National Public Radio. Conservative voices soon appeared, first through the emergence of talk radio featuring personalities like Rush Limbaugh, and through Fox News, under the direction of former Republican political consultant Roger Ailes and his team. That was thirty, even forty years ago.

We've witnessed the wholesale dismissal of the so-called mainstream media by Donald Trump, who recklessly labels these sources "fake news," insisting that only news coming from his own Twitter feeds (and perhaps Fox News) has any legitimacy. Beginning with George Washington, presidents have had a tumultuous time with the press, but in our era, Trump alone has had the audacity to label the pillars of American journalism (and their reporters) frauds, phonies, and perpetuators of fake news, going so far as to call them "enemies of the people."

Fake news no doubt exists, and in our wide-open world of online communication, it can bombard us with misinformation. It is often a deliberate attempt to hide the truth and sow dissent and discord. It comes in the form of crackpot conspiracy theorists, click-bait come-ons, and false stories dressed up as legitimate news sources, from both homegrown and foreign sources. Some of the online platforms finally responded. From January through March 2018, Facebook took down 837 million pieces of spam content, and it has shut down 538 million fake accounts. Many of those sites were filled with hate speech, violence, or pornography, not just fake political and campaign-related content. Yet a Facebook senior manager acknowledged that artificial intelligence "isn't good enough yet to determine whether someone is pushing hate or describing something that happened to them so they can raise awareness of the issue."[20] Following whistleblower testimony and documents, Facebook in 2021 came under considerable scrutiny in Congress for the way it has managed harmful and provocative materials.

Other online platforms are also addressing the problem of fake news, while trying to balance the right to legitimate free speech and the need to protect citizens, and to keep up with the ever-changing and increasingly sophisticated attempts by countries and secretive organizations determined to interfere with political systems, elections, and campaigning.

At the same time, extremist social media sites, often featuring encryption as a selling feature, are sprouting up, taking the place of mainstream online sites. The tension between free speech and harmful content is constant and never-ending.

Trump was kicked off Twitter, his favorite social media site, and Facebook for his continued efforts to discredit the election and the January 6 insurrection. A year after the election, an organization called the Trump Media and Technology Group stated that it would merge with Digital World, an online site, and develop a new social media platform called Truth Social. This site, former president Trump claimed, would "stand up to the tyranny of Big Tech."[21]

What can individuals do to combat the scourge of fake news? Stick to trusted news sites and don't get suckered into the world of the crazies! We need to be able to discern what is true and what is fake, then act and vote accordingly. The attacks and falsehoods continue, so that's a tall order, but it is one of the imperative challenges of our democracy.

Do plutocrats control our elections?

One of the major threats to our election system is the big money from a small group of mega-donors that can overwhelm an election. A $25 million infusion of money from one individual or a small group of wealthy people can make a difference in a tight Senate race. The money can go toward flooding the airwaves with both negative and positive campaign ads and providing ground troops, telephone banks, data analysis, and other essential tools. Based on a wink and a nod, we are expected to believe that these weapons are not attached directly to a campaign but can be crucial in the crunch of a tight campaign. Considering how few people give money to campaigns (generously estimated at 4 percent of the total population), it is almost impossible for individuals to match or even come close to mega-donor giving. These heated and expensive contests invariably become contests between well-financed interest groups and well-heeled individuals.

Many consider the current campaign-financing system to be a mess. Is there any way to reform it?

There are ways to reform the campaign-financing system, but bringing about substantive reform is definitely a long shot. As we saw in chapter 8, almost all the safeguards and prohibitions found in federal campaign-finance law have been scuttled. This didn't happen in the halls of Congress but came about through federal court decisions and regulatory interpretations. Thanks to recent Supreme Court decisions, campaign spending is now wide open; thanks to federal regulations, much of that spending doesn't have to be reported. Ever since *Buckley v. Valeo* in 1976, the court has decided that spending money for one's own campaign amounts to an extension of free speech; now that extends to corporations, labor unions, and especially mega-donors and their special-interest groups.

A fundamental change would require the court to reverse itself on *Citizens United v. FEC* and to reconsider *SpeechNow.org v. FEC*. That's probably not going to happen, given the current makeup of the Supreme Court. And don't count on Congress to make the changes. We've seen how difficult it has been to change campaign-finance law, particularly when the changes would impact one party's ability to reap the rewards from unlimited funds. (Mitch McConnell's "until hell freezes over" comment comes to mind). We've also seen how ineffective the Federal Election Commission is, locked in partisan deadlock with commissioners who are unwilling to make tough rulings and decisions.

Could a constitutional amendment outlawing or curtailing campaign spending do the trick? It could, but there's no appetite for it, no groundswell of citizen anger demanding such a change. And, of course, amending the Constitution is extraordinarily difficult to do.

The bottom line: it would take a fundamental political transformation to change our current campaign-finance system. It would require a reconsideration of Supreme Court rulings, re-examination of federal laws and regulations, or an end run around the whole federal apparatus with a constitutional amendment. It's just not going to happen. Big money, wealthy donors, and powerful interests have won this game.

How can citizens find out which groups gave money to political candidates? For example, who received money from tobacco companies, pro-choice organizations, unions, or the National Rifle Association?

There are several really good resources for finding out which candidates received money from interest groups, how much money they received altogether, and, if you want to dig further, where they spent their campaign money. Thanks to the Federal Election Campaign Act, we know a lot about where money comes from. Unfortunately, as we saw in chapter 8, although "dark money" sources must report how much money they contribute, we still don't know who those individuals or organizations are that make the contributions. And unless Congress tightens up regulations and reporting requirements for dark money, we'll never know.

For federal candidates—that is, candidates running for Congress, the Senate, or the presidency—the best place to go is the website OpenSecrets.org, which is maintained and updated by the Center for Responsive Politics, a nonpartisan organization that collects information from Federal Election

Commission campaign reports, puts it into useful databases, and makes it available to the public. You can easily find out, for example, who has given money to your member of Congress or to candidates running for Congress in your district. Maybe you want to know the names of all congressional candidates who received money from a certain interest group or business. Go to http://www.OpenSecrets.org as your best source for federal candidates.

At the state level, the task of finding out about contributions and the recipients of campaign money gets a little trickier, simply because the states do not have a central system, and reporting and contribution requirements vary from state to state. But it is still possible to find out a lot about where money is raised and which candidate it goes to. The best place to find out what money was spent and who received it in your state is at the website FollowtheMoney.org (https://www.followt hemoney.org), which is maintained by the National Institute of Money in State Politics.

A third good resource, especially for finding out how much money was spent on ballot issues and who put up money to defend or defeat them, is Ballotpedia.org, an online encyclopedia of American politics. Ballotpedia has a wealth of useful information on all sorts of state, local, and federal political issues and politics, gathered by professional writers, researchers, and election analysts.

Another solid resource, particularly if you want to probe more deeply into federal and state campaign financing, is the nonpartisan Campaign Finance Institute (CFI) based in Washington, DC. It publishes reports on federal and state campaign financing, maintains an extensive bibliography of academic works on campaigns and money, and has an extensive database of state campaign laws. Want to find out what contribution limits are in your state, or how the laws have changed since *Citizens United*, or whether your state offers public financing of elections? All this and more can be found on their website, http://www.cfinst.org.

Throughout American history, we have endured challenges, doubts, and tribulations, yet we have endured and grown stronger. Today, we are going through a difficult time, characterized by increased polarization and tribalism, profound cultural changes that threaten the old order, a rapidly changing demographic, the challenges of globalism and immigration, and new questions about America's place in the world. Our system of campaigns and elections should be a bulwark of democracy, and in many ways it has been. But we also face some serious questions about campaigns and elections and the threat to democracy, and hopefully through this book, we can better understand the realities of elections, the threats, the challenges ahead, and the opportunities for reform and resolution.

NOTES

Chapter 1

1 Alexander Keyssar, *The Right to Vote: The Contested History of Democracy in the United States*, rev. ed. (New York: Basic Books, 2009), 2.

2 Charles Aycock, Speech delivered to the North Carolina Society, Baltimore, Maryland, December 18, 1903, reprinted in Anchor: A North Carolina History Online Resource, https://www.ncpedia. org/anchor/governor-aycock-negro (accessed May 25, 2018); and Mike DeBonis, "A Field Guide to the Racists Commemorated inside the U.S. Capitol," *Washington Post*, June 23, 2015, https:// www.washingtonpost.com/news/post-politics/wp/2015/06/ 23/a-field-guide-to-the-racists-commemorated-inside-the-u-s-capitol/?utm_term=.b9489619000a (accessed May 24, 2018).

3 Carrie Chapman Catt and Nettie Rogers Shuler, *Woman Suffrage and Politics: The Inner Story of the Suffrage Movement* (New York: Charles Scribner's Sons, 1926), 472.

4 Bernard Grofman, Lisa Handley, and Richard G. Niemi, *Minority Representation and the Quest for Voting Equality* (New York: Cambridge University Press, 1992), 18.

5 Kevin J. Coleman, "The Voting Rights Act of 1965: Background and Overview," Congressional Research Service Report R43626 (July 20, 2015), 11–12.

6 Shelby County v. Holder, 570 U.S. 529___ (2013), https://supr eme.justia.com/cases/federal/us/570/12-96/#tab-opinion-1970 750 (accessed August 18, 2018).

7   Amy Howe, "We Gave You a Chance: Today's Shelby County Decision in Plain English," *SCOTUSblog*, June 25, 2013, http://www.scotusblog.com/2013/06/we-gave-you-a-chance-tod ays-shelby-county-decision-in-plain-english/ (accessed May 29, 2018).

8   Dana Liebelson, "The Supreme Court Gutted the Voting Rights Act. What Happened Next in These 8 States Will Not Shock You," *Mother Jones*, April 8, 2014, https://www.motherjones.com/ politics/2014/04/republican-voting-rights-supreme-court-id/ (accessed August 2, 2018).

9   Brnovich, Attorney General v. Democratic National Committee, 594 U.S. ___ (2021), https://supreme.justia.com/cases/federal/ us/594/19-1257/#tab-opinion-4446158. Alito and Kagan quotes from this document.

10   Biden quoted in Adam Liptak, "Supreme Court Upholds Arizona Voting Restrictions," *New York Times*, July 1, 2021.

11   "Gender Differences in Voter Turnout," Center for Women and Politics, Rutgers University, July 20, 2017, http://www.cawp. rutgers.edu/sites/default/files/resources/genderdiff.pdf (accessed May 19, 2018).

12   Danielle Paquette, "The Unexpected Voters behind the Widest Gender Gap in Recorded Election History," *Washington Post*, November 9, 2016.

13   Richard Fry, "Millennials and Gen Xers Outvoted Boomers and Older Generations in 2016 Election," Fact Tank, Pew Research Center, July 31, 2017, http/www.pewresearch.org/fact-tank/ 2017/07/31/millennials-and-gen-xers-outvoted-boomers-and-older-generations-in-2016-election/ (accessed May 24, 2018).

14   Ruth Igielnik and Abby Budiman, "The Changing Racial and Ethnic Composition of the US Electorate," Pew Research Center, September 23, 2020, https://www.pewresearch.org/2020/09/ 23/the-changing-racial-and-ethnic-composition-of-the-u-s-ele ctorate/ (accessed September 27, 2021).

15   Ruth Igielnik, Scott Keeter, and Hannah Hartig, "Behind Biden's 2020 Victory," Pew Research Center, June 30, 2021, https://www. pewresearch.org/politics/2021/06/30/behind-bidens-2020-vict ory/ (accessed September 27, 2021).

16   "2017 National Population Projection Tables," US Census Bureau, https://www.census.gov/data/tables/2012/demo/popproj/ 2012-summary-tables.html (accessed May 19, 2018); and Alec

Tyson and Shiva Maniam, "Behind Trump's Victory: Divisions by Race, Gender, Education," Fact Tank, Pew Research Center, November 9, 2016, http://www.pewresearch.org/fact-tank/2016/11/09/behind-trumps-victory-divisions-by-race-gender-education/ (accessed May 28, 2018).

17 Rep. David Lewis, quoted in Robert Barnes, "Supreme Court Sends Case on North Carolina Gerrymandering Back to Lower Court," *Washington Post*, June 25, 2018, https://www.washingtonpost.com/politics/courts_law/supreme-court-sends-case-on-north-carolina-gerrymandering-back-to-lower-court/2018/06/25/03c1119e-787e-11e8-93cc-6d3beccdd7a3_story.html?utm_term=.e6fdf0e86d7e (accessed June 25, 2018).

18 Chris Uggen, Ryan Larson, and Sarah Shannon, "6 Million Lost Voters: State-Level Estimates of Felony Disenfranchisement, 2016," Sentencing Project, Washington, DC, October 6, 2016, https://www.sentencingproject.org/publications/6-million-lost-voters-state-level-estimates-felony-disenfranchisement-2016/ (accessed April 22, 2018).

19 Who Votes for Mayor? Portland State University, OR, 2016, see "About the Project," http://www.whovotesformayor.org/about (accessed March 30, 2018).

20 Kriston Capps, "In the U.S., Almost No One Votes in Local Elections," City Lab, November 1, 2016, https://www.citylab.com/equity/2016/11/in-the-us-almost-no-one-votes-in-local-elections/505766/ (accessed March 30, 2018).

21 Drew DeSilver, "U.S. Voter Turnout Trails Most Developed Countries," Fact Tank, Pew Research Center, May 15, 2017, http://www.pewresearch.org/fact-tank/2017/05/15/u-s-voter-turnout-trails-most-developed-countries/ (accessed May 10, 2018).

22 Anthony Fowler, "Electoral and Policy Consequences of Voter Turnout: Evidence from Compulsory Voting in Australia," *Quarterly Journal of Political Science* 8 (2013): 159–82, available at http://projects.iq.harvard.edu/files/westminster_model_democracy/files/fowler_compulsoryvoting.pdf (accessed May 12, 2018).

23 Barack Obama, quoted in Chris Weller, "Half of Americans Probably Won't Vote—but Requiring Them to Would Change That," *Business Insider*, November 7, 2016, http://www.business

insider.com/compulsory-voting-what-if-americans-have-to-vote-2016-11 (accessed May 12, 2018).

24 Kim Zetter, "The Crisis in Election Security," *New York Times*, September 26, 2018, https://www.nytimes.com/2018/09/26/magazine/election-security-crisis-midterms (accessed September 29, 2018).

25 "2018 HAVA Election Security Funds," US Election Assistance Commission, n.d., https://www.eac.gov/2018-hava-election-security-funds/ (accessed May 19, 2018).

26 Derek Hawkins, "The Cybersecurity 202: How Colorado Became the Safest State to Cast a Vote," *Washington Post*, May 10, 2018, https://www.washingtonpost.com/news/powerpost/paloma/the-cybersecurity-202/2018/05/10/the-cybersecurity-202-how-colorado-became-the-safest-state-to-cast-a-vote/5af317c930fb0 42db5797427/?utm_term=.afc31ebf59cd (accessed May 25, 2018).

27 "Inaccurate, Costly, and Inefficient: Evidence That America's Voting Registration System Needs an Upgrade," Pew Center on the States, February 2012, http://www.pewtrusts.org/~/media/legacy/uploadedfiles/pcs_assets/2012/pewupgradingvoterregi strationpdf.pdf (accessed May 25, 2018).

28 Jonathan Brater, Kevin Morris, Myrna Pérez, and Christopher Deluzio, *Purges: A Growing Threat to the Right to Vote*, Brennan Center for Justice, New York University Law School, 2018, https://www.brennancenter.org/publication/purges-growing-threat-right-vote#Embed (accessed August 18, 2018).

29 Husted, Ohio Secretary of State v. A. Philip Randolph Institute, https://www.supremecourt.gov/opinions/17pdf/16-980_f 2q3.pdf.

30 Adam Liptak, "Supreme Court Upholds Ohio's Purge of Voting Rolls," *New York Times*, June 11, 2018, https://www.nytimes.com/2018/06/11/us/politics/supreme-court-upholds-ohios-purge-of-voting-rolls.html?hp&action=click&pgtype=Homepage&clickSource=story-heading&module=first-column-region&region=top-news&WT.nav= top-news (accessed June 11, 2018).

31 Wendy Underhill, "All-Mail Elections," National Conference of State Legislatures, January 12, 2017, http://www.ncsl.org/research/elections-and-campaigns/all-mail-elections.aspx#Dis (accessed May 24, 2018), contains all the current mail-in requirements of the states.

32 "Absentee Ballot Rules," Vote.org, https://www.vote.org/absen
    tee-voting-rules/ (accessed May 24, 2018). The Vote.org website
    contains the current absentee ballot rules of all the states.

33 Drew Desilver and Abigail Geiger, "For Many Americans,
    Election Day Is Already Here," Pew Research Center, October
    21, 2016, http://www.pewresearch.org/fact-tank/2016/10/21/
    for-many-americans-election-day-is-already-here/ (accessed
    December 10, 2018).

34 Justin Levitt, "The Truth about Voter Fraud," Brennan Center for
    Justice, New York University School of Law, November 9, 2007,
    https://www.brennancenter.org/publication/truth-about-voter-
    fraud (accessed May 24, 2018); and Levitt, "A Comprehensive
    Investigation of Voter Impersonation Finds 31 Credible Incidents
    Out of 1 Billion Ballots Cast," *Washington Post*, https://www.was
    hingtonpost.com/news/wonk/wp/2014/08/06/a-comprehens
    ive-investigation-of-voter-impersonation-finds-31-credible-incide
    nts-out-of-one-billion-ballots-cast/?utm_term=.f488cb99341c
    (accessed May 24, 2018).

35 Gupta and Hasen, quoted in Michael Thackett and Michael
    Wines, "Trump Disbands Commission on Voter Fraud," *New York
    Times*, January 3, 2018, https://www.nytimes.com/2018/01/
    03/us/politics/trump-voter-fraud-commission.html (accessed
    May 10, 2018). See also the responses of state election officials,
    "In Their Own Words: Officials Refuting False Claims of Voter
    Fraud," Brennan Center for Justice, April 13, 2017, http://
    www.brennancenter.org/quotes-on-voter-fraud (accessed May
    30, 2018).

36 Eli Rosenberg, "'The Most Bizarre Thing I've Ever Been a Part
    Of': Trump Panel Found No Widespread Voter Fraud, Ex-
    member Says," *Washington Post*, August 3, 2018, https://www.
    washingtonpost.com/news/politics/wp/2018/08/03/the-
    most-bizarre-thing-ive-ever-been-a-part-of-trump-panel-found-
    no-voter-fraud-ex-member-says/?utm_term=.fb3d61aeb07f
    (accessed August 5, 2018).

37 Amy Gardner and Beth Reinhard, "N.C. Election Officials
    Sounded Alarm about Alleged Election Fraud to Federal
    Prosecutors in January 2017," *Washington Post*, December 21,
    2018, https://www.washingtonpost.com/politics/nc-elect
    ion-officials-sounded-alarm-about-alleged-election-fraud-
    to-federal-prosecutors-in-january-2017/2018/12/21/240e0

9a0-0539-11e9-b5df-5d3874f1ac36_story.html?utm_term=.0fa3f 8f8aa48 (accessed December 21, 2018).

Chapter 2

1 "Computing Apportionment," US Census Bureau, n.d., https:// www.census.gov/population/apportionment/about/comput ing.html (accessed May 30, 2018).

2 Source: Geoffrey Skelly, "How the House Got Stuck at 435 Seats," *FiveThirtyEight*, August 12, 2021, https://fivethirtyeight.com/ features/how-the-house-got-stuck-at-435-seats/?cid=referral_t aboola_feed (accessed September 1, 2021). Population estimates for 2020.

3 Baker v. Carr, 369 U.S. 186 (1962), https://www.law.cornell.edu/ supremecourt/text/369/186; Reynolds v. Sims, 377 U.S. 533 (1964), https://supreme.justia.com/cases/federal/us/377/533/ case.html; and Wesberry v. Sanders, 376 U.S. 1 (1964), https:// supreme.justia.com/cases/federal/us/377/533/case.html (accessed June 1, 2018).

4 See Evenwel v. Abbott, 578 U.S. ___ (2016), https://supreme.jus tia.com/cases/federal/us/578/14-940/ (accessed June 1, 2018); and Garrett Epps, "Who Gets to Be Represented in Congress," *The Atlantic*, December 3, 2015, https://www.theatlantic.com/ politics/archive/2015/12/evenwel-supreme-court-districting/ 418437/ (accessed June 1, 2018).

5 Justin Levitt, "All about Redistricting" (website), Loyola School of Law, Los Angeles, March 24, 2018, http://redistricting.lls.edu/ index.php (accessed June 4, 2018).

6 Levitt, "All about Redistricting."

7 Jennifer Davis, "Elbridge Gerry and the Monstrous Gerrymander," *In Custodia Legis*, the blog of the Law Librarians, Library of Congress, February 10, 2017, https://blogs.loc.gov/ law/2017/02/elbridge-gerry-and-the-monstrous-gerrymander/ (accessed May 31, 2018).

8 Justice O'Connor, Opinion of the Court, Shaw v. Reno, 509 U.S. 630, 643 (1993).

9 Cooper v. Harris, 581 U.S. ___ (2017), https://www.supremeco urt.gov/opinions/16pdf/15-1262_db8e.pdf (accessed June 19, 2018). Justice Elena Kagan delivered the 5–3 opinion.

10 Gene Nichol, "N.C. Has the Worst Gerrymander in U.S. History. What Else Is New?," *News and Observer* (Raleigh), February 1,

2018, http://www.newsobserver.com/opinion/op-ed/article19
7852639.html (accessed May 31, 2018).

11 Abbot v. Perez, 585 U.S. ___ (2018), https://www.supremecourt.
gov/opinions/17pdf/17-586_o7kq.pdf (accessed June 26, 2018).

12 Levitt, "All about Redistricting."

13 Adam Liptak, "Smaller States Find Outsize Clout Growing
in Senate," New York Times, March 11, 2013, http://archive.
nytimes.com/www.nytimes.com/interactive/2013/03/11/
us/politics/democracy-tested.html?_r%25E2%2580%25B0=
%25E2%2580%25B00#/#smallstate (accessed May 30, 2018).

14 "National Population Projections," Weldon Cooper Center for
Public Service, University of Virginia, n.d., https://demograph
ics.coopercenter.org/national-population-projections (accessed
July 16, 2018).

Chapter 3

1 Earl Black and Merle Black, The Rise of Southern Republicans
(Cambridge, MA: Belknap Press of Harvard University Press,
2003), 2–3.

2 "Political Typology Reveals Deep Fissures on the Right and
Left," Pew Research Center, October 24, 2017, http://www.peo
ple-press.org/2017/10/24/political-typology-reveals-deep-fissu
res-on-the-right-and-left/ (accessed July 12, 2018).

3 Quoted in Dana Milbank, "The Trump Albatross," Washington
Post, September 14, 2018.

4 Amina Dunn, "Two-Thirds of Republicans Want Trump to Retain
Major Political Role; 44% Want Him to Run Again in 2021," Pew
Research Center, October 6, 2021, https://www.pewresearch.
org/fact-tank/2021/10/06/two-thirds-of-republicans-want-
trump-to-retain-major-political-role-44-want-him-to-run-again-
in-2024/ (accessed October 12, 2021).

5 "Political Polarization in the American Public," Pew Research
Center, June 12, 2014, http://www.people-press.org/2014/06/
12/political-polarization-in-the-american-public/ (accessed July
12, 2018).

6 Wilson, quoted in David Blankenhorn, "Why Polarization
Matters," American Interest, December 22, 2015, https://www.
the-american-interest.com/2015/12/22/why-polarization-matt
ers/ (accessed July 12, 2018).

7 Blankenhorn, "Why Polarization Matters."

8 Bill Bishop, *The Big Sort: Why the Clustering of Like-Minded America Is Tearing Us Apart* (New York: First Mariner Books, 2009).

9 "New Initiative Explores the Deep, Persistent Divides between Biden and Trump Voters," University of Virginia Center for Politics, September 30, 2021, https://centerforpolitics.org/crys talball/articles/new-initiative-explores-deep-persistent-divides-between-biden-and-trump-voters/ (accessed October 13, 2021).

10 "Party Affiliation," Gallup Poll, 2004–, https://news.gallup. com/poll/15370/party-affiliation.aspx (accessed July 5, 2018).

11 Jeffrey M. Jones, "Quarterly Gap in Party Affiliation Largest since 2012," Gallup, April 7, 2021, https://news.gallup.com/poll/343 976/quarterly-gap-party-affiliation-largest-2012.aspx (accessed October 22, 2021).

12 See Nate Silver, "There Is No 'Blue Wall,'" FiveThirtyEight.com, May 12, 2015, https://fivethirtyeight.com/features/there-is-no-blue-wall/ (accessed June 5, 2018).

13 Steven E. Billet, "The Rise and Impact of Monster PACs," in Dennis W. Johnson, ed., *Routledge Handbook on Political Management* (New York: Routledge, 2009), 135–50.

14 John K. White and Matthew R. Kerbel, *Party On! Political Parties from Hamilton and Jefferson to Trump*, 2nd ed. (New York: Routledge, 2018), 5.

Chapter 4

1 Data are from Jennifer L. Lawless, *Becoming a Candidate: Political Ambition and the Decision to Run for Office* (New York: Cambridge University Press, 2012), 33.

2 Campaign Finance Institute, "Historical Database of State Campaign Finance Laws," https://cfinst.github.io/#contribut ion-limits?question=IndividualToCandLimit_H_Max&year=2016 (accessed April 13, 2018).

3 Quoted in Charlotte Alter, "A Year Ago They Marched. Now a Record Number of Women Are Running for Office," *Time*, January 18, 2018, http://time.com/5107499/record-number-of-women-are-running-for-office/ (accessed May 9, 2018).

4 "Women in National Parliaments," International Parliamentary Union (website), April 1, 2018, http://archive.ipu.org/wmn-e/classif.htm (accessed May 9, 2018).

5 Jennifer L. Lawless and Richard L. Fox, *It Takes a Candidate: Why Women Don't Run for Office* (New York: Cambridge University

Press, 2005). The second edition of this book is titled *It Still Takes a Candidate* (2010). See also Susan J. Carroll and Kira Sanbonmatsu, *More Women Can Run: Gender and Pathways to the State Legislatures* (New York: Oxford University Press, 2013).

6 "Over 34,000 Women Want to Run for Office," press release, EMILY's List, February 27, 2018, https://www.emilyslist.org/news/entry/over-34000-women-want-to-run-for-office (accessed May 9, 2018). EMILY is an acronym for Early Money Is Like Yeast.

7 Denise Lu and Kate Zernike, "Women Have Won More Primaries Than Ever Before. Will They Set a Record in November?," *New York Times*, September 17, 2018.

8 "Women in State Legislatures 2021," https://cawp.rutgers.edu/women-state-legislature-2021 (accessed September 28, 2021).

9 National Institute on Money and State Politics, 2016 data, https://www.followthemoney.org/tools/election-overview (accessed March 12, 2018).

10 Jesse McKinley and Kirk Johnson, "Mormons Tip Scale on Ban on Gay Marriage," *New York Times*, November 14, 2008.

11 Obergefell et al. v. Hodges, Director, Ohio Department of Health, 576 U.S. ___ (2015), https://www.supremecourt.gov/opinions/14pdf/14-556_3204.pdf (accessed July 17, 2018).

12 See Dennis W. Johnson, *Political Consultants and American Elections* (New York: Routledge, 2016), 208–41.

13 "Pritzker Price Tag: Victory in Gov. Race Costly, No Matter How You Slice It," *Chicago Tribune*, November 7, 2018, https://chicago.suntimes.com/news/illinois-governor-results-j-b-pritzker-price-tag-victory-race-cost-per-vote-bruce-rauner-self-finance/ (accessed December 12, 2018).

14 "Overview of State Laws on Public Financing," National Council of State Legislatures, n.d., http://www.ncsl.org/research/elections-and-campaigns/public-financing-of-campaigns-overview.aspx (accessed April 9, 2018).

15 "Judicial Selection in the States," Ballotpedia, n.d., https://ballotpedia.org/Judicial_selection_in_the_states (accessed August 31, 2018).

16 Dennis W. Johnson, *Democracy for Hire: A History of American Political Consulting* (New York: Oxford University Press, 2017), 241–42.

17 "New Politics of Judicial Elections," National Institute of Money in State Politics, 2012; and Johnson, *Democracy for Hire*, 241–42.

18 "Re-election Rates over the Years" (1964–2018), Opensecrets.org,
    https://www.opensecrets.org/overview/reelect.php (accessed
    May 10, 2018).
19 Chris Cillizza, "People Hate Congress. But Most Incumbents
    Get Re-elected. What Gives?," *Washington Post*, May 19, 2013,
    https://www.washingtonpost.com/news/the-fix/wp/2013/05/
    09/people-hate-congress-but-most-incumbents-get-re-elected-
    what-gives/?utm_term=.ec4b634b1338 (accessed July 19, 2018).

Chapter 5

1 Domenico Montanaro, "How Exactly Do Iowa Caucuses Work?,"
   National Public Radio, January 30, 2016, https://www.npr.
   org/2016/01/30/464960979/how-do-the-iowa-caucuses-work
   (accessed June 22, 2018).
2 Elaine Kamarck, "Why Is New Hampshire the First Primary in
   the Nation?," Brookings Institution, February 5, 2016, https://
   www.brookings.edu/blog/fixgov/2016/02/05/why-is-new-
   hampshire-the-first-primary-in-the-nation/ (accessed June
   18, 2018).
3 Michael Scherer, "Democrats Edge toward Dumping Iowa's
   Caucuses as First Presidential Vote," *Washington Post*, October
   9, 2021.
4 Akhil Reed Amar, "The Troubling Reason the Electoral College
   Exists," *Time*, November 10, 2016, http://time.com/4558510/
   electoral-college-history-slavery/ (accessed June 7, 2018). See also
   Amar's book-length treatment, *The Constitution Today: Timeless
   Lessons for the Issues of Our Era* (New York: Basic Books, 2016).
5 Chiafalo v. Washington (2020), https://www.supremecourt.
   gov/opinions/19pdf/19-465_i425.pdf. Eight justices were in the
   majority; Justice Thomas concurred.
6 Thomas H. Neale, "Presidential and Vice Presidential
   Succession: Overview and Current Law" (CRS Report to
   Congress RL31761, Washington, DC: Congressional Research
   Service, September 27, 2004), https://fas.org/sgp/crs/misc/
   RL31761.pdf (accessed June 13, 2018).
7 Bob Woodward and Robert Costa, *Peril* (New York: Simon &
   Schuster, 2021), 209–12, quote at 211.
8 Peter Fenn, "Has the Electoral College Outlived Its Usefulness?,"
   Thomas Jefferson Street (opinion blog), *U.S. News & World Report*,
   October 11, 2012, https://www.usnews.com/opinion/blogs/

peter-fenn/2012/10/11/electoral-college-lets-obama-romney-ign
ore-80-percent-of-america (accessed July 16, 2018).

9   Amisa Ratliff, "12 Numbers to Know about the Money in the
2020 Presidential Election," *Issue One*, December 14, 2020,
https://www.issueone.org/12-numbers-to-know-about-the-
money-in-the-2020-presidential-election/ (accessed October
22, 2021).

10   See, for example, John Haskell, "Reforming Presidential
Primaries: Three Steps for Improving the Campaign
Environment," *Presidential Studies Quarterly* 26, no. 2 (Spring
1996): 380–90.

11   "U.S. Electoral College," National Archives and Records
Administration, https://www.archives.gov/federal-register/
electoral-college/faq.html#changes (accessed June 18, 2018).

12   Art Swift, "Americans' Support for Electoral College Rises
Sharply," Gallup Poll, December 2, 2016, https://news.gallup.
com/poll/198917/americans-support-electoral-college-rises-shar
ply.aspx (accessed June 18, 2018).

Chapter 6

1   Zeeshan Aleem, "Rep. Jim Clyburn's Endorsement Gave Biden
Some Serious Momentum in South Carolina," *Vox*, March 1,
2020.

2   Rayshawn Ray, "How Black Americans Saved Biden and
American Democracy," Brookings, November 24, 2020, https://
www.brookings.edu/blog/how-we-rise/2020/11/24/how-
black-americans-saved-biden-and-american-democracy/
(accessed August 5, 2021).

3   Elaine Karmack, Yousef Ibreak, Amanda Powers, and Chris
Stewart, "Voting by Mail in a Pandemic: A State-by-State
Scorecard," Brookings, October 2020, https://www.brookings.
edu/research/voting-by-mail-in-a-pandemic-a-state-by-state-
scorecard/ (accessed September 22, 2021).

4   Bob Woodward and Robert Costa, *Peril* (New York: Simon &
Schuster, 2021), 132.

5   Nicholas Riccardi, "Here's the Reality behind Trump's Claim of
Mail Voting," Associated Press, September 30, 2020, https://apn
ews.com/article/virus-outbreak-joe-biden-election-2020-donald-
trump-elections-3e8170c3348ce3719d4bc7182146b582 (accessed
September 24, 2021).

6 William H. Frey, "Biden-Won Counties Are Home to 67 Million More Americans Than Trump-Won Counties," Brookings, January 21, 2021, https://www.brookings.edu/blog/the-ave nue/2021/01/21/a-demographic-contrast-biden-won-551-count ies-home-to-67-million-more-americans-than-trumps-2588-count ies/ (accessed August 4, 2021).

7 Louis Jacobsen, "How Democrats Are Losing the War for Counties," *Sabato's Crystal Ball*, University of Virginia Center for Politics, October 2021, https://centerforpolitics.org/crys talball/articles/how-democrats-are-losing-the-war-for-counties (accessed October 13, 2021).

8 Trump quoted in Chris Cillizza, "Donald Trump Just Kind-of Endorsed Stacey Abrams for Governor," *CNN Politics*, September 27, 2021, https://www.cnn.com/2021/09/27/politics/donald- trump-brian-kemp-stacey-abrams/index.html (accessed October 13, 2021).

9 Sterling quoted from CNN interview in Daniel Funke, "Fact Check: No Evidence of Fraud in Georgia Election Results," *USA Today*, June 1, 2021, https://www.usatoday.com/story/news/ factcheck/2021/06/01/fact-check-georgia-audit-hasnt-found-30- 000-fake-ballots/5253184001/ (accessed October 6, 2021).

10 A good summary of the problems with the Arizona Cyber Ninja audit is found in Ralph Neas, Richard A. Gephardt, Timothy E. Wirth, Gary Hart, and Anthony Essaye, "The Truth behind the Results of the Maricopa County Election Audit," *Century Fund*, September 27, 2021, https://tcf.org/content/commentary/ truth-behind-results-maricopa-county-election-audit/?agreed=1 (accessed October 5, 2021).

11 Scott Bauer, "Wisconsin Audit Finds Elections Are 'Safe and Secure,'" *Associated Press*, October 22, 2021, https://apnews. com/article/joe-biden-wisconsin-presidential-elections-state- elections-madison-9a2f172dd8074668ded26bd5b0b41fbb (accessed October 22, 2021).

12 Wray quoted in "It's Official: The Election Was Secure," Brennan Center for Justice, New York University, December 11, 2020, https://www.brennancenter.org/our-work/research-reports/its- official-election-was-secure (accessed July 17, 2021).

13 "Joint Statement from Elections Infrastructure Government Coordinating Council & the Election Infrastructure Sector Coordinating Executive Committees," Cybersecurity and

Infrastructure Security Agency, November 12, 2020, https://
www.cisa.gov/news/2020/11/12/joint-statement-elections-inf
rastructure-government-coordinating-council-election (accessed
July 13, 2021).

14 King quoted in David E. Sanger and Nicole Perlroth, "Trump
Fires Christopher Krebs, Official Who Disputed Election Fraud
Claims," *New York Times*, November 17, 2020.

15 "It's Official: The Election Was Secure," Brennan Center for
Justice, New York University, December 11, 2020, https://www.
brennancenter.org/our-work/research-reports/its-official-elect
ion-was-secure (accessed July 17, 2021).

16 Jonathan D. Karl, "Inside William Barr's Breakup with Trump,"
The Atlantic, June 27, 2021.

17 See Woodward and Costa, *Peril*.

18 "Foreign Threats to the 2020 US Federal Elections," National
Intelligence Council, declassified March 15, 2021, https://int.
nyt.com/data/documenttools/2021-intelligence-community-
election-interference-assessment/abd0346ebdd93e1e/full.pdf
(accessed October 15, 2021).

Chapter 7

1 Zachary Jonathan Jacobson, "Many Are Worried About the
Return of the 'Big Lie.' They're Worried About the Wrong Thing,"
Washington Post, May 21, 2018. This was written well before the
2020 Big Lie became a familiar part of our political lexicon.

2 Snyder quoted in Brian Stelter, "Experts Warn That Trump's Big
Lie Will Outlast His Presidency," CNN, January 11, 2021, https://
www.cnn.com/2021/01/11/media/trump-lies-reliable-sources/
index.html (accessed October 21, 2021).

3 Zachary B. Wolf, "The Five Key Elements of Trump's Big Lie and
How It Came About," *CNN Politics*, May 19, 2021, https://www.
cnn.com/2021/05/19/politics/donald-trump-big-lie-explainer/
index.html (accessed October 21, 2021).

4 Opinion article by Jamelle Bouie, "'Stop the Steal' Didn't Start
with Trump," *New York Times*, January 15, 2021.

5 "#StoptheSteal: Timeline of Social Media and Extremist Activities
Leading to 1/6 Insurrection," Digital Forensic Research Lab,
Atlantic Council, February 10, 2021, https://www.justsecurity.
org/74622/stopthesteal-timeline-of-social-media-and-extremist-
activities-leading-to-1-6-insurrection/ (accessed August 11, 2021).

6 Trump quoted in Jonathan Martin, "Donald Trump's Heated Barrage Has Little Precedent," *New York Times*, October 15, 2016; Karen Tumulty and Philip Rucker, "At Third Debate, Trump Won't Commit to Election Results if He Loses," *Washington Post*, October 19, 2016.

7 Matthew Rosenberg and Jim Rutenberg, "Key Takeaways from Trump's Effort to Overturn the Election," *New York Times*, February 1, 2021, https://www.nytimes.com/2021/02/01/us/politics/trump-election-results.html (accessed October 12, 2021).

8 "#StoptheSteal," citing research by Buzzsumo.

9 Eric Wemple, "Sean Hannity, America's No. 2 Threat to Democracy: An A to Z Guide," *Washington Post*, December 14, 2020.

10 Lis Power, "In 2 Weeks after It Called the Election, Fox News Cast Doubts on the Results Nearly 800 Times," Media Matters for America, January 14, 2021, https://www.mediamatters.org/fox-news/2-weeks-after-it-called-election-fox-news-cast-doubt-resu lts-nearly-800-times (accessed January 20, 2021). Erik Wemple, "Never Forget Fox News' Promotion of the 'Big Lie,'" *Washington Post*, January 19, 2021.

11 "'The Big Lie': Most Republicans Believe the 2020 Election Was Stolen," Public Religion Research Institute, May 12, 2021, https://www.prri.org/spotlight/the-big-lie-most-republic ans-believe-the-2020-election-was-stolen/ (accessed October 13, 2021). The Public Religion Research Institute is a nonprofit, nonpartisan organization.

12 Cheney quoted in Caroline Kelly, "Cheney: Trump Inciting January 6 Riot 'the Most Dangerous Thing' a President Has Done," *CNN Politics*, June 6, 2021, https://www.cnn.com/2021/06/06/politics/cheney-trump-dangerous-thing-axe-files/index.html (accessed October 21, 2021).

13 Ronna McDaniel, Republican National Committee chair, later tried to make a distinction between the Capitol Hill rioters and innocent protestors. "Liz Cheney and Adam Kinzinger crossed a line," McDaniel said. "They chose to join Nancy Pelosi in a Democrat-led persecution of ordinary citizens who engaged in legitimate political discourse that had nothing to do with violence at the Capitol." But McDaniel's uncle, Senator Mitt Romney, tweeted, "Shame falls on a party that would censure persons of conscience, who seek truth in the face of vitriol. Honor

attaches to Liz Cheney and Adam Kinzinger for seeking truth
even when doing so comes at great personal cost." Brittany
Shepherd and Will Steakin, "RNC Votes to Censure Cheney,
Kinzinger for Roles in House Jan. 6 Committee," ABC News,
February 4, 2022, https://abcnews.go.com/Politics/rnc-vote-
censure-cheney-kinzinger-roles-jan-committee/story?id=82671
994 (accessed February 5, 2022).

14 Press release, "Romney Condemns Insurrection at US Capitol,"
Office of Senator Mitt Romney, January 6, 2021, https://www.
romney.senate.gov/romney-condemns-insurrection-us-capitol
(accessed October 12, 2021). McConnell quoted in Lisa Mascaro
and Mary Clare Jalonick, "McConnell Blames Trump," *Denver
Post*, January 20, 2021.

15 Transcript of interview, with Lesley Stahl, "Liz Cheney on Being
a Republican while Opposing Donald Trump," *60 Minutes*, CBS,
September 26, 2021, https://www.cbsnews.com/news/liz-che
ney-donald-trump-wyoming-60-minutes-2021-09-26/ (accessed
October 12, 2021).

16 Katie Benner, "Trump Pressed Justice Department to Declare
Election Results Corrupt, Notes Show," *New York Times*, October
13, 2021.

17 "Subverting Justice: How the Former President and His Allies
Pressured DOJ to Overturn the 2020 Election," Senate Committee
on the Judiciary, Majority Staff Report; Senator Dick Durbin
(D-Illinois), chair, October 6, 2021, https://www.judiciary.sen
ate.gov/imo/media/doc/Interim%20Staff%20Report%20FI
NAL.pdf. The Republican viewpoint was that Trump had done
nothing wrong and was just trying to determine if any fraud
had been committed: "In Their Own Words: A Factual Summary
of Testimony from Senior Justice Department Officials Relating
to Events from December 14, 2020 to January 3, 2021," Senate
Committee on the Judiciary, Minority Report, Senator Charles
Grassley (R-Iowa), October 7, 2021, https://www.judiciary.
senate.gov/imo/media/doc/in_their_own_words_a_factual_
summary_of_testimony_from_senior_justice_department_
officials_relating_to_events_from_december_14_2020_to_january
_3_2021.pdf (accessed October 13, 2021). Kate Brenner, "Trump
and Justice Dept. Lawyer Said to Have Plotted to Oust Acting
Attorney General," *New York Times*, January 22, 2021; Jess Bravin
and Sadie Gurman, "Trump Pressed Justice Department to Go

Directly to Supreme Court to Overturn Election," *Wall Street Journal*, January 23, 2021.

18   Eric Bradner, "Trump's Big Lie about 2020 Election Results Suffers Legal and Political Blows in Key Swing States," *CNN Politics*, June 27, 2021, https://www.cnn.com/2021/06/27/politics/2020-election-falsehoods-voting/index.html (accessed October 23, 2021).

19   Transcript of conversation between Trump and Raffensperger in Amy Gardner and Paulina Firozi, "Here's the Full Transcript and Audio of the Call between Trump and Raffensperger," *Washington Post*, January 5, 2021, https://www.washingtonpost.com/politics/trump-raffensperger-call-transcript-georgia-vote/2021/01/03/2768e0cc-4ddd-11eb-83e3-322644d82356_story.html (accessed October 12, 2021).

20   Philip Bump, "This Is How Embarrassing Trump's 'Fraud' Claims Have Gotten," *Washington Post*, September 17, 2021.

21   See Editorial, "January 6th Was a Warning. Will Lawmakers Do Anything to Protect the 2024 Election?," *New York Times*, February 5, 2022, https://www.nytimes.com/2022/02/05/opinion/electoral-count-act-congress.html; Edward B. Foley, "Preparing for a Disputed Presidential Election: An Exercise in Election Assessment and Risk Management," *Loyola University Chicago Law Journal* 51 (2019): 309–62, https://www.luc.edu/media/lucedu/law/students/publications/llj/pdfs/vol-51/issue-2/7_Foley%20(309-362).pdf (accessed February 4, 2022).

22   "Election Administration at State and Local Levels," National Conference of State Legislatures, February 3, 2020, https://www.ncsl.org/research/elections-and-campaigns/elect ion-administration-at-state-and-local-levels.aspx (accessed October 23, 2021). Kathleen Hale, Robert Montjoy, and Mitchell Brown, *Administering Elections: How American Elections Work* (New York: Palgrave Macmillan, 2015).

23   "Election Officials under Attack," Brennan Center for Justice, New York University Law School, June 16, 2021, https://www.brennancenter.org/sites/default/files/2021-06/BCJ-129%20Elect ionOfficials_v7.pdf (accessed October 22, 2021).

24   Glenn Kessler, Salvador Rizzo, and Meg Kelly, "Trump's False or Misleading Claims Total 30,573 over 4 Years," *Washington Post*, January 24, 2021.

25 Rosenberg and Rutenberg, "Key Takeaways from Trump's Effort to Overturn the Election."

26 Bibas quoted in Zoe Tillman, "Trump and His Allies Have Lost Nearly 60 Election Fights in Court (and Counting)," *BuzzFeed News*, December 14, 2020, https://www.buzzfeednews.com/article/zoetillman/trump-election-court-losses-electoral-college (accessed October 15, 2021).

27 Rosalind S. Helderman and Elise Viebeck, " 'The Last Wall': How Dozens of Judges across the Political Spectrum Rejected Trump's Efforts to Overturn the Election," *Washington Post*, December 12, 2020, https://www.washingtonpost.com/politics/judges-trump-election-lawsuits/2020/12/12/e3a57224-3a72-11eb-98c4-25dc9f4987e8_story.html (accessed October 23, 2021).

28 Nicolai quoted in Rosenberg and Rutenberg, "Key Takeaways from Trump's Effort to Overturn the Election."

29 *Texas v. Pennsylvania et al.*, 592 U.S. ____ (2020), December 11, 2020, https://www.supremecourt.gov/orders/courtorders/121120zr_p860.pdf (accessed October 23, 2021).

30 Nicole Hong, William K. Rashbaum, and Ben Protess, "Court Suspends Giuliani Law License, Citing Trump Election Lies," *New York Times*, June 24, 2021. The court's opinion is found in https://www.nytimes.com/interactive/2021/06/24/us/giuliani-law-license-suspension.html (accessed October 14, 2021).

31 Quoted in Bradner, "Trump's Big Lie."

32 Pepper quoted in Tillman, "Trump and His Allies Have Lost Nearly 60 Election Fights."

33 Jan Wolfe, " 'Profound Abuse': Judge Disciplines Pro-Trump Lawyers over Election Dispute," Reuters, August 26, 2021, https://www.reuters.com/world/us/judge-sanctions-sidney-powell-other-pro-trump-lawyers-who-claimed-voter-fraud-2021-08-25/ (accessed October 13, 2021).

34 Lateshia Beachum and Maria Luisa Paúl, "Dominion's Lawsuit against Trump Allies Can Move forward after Judge Rejects Arguments," *Washington Post*, August 12, 2021.

35 Dominion Voting website, https://www.dominionvoting.com/legal-updates-learn-how-we-are-defending-dominion/ (accessed October 13, 2021).

36 Chris Cillizza, "Here's Even More Evidence That Widespread Voter Fraud Isn't a Thing," *CNN Politics*, February 2, 2022,

https://www.cnn.com/2022/02/02/politics/voter-election-fraud-trump/index.html (accessed February 4, 2022).

37 Peter Carlson, "Another Race to the Finish," *Washington Post*, November 17, 2000.

38 Edmund F. Kallina Jr., *Kennedy v. Nixon: The Presidential Election of 1960* (Gainesville: University of Florida Press, 2010).

39 Gore quoted in Andrew Glass, "Gore Concedes Presidential Election to Bush, December 13, 2000," *Politico*, December 13, 2017.

40 Jena McGregor, "Hillary Clinton Didn't Give Her Concession Speech on Election Night. Now We See One Reason Why," *Washington Post*, November 9, 2016, https://www.washingtonp ost.com/news/on-leadership/wp/2016/11/09/hillary-clinton-didnt-give-her-concession-speech-on-election-night-now-we-see-one-reason-why/ (accessed October 23, 2021).

Chapter 8

1 Robert Caro, *The Years of Lyndon Johnson: Master of the Senate* (New York: Alfred A. Knopf, 2002), 403–13; and Johnson, *Democracy for Hire*, 130–31.

2 John Kenneth White and Matthew R. Kerbel, *Party On! Political Parties from Hamilton and Jefferson to Trump*, 2nd ed. (New York: Routledge, 2018), 142.

3 Buckley v. Valeo, 424 U.S. 1 (1976), https://supreme.justia.com/ cases/federal/us/424/1/ (accessed June 26, 2018). Wealthy US Senate candidate James Buckley wanted to spend his own money but was prohibited from doing so by the FECA. He argued that it was a matter of free speech to spend as much as he wanted out of his own pocket.

4 See, generally, Dennis W. Johnson, *No Place for Amateurs: How Political Consultants Are Reshaping American Democracy*, 2nd ed. (New York: Routledge, 2009), chap. 8.

5 "Total Number of Political Action Committees (PACs) in the United States from 1990 to 2015," Statista (website), n.d., https:// www.statista.com/statistics/198132/total-number-of-us-politi cal-action-committees-since-1990/ (accessed April 10, 2018).

6 Steve Kroft, "Washington's Open Secrets: Profitable PACs," *60 Minutes*, November 2013, https://www.youtube.com/watch?v= O-CTQ0X47iw (accessed April 10, 2018). The segment was based in part on the research conducted by the nonpartisan watchdog organization Citizens for Responsibility and Ethics in Washington

and Peter Schweizer, a fellow at the Hoover Institute, whose book *Extortion: How Politicians Extract Your Money, Buy Votes, and Line Their Own Pockets* (New York: Houghton Mifflin, 2013), outlined much of the abuse by members of Congress.

7 Terry M. Neal, "Fired-Up and Financially Flush, Forbes Prepares to Run Ads in Key States," *Washington Post*, April 11, 1996, A16.

8 Center for Responsive Politics, "The Top 50 Federally Focused Organizations" (for 2014 election cycle), OpenSecrets.org, https://www.opensecrets.org/527s/527cmtes.php?level= C&cycle=2014 (accessed April 22, 2018).

9 Citizens United v. Federal Election Commission, 558 U.S. 310 (2010), https://www.law.cornell.edu/supct/html/08-205. ZS.html (accessed April 23, 2018).

10 McCain, quoted in Howard Kurtz, "John McCain Rips Super PACs," Daily Beast, March 27, 2012, https://www.thedailybe ast.com/john-mccain-rips-super-pacs?ref=scroll; and President Barack Obama, "Remarks by the President in State of the Union Address," White House, January 27, 2010, http://whitehouse. gov/the-press-office/remarks-president-state-union-address (accessed April 23, 2018).

11 McCutcheon et al. v. Federal Election Commission, 572 U.S. 185_ __ (2013), https://www.supremecourt.gov/opinions/13pdf/12-536_e1pf.pdf (accessed April 23, 2018).

12 On the political activity of 501(c) organizations, see John Francis Reilly and Barbara A. Braig Allen, "Political Campaign and Lobbying Activities of IRC 501(c)(4), (c)(5), and (c)(6) Organizations," Internal Revenue Service, 2003, https://www. irs.gov/pub/irs-tege/eotopicl03.pdf (accessed April 24, 2018).

13 Ashley Balcerzak, "Inside Donald Trump's Super PACs and MAGA Nonprofits," Center for Public Integrity, February 18, 2019, https://publicintegrity.org/politics/donald-trump-army-super-pacs-maga-nonprofits/ (accessed September 24, 2021).

14 Karl Evers-Hillstrom, "Outside Spending Reaches Record $2 Billion as Super PACs Hammer Trump," Opensecrets.org, October 9, 2020, https://www.opensecrets.org/news/2020/10/ super-pacs-hammer-trump/ (accessed September 23, 2021).

15 Chris Cillizza, "How Citizens United Changed Politics, in 7 Charts," *Washington Post*, January 22, 2014.

16 Kenneth P. Vogel, "Koch World 2014," *Politico*, January 24, 2014, https://www.politico.com/story/2014/01/koch-broth

ers-2014-elections-102555_Page2.html (accessed April 29, 2018).
See also Johnson, *Democracy for Hire*, 452–54.

17 Anthony Corrado and Tassin Braverman, "Presidential
Campaign Fundraising: An Exception to the Rule?," in Dennis
W. Johnson and Lara M. Brown, eds., *Campaigning for President
2016: Strategy and Tactics* (New York: Routledge, 2017), 112.
Numbers are from FEC data, June 2016.

18 Center for Responsive Politics, "Donor Demographics," 2016
elections, Opensecrets.org, https://www.opensecrets.org/overv
iew/donordemographics.php?cycle=2016&filter=A (accessed
December 18, 2018).

19 Karl Evers-Hillstrom, "Most Expensive Ever: 2020 Election
Cost $14.4 Billion," Opensecrets.org, https://www.opensecrets.
org/news/2021/02/2020-cycle-cost-14p4-billion-doubling-16/
(accessed October 22, 2021).

20 Shane Goldmacher, "Trump's Repeating Donation Tactics Led to
Millions in Refunds into 2021," *New York Times*, August 7, 2021.

21 Fred Wertheimer and Don Simon, "The FEC: The Failure to
Enforce Commission," American Constitutional Society for Law
and Policy, January 2013, 4, http://www.democracy21.org/wp-
content/uploads/2013/02/Wertheimer-and-Simon-The-Failure-
to-Enforce-Commission-.pdf (accessed April 28, 2018).

22 See also David Levinthal, "Another Massive Problem with U.S.
Democracy: The FEC Is Broken," *The Atlantic*, December 17, 2013,
https://www.theatlantic.com/politics/archive/2013/12/anot
her-massive-problem-with-us-democracy-the-fec-is-broken/282
404/ (accessed April 28, 2018).

23 Alan Rappeport, "In Targeting Political Groups, I.R.S. Crossed
the Line," *New York Times*, October 5, 2017.

24 Ollie Gratzinger, "Four Out of Ten Most Expensive House
Races of All Time," Opensecrets.org, December 8, 2020, https://
www.opensecrets.org/news/2020/12/house-races-four-of-10/
(accessed September 24, 2021).

Chapter 9

1 On the history of the political consulting business, see Johnson,
Democracy for Hire.

2 See Dennis W. Johnson, "Campaign Consultants," in Michael
Kazin, ed., *The Concise Princeton Encyclopedia of American Political
History* (Princeton, NJ: Princeton University Press, 2011), 56–59.

3 Sue Halpern, "Cambridge Analytica and the Perils of Psychographics," *New Yorker*, March 30, 2018, https://www.newyorker.com/news/news-desk/cambridge-analytica-and-the-perils-of-psychographics (accessed July 30, 2018).

4 See, for example, Johnson and Brown, *Campaigning for President 2016*.

5 Matt Rhoades managed Romney's 2012 campaign; Jim Messina managed Obama's 2012 re-election campaign; and Robby Mook managed Hillary Clinton's 2016 campaign.

6 Michael Moore, "Five Reasons Why Trump Will Win," MichaelMoore.com, July 2016, http://michaelmoore.com/trump willwin/ (accessed July 31, 2018); and Moore, in a speech at the Murphy Theatre, Wilmington, Ohio, October 24, 2016, featured in his movie *Michael Moore in TrumpLand*, selections aired on "Morning Joe" show, MSNBC, November 4, 2016, http://www.youtube.com/watch?v=kiyqlOfSOjM (accessed July 31, 2018).

Chapter 10

1 "Initiative, Referendum and Recall," National Conference of State Legislatures, September 20, 2012, http://www.ncsl.org/research/elections-and-campaigns/initiative-referendum-and-recall-overview.aspx (accessed August 10, 2018). Question 5, Maine referendum found at Bureau of Corporations, Elections and Commissions, State of Maine, https://www.maine.gov/sos/cec/elec/upcoming/index.html (accessed October 10, 2018).

2 States permitting recall elections: Alaska, Arizona, California, Colorado, Georgia, Idaho, Illinois, Kansas, Louisiana, Michigan, Minnesota, Montana, Nevada, New Jersey, North Dakota, Oregon, Rhode Island, Washington, and Wisconsin. The District of Columbia also permits recall.

3 Shawn Hubler, "The California Recall, Untangled," *New York Times*, July 13, 2021.

4 "Recall of State Officials," National Conference of State Legislatures, March 8, 2016, http://www.ncsl.org/research/electi ons-and-campaigns/recall-of-state-officials.aspx (accessed May 1, 2018).

5 Nelson, quoted in "Media and the Initiative Campaign," *Campaigns and Elections*, January 1992, 35.

6 Johnson, *Democracy for Hire*, 248.

7   John Diaz, "A Long Way from the Grassroots," SFGate.com, October 12, 2008, https://www.sfgate.com/opinion/article/A-long-way-from-the-grassroots-3190565.php (accessed June 29, 2018).

8   Nicholas Confessore, "The Unlikely Activist Who Took on Silicon Valley—and Won," *New York Times Magazine*, August 14, 2018, https://www.nytimes.com/2018/08/14/magazine/facebook-google-privacy-data.html (accessed August 14, 2018).

9   Johnson, *Democracy for Hire*, 245–46.

10   Ballotpedia, https://ballotpedia.org/2016_ballot_measures (accessed May 8, 2018).

11   "2020 Ballot Measures," Ballotpedia, https://ballotpedia.org/2020_ballot_measures (accessed September 24, 2021).

12   Ned Augenblick and Scott Nicholson, "Ballot Position, Choice Fatigue, and Voting Behaviour," *Review of Economic Studies* 82, no. 2 (April 2016): 460–80, in Simon Hedlin, "Do Longer Ballots Offer Too Much Democracy?," *The Atlantic*, November 3, 2015, https://www.theatlantic.com/politics/archive/2015/11/long-ballots-democracy/413701/ (accessed August 10, 2018).

13   U.S. Term Limits, Inc. v. Thornton, 514 U.S. 779 (1995), https://www.law.cornell.edu/supct/html/93-1456.ZO.html (accessed August 10, 2018).

14   "Expulsion and Censure," US Senate website, n.d., https://www.senate.gov/artandhistory/history/common/briefing/Expulsion_Censure.htm (accessed May 2, 2018).

Chapter 11

1   Andrew Wallenstein, "Media Trends That Will Define 2018," *Variety Premier*, in Morgan Stanley media blog, https://fa.morganstanley.com/balog/mediahandler/media/111219/2018%20Entertainment%20Industry%20Trends.Variety%20Thought%20Leaders.pdf (accessed August 13, 2018).

2   Todd Spangler, "Cord-Cutting Keeps Churning: US Pay-TV Cancelers to Hit 33 Million in 2018 (Study)," *Variety*, July 24, 2018, https://variety.com/2018/digital/news/cord-cutting-2018-estimates-33-million-us-study-1202881488/ (accessed December 18, 2018).

3   "2018 Global Mobile Consumer Survey: US Edition," Deloitte Global, n.d., https://www2.deloitte.com/content/dam/Deloitte/us/Documents/technology-media-telecommunications/

us-tmt-global-mobile-consumer-survey-exec-summary-2018.pdf
(accessed December 18, 2018).

4 Ad Hoc Committee on 2016 Election Polling, "An Evaluation
   of 2016 Election Polls in the U.S.," American Association for
   Public Opinion Research, n.d., https://www.aapor.org/Educat
   ion-Resources/Reports/An-Evaluation-of-2016-Election-Polls-
   in-the-U-S.aspx; and Nate Cohn, "A 2016 Review: Why Key State
   Polls Were Wrong about Trump," *New York Times*, May 31, 2017,
   https://www.nytimes.com/2017/05/31/upshot/a-2016-review-
   why-key-state-polls-were-wrong-about-trump.html (accessed
   August 20, 2018).

5 Dennis W. Johnson, *Campaigning in the Twenty-First
   Century: Activism, Big Data, and Dark Money*, 2nd ed.
   (New York: Routledge, 2016), 64–76.

6 Drew DeSilver and Abigail Geiger, "For Many Americans,
   Election Day Is Already Here," Fact Tank, Pew Research Center,
   October 21, 2016, http://www.pewresearch.org/fact-tank/
   2016/10/21/for-many-americans-election-day-is-already-here/
   (accessed August 20, 2018); and Zach Montellaro, "A Staggering
   36 Million People Have Voted Early, Setting the Stage for Big
   Midterm Turnout," *Politico*, November 5, 2018, https://www.
   politico.com/story/2018/11/05/early-voting-turnout-2018-electi
   ons-midterms-963149 (accessed December 21, 2018).

7 Abram Brown, "Meet the Billionaires behind Signal and
   Telegram, Two New Online Homes for Angry Conservatives,"
   Forbes, January 13, 2021, https://www.forbes.com/sites/abr
   ambrown/2021/01/13/meet-the-billionaires-behind-signal-and-
   telegram-two-potential-new-online-homes-for-angry-conservati
   ves/?sh=e892e8d7edaf (accessed October 20-, 2021).

8 Johnson, *Campaigning in the Twenty-First Century*, 2–11.

Chapter 12

1 Jennifer Agiesta and Ariel Edwards-Levy, "CNN Poll: Most
   Americans Feel Democracy Is under Attack in US," CNN,
   September 15, 2021, https://www.cnn.com/2021/09/15/polit
   ics/cnn-poll-most-americans-democracy-under-attack/index.
   html (accessed October 11, 2021).

2 Agiesta and Edwards-Levy, "CNN Poll."

3 Megan Brenan, "American's Confidence in Major US Institutions
   Dips," Gallup, July 14, 2021, https://news.gallup.com/poll/352

316/americans-confidence-major-institutions-dips.aspx (accessed October 22, 2021).

4   Kevin Freking, "Trump Joins a Select Few in Skipping Biden Inauguration," *AP News*, January 8, 2021.

5   Vann R. Newkirk II, "Voter Suppression Is Warping Democracy," *The Atlantic*, July 17, 2018, https://www.theatlantic.com/polit ics/archive/2018/07/poll-prri-voter-suppression/565355/ (accessed August 29, 2018).

6   Newkirk, "Voter Suppression Is Warping Democracy."

7   "Voting Laws Roundup, July 2021," Brennan Center for Justice, July 22, 2021, https://www.brennancenter.org/our-work/resea rch-reports/voting-laws-roundup-july-2021 (accessed October 1, 2021).

8   Jane Mayer, "The Big Money behind the Big Lie," *New Yorker*, August 9, 2021;

9   Mayer, "The Big Money behind the Big Lie," Mitchell quote at 34.

10   "Text of the President's Statement," *New York Times*, November 7, 1981, https://www.nytimes.com/1981/11/07/us/text-of-presid ent-s-statement.html (accessed October 10, 2018).

11   Sewell quoted in Marty Johnson, "House Approves John Lewis Voting Rights Measure," *The Hill*, August 24, 2021, https://theh ill.com/homenews/house/569217-house-approves-john-lewis-voting-rights-measure (accessed October 23, 2021).

12   McConnell quoted in Steven Nelson, "McConnell Vows Senate Republicans Will Resist 'Power Grab' HR 1 Election Bill," *New York Post*, May 10, 2021, https://nypost.com/2021/05/10/ senate-democrats-hold-hearing-over-hr1-voting-bill/ (accessed October 23, 2021).

13   Tal Kopan, "DHS Officials: 21 States Potentially Targeted by Russian Hackers Pre-election," CNN, July 18, 2017, https:// www.cnn.com/2017/06/21/politics/russia-hacking-hearing-sta tes-targeted/index.html (accessed August 27, 2018).

14   US Senate Select Committee on Intelligence, "Russian Targeting of Election Infrastructure during the 2016 Election: Summary of Initial Findings and Recommendations," May 8, 2018, https:// www.burr.senate.gov/imo/media/doc/RussRptInstlmt1-%20ElecSec%20Findings,Recs2.pdf (accessed June 12, 2018). The committee was chaired by Senator Richard M. Burr (Republican-North Carolina).

15 New Knowledge, *The Tactics and Tropes of the Internet Research Agency*, n.d. (report to the US Senate Select Committee on Intelligence, Washington, DC); and Computational Propaganda Research Project, *The IRA, Social Media and Political Polarization in the United States, 2012–2018*, n.d., ed. Philip N. Howard, Bharath Ganesh, Dimitri Liotsiou (Oxford: Oxford University Press) together with John Kelly and Camille Françoise (Graphika).

16 Derek Hawkins, "The Cybersecurity 202: We Surveyed 100 Security Experts. Almost All Said State Election Systems Were Vulnerable," *Washington Post*, May 21, 2018, https://www.was hingtonpost.com/news/powerpost/paloma/the-cybersecur ity-202/2018/05/21/the-cybersecurity-202-we-surveyed-100-security-experts-almost-all-said-state-election-systems-were-vul nerable/5b0189b030fb0425887995e2/?utm_term=.1b2fc8032065 (accessed August 28, 2018).

17 "Same Day Voter Registration," National Conference of State Legislatures, March 27, 2018, http://www.ncsl.org/research/ elections-and-campaigns/same-day-registration.aspx (accessed August 27, 2018); see research studies that are cited in this article.

18 Amy B. Wang, "Taylor Swift's Endorsement of Democrats Is Followed by a Spike in Voter Registrations," *Washington Post*, October 9, 2018.

19 Juliet Lapidos, "Doing Democracy Right," Slate, October 17, 2008, http://www.slate.com/articles/news_and_politics/how _they_do_it/2008/10/doing_democracy_right.html (accessed August 27, 2018).

20 Andrew Griffin, "Facebook Shuts Down 583 Million Fake Accounts as It Reveals It Is Packed with Abusive Content," *The Independent* (UK), May 15, 2018, https://www.independent. co.uk/life-style/gadgets-and-tech/news/facebook-fake-accou nts-removed-deleted-spam-abusive-content-latest-a8353021.html (accessed August 31, 2018).

21 Brian Pietsch, "Marjorie Taylor Greene Buys Up to $50,000 Worth of Trump SPAC Stock During Week of Wild Fluctuation," *Washington Post*, October 28, 2021, https://www.washingtonp ost.com/politics/2021/10/28/marjorie-taylor-greene-trump-spac-dwac/ (accessed October 29, 2021).

FURTHER READING

Bishop, Bill. *The Big Sort: Why the Clustering of Like-Minded America Is Tearing Us Apart.* New York: First Mariner Books, 2009.

Blankenhorn, David. "Why Polarization Matters." *American Interest,* December 22, 2015. https://www.the-american-interest.com/2015/12/22/why-polarization-matters/.

Gerhart, Ann. "Election Results under Attack: Here Are the Facts." *Washington Post,* March 11, 2021, https://www.washingtonpost.com/elections/interactive/2020/election-integrity/.

Hasen, Richard L. *Plutocrats United: Campaign Money, the Supreme Court, and the Distortion of American Elections.* New Haven, CT: Yale University Press, 2016.

Jacobson, Gary C., and Jamie L. Carson. *The Politics of Congressional Elections.* 9th ed. Lanham, MD: Rowman and Littlefield, 2015.

Johnson, Dennis W. *Campaigning in the Twenty-first Century: Activism, Big Data, and Dark Money.* 2nd ed. New York: Routledge, 2016.

Johnson, Dennis W. *Democracy for Hire: A History of American Political Consulting.* New York: Oxford University Press, 2017.

Keyssar, Alexander. *The Right to Vote: The Contested History of Democracy in the United States.* Rev. ed. New York: Basic Books, 2009.

Lawless, Jennifer L. *Becoming a Candidate: Political Ambition and the Decision to Run for Office.* New York: Cambridge University Press, 2012.

Leonnig, Carol, and Philip Rucker. *I Alone Can Fix It: Donald J. Trump's Catastrophic Final Year.* New York: Penguin Press, 2021.

Nelson, Candice J., and James A. Thurber, eds. *Campaigns and Elections American Style: The Changing Landscape of Political Campaigns.* 5th ed. New York: Routledge, 2018.

Newkirk, Vann R., II. "Voter Suppression Is Warping Democracy." *The Atlantic,* July 17, 2018. https://www.theatlantic.com/politics/arch ive/2018/07/poll-prri-voter-suppression/565355/.

"Political Polarization in the American Public." Pew Research Center, June 12, 2014. http://www.people-press.org/2014/06/12/political-polarization-in-the-american-public/.

Shane, Scott, and Mark Mazetti. "The Plot to Subvert an Election." *New York Times Magazine,* September 20, 2018. https://www.nyti mes.com/interactive/2018/09/20/us/politics/russia-interfere nce-election-trump-clinton.html?action=click&module=Top%20Stor ies&pgtype=Homepage.

Sides, John, Daron Shaw, Matt Grossman, and Keena Lipsitz. *Campaigns and Elections.* 3rd ed. New York: W. W. Norton, 2018.

White, John Kenneth, and Matthew R. Kerbel. *Party On! Political Parties from Hamilton and Jefferson to Trump.* 2nd ed. New York: Routledge, 2018.

Wolff, Michael. *Landslide: The Final Days of the Trump Presidency.* New York: Henry Holt, 2021.

Woodward, Bob, and Robert Costa. *Peril.* New York: Simon and Schuster, 2021.

Zetter, Kim. "The Crisis in Election Security." *New York Times,* September 26, 2018. https://www.nytimes.com/2018/09/26/magazine/election-security-crisis-midterms.html.

INDEX